A Burning Issue

The Political Economy Forum

Sponsored by the Political Economy Research Center (PERC)
Series Editor: Terry L. Anderson

A Burning Issue

A Case for Abolishing the U.S. Forest Service

Robert H. Nelson

ROWMAN & LITTLEFIELD PUBLISHERS, INC.
Lanham • Boulder • New York • Oxford

ROWMAN & LITTLEFIELD PUBLISHERS, INC.

Published in the United States of America
by Rowman & Littlefield Publishers, Inc.
4720 Boston Way, Lanham, Maryland 20706
http://www.rowmanlittlefield.com

12 Hid's Copse Road
Cumnor Hill, Oxford OX2 9JJ, England

British Library Cataloguing in Publication Information Available

Library of Congress Cataloging-in-Publication Data

Nelson, Robert H. (Robert Henry), 1944–
    A burning issue : a case for abolishing the U.S. Forest Service / Robert H. Nelson
    p.   cm.—(The political economy forum)
    Includes bibliographical references (p.).
    ISBN 0-8476-9734-7 (cloth : alk. paper)—ISBN 0-8476-9735-5 (pbk. : alk. paper)
    1. United States. Forest Service—Management. 2. Forest policy—West (U.S.) 3. Fire
management—Government policy—West (U.S.) I. Title. II. Series.
SD565.N46 2000
333.75'0973—dc21   99-057704

Printed in the United States of America

∞™ The paper used in this publication meets the minimum requirements of
American National Standard for Information Sciences—Permanence of Paper for
Printed Library Materials, ANSI/NISO Z39.48–1992.

For Martha

Contents

Figures and Tables

Preface

It is time to abolish the U.S. Forest Service. I do not make this recommendation lightly. For many years the Forest Service was considered a model federal agency. In 1952, *Newsweek* magazine declared that the agency was "one of Uncle Sam's soundest and most business-like investments."[1] Herbert Kaufman famously studied the administrative workings of the Forest Service of the 1940s and 1950s as an example of an organization succeeding very well at its job.[2] The Forest Service is still held in high regard by much of the American public. Those who interact with the Forest Service are often impressed with its many capable and dedicated employees.*

Yet, the earlier successes of the Forest Service were exaggerated then and in any case now lie well in the past. In the present, the agency is a model not of administrative efficiency but of administrative gridlock. A group of twenty leading academics, environmentalists, and spokesmen for commodity groups, gathered to discuss the future of the agency, recently stated that "fifty years ago, the Forest Service was one of the most highly regarded agencies in government. Today, the agency is besieged from without, demoralized within, and many wonder whether it will survive to see its centennial in 2005."[3]

Idaho has a higher percentage of its land in the national forest system than any other state, 40 percent of the area of the state. From a western

---

* My own experiences with the Forest Service date back to the 1970s. I joined the Economics Staff of the Office of Policy Analysis, located in the Office of the Secretary of the U.S. Department of the Interior, in 1975. I remained in this office until 1993, when I left to become a professor of environmental policy in the School of Public Affairs of the University of Maryland. During my years at Interior, I often had occasion to deal with the Forest Service. Like many people, I often had the reaction—how could such a nice group of people end up producing such a dysfunctional agency? Of course, as analyzed in this book, the answer has to do with the deficiencies of the legal, political, and organizational environment in which the employees of the Forest Service must function.

state perspective, a Federal Lands Task Force, convened by the Idaho State Board of Land Commissioners, declared in 1998 that its starting point for discussion was the failure of the current public land system, including the management of the national forests. "The current processes of federal land management have resulted in uncertain decision making, destabilization of resource dependent communities, and deterioration in environmental quality on federal lands. In short, the system is broken."[4] The view from the federal level is not much different. In testimony to Congress in 1997, the General Accounting Office concluded that "in summary, . . . the Forest Service's decision-making process is broken."[5]

In 1974 and 1976, Congress enacted legislation providing a new statutory foundation for national forest management.[6] A principal requirement of this legislation was that management of the national forests should be based on land use and other formal plans. The legitimacy of Forest Service management actions henceforth would rest on the quality and acceptability of land use and other planning. Yet, almost twenty-five years later there is general agreement that forest planning has been a large failure. In 1997, Secretary of Agriculture Dan Glickman appointed a Committee of Scientists to review the planning system and other elements of the decision-making process of the Forest Service. The 1999 report of the committee—recommending the development of a whole new approach to planning—declared that "the Forest Service is in a time of great change," partly because "trust in the Forest Service and among the many groups and individuals that care about the national forests and grasslands has diminished after years of a planning process that has been both divisive and disillusioning for all involved."[7]

The Forest Service land-use plans in the 1980s had involved a "massive effort that went for naught because the plans were built on an unsound foundation."[8] The full costs of Forest Service planning during the 1980s are estimated at $3 billion.[9] Yet, close scrutiny would later reveal the knowledge base for most individual forest plans, as the Committee of Scientists concluded, "to be inadequate and to lack scientific credibility. As this foundation disintegrated, the plans that had been built on them also collapsed," and the Forest Service was left unable to give the American public any clear rational explanation for its resource management decisions. In retrospect, given the problems that had to be overcome, the Committee of Scientists was now of the opinion that "it is doubtful" that the land-use planning process laid out in the National Forest Management Act of 1976 "ever stood a chance of succeeding." Outside the Forest Service, "many public participants are burned out, wary, fatigued, and disillusioned" with the agency manner of decision making; within the Forest Service, "planning is [now] disdained by many in the agency."[10]

At the national level the Resources Planning Act (RPA) Program, mandated by the Resources Planning Act of 1974 and intended to be another key element of Forest Service planning and decision making, "has rarely worked as intended in the 25 years since its passage." The Committee of Scientists found that it is not only "presidents and legislatures [who] have largely ignored" national level planning but also Forest Service "regions and their individual national forests and grasslands have largely ignored the RPA Program in planning."[11]

It is not that the planning activities of the Forest Service have had no impact. Outside groups have utilized the many procedural handles provided by the planning system to pursue their own agendas. Rather than generate agreement on a future course of action for forest management, the process of plan preparation has instilled distrust of the agency and promoted adversarial relationships among user groups. The Forest Service has had to commit large resources to land-use planning even while the inability to develop a workable planning system has tied the agency in knots. Planning has thus had the very opposite of the original intent of providing a clear and open basis for rational decision making on the national forests.

One reason for the failure of planning has been the inability of the Forest Service to define its mission in a time of rapid cultural and value shifts in American society. The Forest Service once believed that a main purpose for its existence was to supply timber to meet the material needs for wood of an expanding national economy.[12] Yet, in the past ten years timber harvests on the national forests have plummeted from 12 billion board feet per year to less than 4 billion board feet. Even those timber harvests that remain are undertaken in significant part for other purposes such as removal of excess fuels that pose a large fire hazard.

The end of timber harvesting as a main goal of the agency has also radically altered another central purpose of the agency in the past, actions to suppress forest fire.[13] (Historically, timber management and fire management have often absorbed as much as two-thirds of the budget of the Forest Service.) Fire was such a high priority in significant part because it meant protecting a valuable economic resource, the large stores of marketable timber of the national forests. If little of this timber is now to be harvested, a central purpose of the agency no longer exists. Indeed, the suppression of forest fire is now often seen as intrinsically undesirable; it is an interference with the "natural order" of the forests. Protection of human lives and structures does still frequently require suppression of the natural fire regime. However, this is now seen by many people as an unfortunate if perhaps necessary compromise with the highest ideals for the management of the natural forests.

The provision of forage for livestock grazing is now much contested, even as the actual levels of grazing decline. Another traditional important use of the national forests—production of oil and gas, coal, copper, silver, and other minerals—is facing new barriers. One historic function of the national forests that remains is to serve as a watershed and source of water for the rivers and streams of the nation. Yet, there are few management actions required to serve this water supply purpose, and by itself this goal offers little justification for a large administrative organization such as the Forest Service.

What, then, is the Forest Service to do? The one area of rapidly increasing use of the forests has been recreation. Recreational visits to the national forests have risen from 25 million visitor days in 1950 to 250 million visitor days in 1992. The Forest Service serves as a provider of many campgrounds, ski resort sites, hunting and fishing opportunities, and other recreation activities. Yet there is little in the history of the agency that sees its central mission in recreation. The founding father of the Forest Service, Gifford Pinchot, was notoriously indifferent to the recreational uses of the national forests.[14] The management of wildlife populations for hunting has traditionally been the province of state fish and game departments. Provision of campgrounds and resort sites may involve little more than the real estate function of issuing and monitoring leases to private operators. The most common recreational use of the national forests is simply the act of many millions of people driving an automobile along roads that traverse the forests.

The intensive recreation that involves the largest number of people fits uncomfortably with the current "ecosystem" goals for the national forests. Expansion of popular recreation sites such as ski areas is increasingly resisted. The ecosystem goals for the forests will more and more require limits on public recreation access to wilderness areas. All too often, they are being "loved to death." Indeed, for many people today the goal for the national forests should be to avoid human influences on the "natural" functioning of the forest ecosystem. The national forests should serve, as this widely held view suggests, as a biodiversity and general ecological reserve for the nation.[15] The General Accounting Office reported that "this attention to sustaining wildlife and fish will likely constrain future use of the national forests such as recreation."[16]

Like wilderness, and recognizing that many compromises will be necessary, this view suggests that the national forests so far as possible should be places "untrammeled by man." Although this vision is still fiercely contested in American society, it has been gaining ground for twenty-five years, as seen in the sharp declines in timber harvesting, mining, and other traditional uses of the national forests. The Clinton administration has actively sought to instill this ethos as the new core value defining the institutional culture of the Forest Service.

The existing organizational arrangements of the Forest Service, however, were never created to oversee nature with minimal human impacts. Its large administrative apparatus was designed for an opposite purpose, active human management to serve human needs. The agency does not have 35,000 employees and a resource management budget of more than $2 billion per year to build fences around the national forests. What are all these Forest Service personnel and resources to do in the future, if a regime of minimal human interference with forest ecosystems takes hold? At best, they might be required to implement transitional management actions as the national forests shift from production of outputs for human use to a more "natural" mode of functioning. According to the precepts of "ecosystem management," the Forest Service should be gradually working itself out of a job, it would seem, if not disappearing immediately.

Reflecting all these developments, the Forest Service today is an agency that no longer knows why it exists.[17] The original use justifications for creating the agency have been disavowed over the past twenty-five years by important segments of American public opinion and in the 1990s by its own political leadership. Other proposals for a new mission for the Forest Service are strongly advocated but fail to achieve consensus and in any case would imply radical changes from the structure of the current Forest Service administrative organization. The attempts by the Forest Service to sort all this out in order to define a new organizational mission have met with repeated failures, leaving a trail of wide confusion within the agency and among the concerned public. The former secretary of the Interior in the Carter administration and former longtime governor of Idaho, Cecil Andrus, recently declared that the Forest Service is a "federal agency so buffeted by politicians and pressure groups that it cannot chart its own course or fully benefit from the skills of its own people on the ground."[18] Outside forces today push the Forest Service in all directions as they seek—often successfully—to use the agency for their own purposes. Lacking any clear sense of mission, and harsh as it may sound to say, the most important goal remaining for many Forest Service employees has become institutional survival of the agency in order to preserve their own attractive jobs.

Instead, this book will argue that the Forest Service should now be put out of its misery. It should simply be abolished. The Forest Service suffers from a fatal malady. It was founded early in this century on an idea—the "scientific management" of the national forests—that has failed the test of time. No agency can function well when it does not know its purpose. If the Forest Service is unable to identify a valid mission widely acceptable to the American public, there is no longer any reason for the Forest Service to exist. Indeed, the very existence of the Forest Service becomes a hindrance and an obstacle to more imaginative and innovative solutions to the problems of the national forests. The time has come to remove this obstacle.

ACKNOWLEDGMENTS

Terry Anderson of the Political Economy Research Center in Bozeman, Montana, made comments on an earlier draft that helped me to reshape the basic argument of the book. Mary Chapman as usual made a number of useful suggestions. Jonathan Adler, Neil Sampson, Graham Child, Karl Hess, Randal O'Toole, Brad Little, Mark Sagoff, and Carl Spector read various drafts among them and also provided helpful comments. I thank them all and the many other people who have made the study of public land management such an enjoyable subject for me over the past twenty-five years.

NOTES

1. "Fabulous Bear, Famous Service, Fight Annual Billion Dollar Fire," *Newsweek*, June 2, 1952, pp. 50–54.

2. Herbert Kaufman, *The Forest Ranger* (Baltimore: Johns Hopkins University Press, 1960). As recently as 1996, an administrative study of the Forest Service described it as a "bureaucratic superstar," although the authors also noted that the agency was facing newly challenging circumstances. See Jeanne Nienaber Clarke and Daniel C. McCool, *Staking Out the Terrain: Power and Performance Among Natural Resource Agencies* (Albany: State University of New York Press, 1996), pp. 49–66.

3. *Options for the Forest Service 2nd Century: A Report to the American People by the Forest Options Group* (Portland, Ore.: Thoreau Institute, January 1999), p. 1 of introduction. Available at <http://www.ti.org/2c.html>.

4. *New Approaches for Managing Federally Administered Lands*, A Report to the Idaho State Board of Land Commissioners by the Federal Lands Task Force (July 1998), p. 3.

5. General Accounting Office, *Forest Service Decision-Making: Greater Clarity Needed on Mission Priorities*, testimony to Congress by Associate Director Barry T. Hill (Washington, D.C.: February 25, 1997), p. 9.

6. Dennis C. Le Master, *Decade of Change: The Remaking of Forest Service Statutory Authority during the 1970s* (Westport, Conn.: Greenwood Press, 1984).

7. Committee of Scientists, *Sustaining the People's Lands: Recommendations for Stewardship of the National Forests and Grasslands into the Next Century* (Washington, D.C.: U.S. Department of Agriculture, March 15, 1999), pp. 76, 64.

8. Ibid., p. 148.

9. Kathryn A. Kohm and Jerry F. Franklin, "Introduction," in *Creating a Forestry for the 21st Century: The Science of Ecosystem Management*, ed. Kohm and Franklin (Washington, D.C.: Island Press, 1997), p. 4.

10. Ibid., pp. 148, 2, 5.

11. Ibid., p. 115.

12. For an excellent review of the history of American forests, including the national forests, see Douglas W. MacCleery, *American Forests: A History of Resiliency and Recovery* (Durham, N.C.: Forest History Society, 1993). See also Char Miller, ed., *American Forests: Nature, Culture and Politics* (Lawrence: University Press of Kansas, 1997).

13. For a good discussion of the crisis of purpose facing the Forest Service, see *Reinventing the Forest Service*, special issue of *Different Drummer*, edited by Randal O'Toole and published by the Thoreau Institute (Spring 1995).

14. Charles F. Wilkinson, *Crossing the Next Meridian: Land, Water, and the Future of the West* (Washington, D.C.: Island Press, 1992), pp. 129–31.

15. Dyan Zaslowsky and T. H. Watkins, *These American Lands: Parks, Wilderness, and the Public Lands* (Washington, D.C.: Island Press, 1994), p. 102.

16. General Accounting Office, *Forest Service Decision-Making*, p. 8.

17. See Robert H. Nelson, "The Future of the National Forests," *Society* (November/December 1996) and Robert H. Nelson, "The Religion of Forestry: Scientific Management," *Journal of Forestry* (November 1999), pp. 4–8.

18. Cecil D. Andrus and Joel Connelly, *Cecil Andrus: Politics Western Style* (Seattle: Sasquatch Books, 1998), p. 130.

other special interests. Wall Street, it appeared to many, owned the U.S. Congress. In the early twentieth century there was a further general "disillusionment about the rational capacity of the people" in detailed matters of governance. It was thus imperative that objective knowledge, as discovered by physical and social scientists, be applied more directly to the processes of government. As Lee comments, progressive theorists such as Pinchot saw themselves engaged in a project in which the stakes were nothing less than "the survival of American democracy [which] rested on the use of scientific knowledge as a technology of governance."[11]

The professionals in the Forest Service should therefore be left free of political interference to calculate the optimal age of tree harvest, the appropriate level of timber cut, the resources needed for suppressing forest fires, the appropriate level of livestock grazing in the forests, and many other such "technical" matters. Social values, as dictated by the Congress and other parts of the political process, might enter in setting certain broad goals for the use of the national forests. But crass political influences must not enter into the details of forest management by which these goals were realized. The chief of the Forest Service must be a forestry professional, insulated from politics, who would supervise the overall application of scientific forestry knowledge to achieve forest outcomes in the most efficient manner possible.

From this perspective, the mission of federal foresters was to manipulate nature, to make wild nature "perfect" through the application of science. Perfection was defined in terms of serving basic human purposes such as the provision of wood for home building or water for drinking. According to scientific management, as Nancy Langston writes in *Forest Dreams, Forest Nightmares*, a well-managed forest should be "efficient, orderly, and useful." Federal foresters followed in the tradition of European silviculture, which "had as its ideal a waste-free, productive stand: nature perfected by human efficiency" and put to use to serve human needs. The early foresters who set out on this path, and saw the Forest Service as the exemplar of all that it represented, came "with the certainty that they could use science to fix the forests, and that with the help of science, they could do no wrong." They were very "self-conscious of their mission, and proud of their new scientific discipline" of professional forestry.[12]

If the professional practitioners of scientific management regarded knowledge obtained through formal research methods as authoritative, they tended to be dismissive of local knowledge grounded in practical experience. The great advantage of science was that, through the results of expert investigations, it would be possible to eliminate the waste and confusion that had inevitably attended to all the failed local experiments of the past. In short, the newly efficient methods of science would supplant the old haphazard and wasteful methods of local trial and error.

SCIENTIFIC MANAGEMENT OF FIRE

Scientific management of the forests would necessarily have to include the scientific management of forest fire. William Greeley, later to be chief of the Forest Service, said in 1911 that "firefighting is a matter of scientific management, just as much as silviculture or range improvement."[13] Fighting fires has traditionally been a central task of the Forest Service, absorbing major shares of its budget and personnel resources. In the 1920s, as David Clary writes in a history of Forest Service timber harvesting policy, the agency followed a "prescription for what ailed America's forests" that involved "first, 'effective protection against fire.'" In the 1930s, when the Civilian Conservation Corps was put to work on the national forests, "the biggest single employment of the CCC on the national forests was in fire control."[14] In the 1990s, the fire-fighting activities still receive in an average year about one-quarter of the resource management funding for the national forests.

Prevention of fire was necessary first of all to protect the valuable timber supplies of the national forests, saving them for future harvest. But the campaign against fire was also a campaign against nature out of human control. If the forests were to be deliberately managed to achieve goals for human use, the destructive actions of fire would have to be controlled. This would be a task that depended on the application of the expert skills of the forestry professionals newly staffing the Forest Sevice.

Such attitudes were reflected in a 1928 study of U.S. forest policy done for the Brookings Institution. Jenks Cameron, the author of the study, considered that "working toward Order" based on "national policy" and coordination, and overcoming "irreconcilable localisms," were not only desirable but also an inevitable result of inexorable economic and social trends of the time. In "sloughing off parochialism" on the forests of the nation, "the most important thing that took place was a continuing growth of that spirit of cooperative fire protection." It reflected a recognition of the need to protect valuable timber supplies because "lumber was 'King' and will be 'King' for many years to come." The building of an extensive network of roads, also facilitating protection against fire, was another sign of the great rational progress being achieved on the forests of the nation. All in all, Cameron could report in 1928 that "the matter of fire has come to be increasingly recognized in the development of forestal knowledge for what it unquestionably is—the problem of problems in America's working toward a perfect forest order. Conservative foresters today declare that an approximation of fire protection would mean that our forest problem was 75 percent solved."[15]

In the Blue Mountains of northeast Oregon and southeast Washington, for example, the Forest Service knew that local Indians earlier had frequently burned the forests there. Some of the earliest European arrivals had begun to imitate the Indian practice. But the Forest Service in the early twentieth century rejected all this as simplistic and old fashioned. Indeed, as Langston writes, they saw "burning as part of [the old] irresponsible laissez faire logging practices—practices utterly opposed to scientific sustained yield forestry." Moreover, "if light burning was an Indian practice, then by definition it was superstition, not science," and thus could never be an option. Instead, as Langston explains, "scientific control and management . . . were the goals of government scientists." By means of science, the Forest Service would be able to "improve nature," not merely preserve it or protect its environmental quality.[16]

This led federal foresters to reject even the views of many local non-Indians who considered the government plan for eliminating fire to be "absurd." To be sure, there were also self-interested motives at stake. As Langston further comments, "If light burning was accepted, that would threaten the Forest Service's very justification for managing the Forests— a justification which came from its claims to technical and scientific expertise." The Forest Service "was desperate to defend its own authority as manager of the federal forests, and fire suppression was one way to do that."[17]

In his wide-ranging writings on fire policy, Stephen Pyne also explores how Forest Service thinking about forest fires was derived from the broader themes of the progressive era. The aspiration to scientific fire management early in this century involved "nothing peculiar, . . . nothing idiosyncratic to foresters." Rather, it was a natural outgrowth of the prevailing general "precepts of progressivism, the belief that scientific knowledge was essential and adequate, that public policy and public lands should be administered by experts trained in scientific management and shielded from political corruption and public whim." In the progressive gospel, the Forest Service efforts "reified" the widespread hopes to control nature for human use—"to wage a sublimated war on the forces of nature."[18]

A CRISIS OF SCIENTIFIC FAITH

Some years ago, Charles Lindblom and David Cohen made a general distinction across a wide range of professional fields between "professional social inquiry" and "ordinary knowledge." They argued that the members of professional groups exhibited certain general tendencies of thought, treating knowledge as authoritative only when it was the product of formal research, grounded in the application of the scientific method. In the real world, however, Lindblom and Cohen argued that professional methods typically could offer little more than "a supplement to ordinary knowledge."[19]

Moreover, ordinary knowledge was not developed and brought to bear in the formal and systematic fashion expected of professional social inquiry. Rather, it accrued almost haphazardly in the course of various societal and political interactions that somehow came together to yield a decision. Lindblom in an earlier article had famously characterized this form of government decision making as "the science of 'muddling through.'"[20] As Lindblom and Cohen now argued, the tendency of professionals to overestimate the power of their own methods often rendered them incapable of seeing the essential contributions that other forms of knowledge and of less formal decision-making processes could make.[21]

The problems associated with the efforts of professional foresters to manage fire over the course of the twentieth century have served well to illustrate this kind of broader failure of professional thinking and scientific management.[22] As the Forest Service in the 1990s was finally compelled to acknowledge, the fire management practices of the twentieth century put much too great a burden on the knowledge available from the science of forest ecology.[23] Suppressing fire, it was recognized, can be as harmful to forests as letting fire burn. Fire is essential to the normal ecological workings of forests in ways that the Forest Service never understood for many decades. Contrary to the tenets of scientific management, the most important forest fire lessons of the twentieth century were learned through practical experience and trial and error, not through formal research.

Suppressing fire in the past has now led to increased fire risks in the future, owing to the buildup of brush and dense thickets of smaller trees in many forests. As Pyne relates, it took many decades, culminating in the large destructive fires of the past fifteen years, to prove to disbelieving Forest Service eyes that "the decision not to burn can be as ecologically fatal as promiscuous burning." In "removing anthropogenic fire from many environments," the Forest Service committed "less an act of humility than of vandalism."[24]

In 1998, Barry Hill, associate director for energy, resources, and science issues of the General Accounting Office, testified to the Congress that "catastrophic wildfires" were now posing a basic threat to the resource base and the communities of the West. It was the most serious policy issue facing the national forest system. As Hill testified,

The increasing number of large, intense, uncontrollable, and catastrophically destructive wildfires is the most extensive and serious national forest health-related problem in the interior West. Past management practices, especially the Forest Service's decades-old policy of suppressing fire in the national forests, disrupted the historical occurrence of frequent low-intensity fires. As a result, vegetation accumulated, creating high levels of fuels for catastrophic wildfires and transforming much of the region into a tinderbox. The number of large wildfires, and of acres burned by them, has increased over the last decade, as have the costs of attempting to suppress them. These fires not only compromise the forest's ability to provide timber, outdoor recreation, clean water and other resources but they also pose increasingly grave risks to human health, safety and property, especially along the boundaries of forests where population has grown rapidly in recent years.[25]

Facing such problems, after almost a century of actively seeking the suppression of fire, the Forest Service today has reversed course altogether and now seeks to restore the very historic fire regimes that preceded the creation of the national forest system with its failed aspirations for scientific management.

THE FAILURE OF SCIENTIFIC MANAGEMENT

Forest fire is not an isolated story.[26] The progressive-era concepts of scientific management were widely applied to the management of the natural resources of the West. What is striking is the similarity of outcome across a wide range of fields of endeavor. The Bureau of Reclamation was created in 1902, three years before the Forest Service. One of the main reasons for establishing the bureau was to control flooding. Forest fire and floods both represented nature out of control and a menace to human life and property. As Samuel Hays has described, the bureau was founded in the same spirit of technocratic efficiency as the Forest Service fire-fighting program.[27] In short, the methods of scientific management in both cases would have to be applied to bring natural forces under human control.

The management of the flow of the river achieved by a dam would also allow the storage of water to irrigate the lands of the West to feed the American people and the production of electricity to light their homes. Here again, there is a close analogy with control over forest fire, which sought to preserve timber inventories to supply the wood to build the homes of the nation. In the first half of the twentieth century, dams and forest fire management symbolized the rising power of science to confer benefit on mankind. Woodie Guthrie sang ballads celebrating the inspiration he felt in witnessing the construction of Grand Coulee Dam in Washington State, sure evidence of the forward march of human progress.[28] The current headquarters building of the Interior department in Washington, D.C., built in the 1930s, has murals on the walls showing the actions of heroic workers in constructing a large dam. Indeed, no scene was more typical of the art of socialist realism than the site for the construction of a dam. For its part, the Forest Service put its public relations skills to work in its "Smokey Bear" campaign, persuading all Americans that it was doing its part to apply science for human advance in the world.

The construction of dams, however, often turned into boondoggle public works projects. If conservationism had been a "gospel of efficiency," there were few areas of American life that exhibited greater inefficiencies. In the crucible of American politics, the ideals of scientific management could seldom be realized for the water projects of the West. Rather than efficiency, it was the subsidization of favored constituency groups that typically became a driving force for programs that still operated in the name of scientific management.[29] Thus, within a decade the beneficiaries of Bureau of Reclamation projects were pleading that they could not afford to pay back their loans, and the government was responding by forgiving these loans. Over the course of the twentieth century, the federal government would recover only 20 cents of every dollar of capital construction costs for the agricultural components of bureau projects.[30]

Then, in the second half of the twentieth century, the very goal of control over nature would increasingly be challenged by a vocal part of the population.[31] Instead of inspiring a virtual reverence for progress, a dam has now become a leading symbol of evil in the world. David Brower says simply that "I hate all dams," and it has nothing to do with whether the benefit-cost ratio is favorable or not.[32] Economics for him has nothing to do with the undesirability of building a dam because a dam is, simply put, a desecration of nature. To argue for building a dam is like arguing for the institution of slavery because it is economically efficient.

The Wilderness Act of 1964 represented a great turning point in the value symbolism of American life. If a dam had inspired reverence because it symbolized the control given by science over nature, this very control was now coming to be seen by many people as undesirable. Instead of control over nature, a wilderness area represented the very opposite. To experience reverence and awe, Americans now sought to visit areas that were "untrammeled by man." The most sacred sites, the places of greatest spiritual inspiration, were precisely those places on earth where the exercise of human power over nature was at a minimum.[33] If atom bombs and other products of great technological skill now suggested to many that human beings might be able to kill themselves or otherwise do great harm with the instruments of modern science, many people wanted to find refuges where the impacts of science would not be seen or felt.

This new view of the relationship of man and nature—itself a subject of ancient religious significance—has had a major practical impact on federal management of natural resources. There are now more than 100 million acres (about the size of California) in the national wilderness system. On the federal lands, the total acreage of areas set aside for wilderness, wildlife refuges, wild and scenic rivers, and other preservation purposes has risen from 51 million acres in 1964 to 271 million acres in 1993.[34] Lands set aside for preservation purposes now represent about 45 percent of the combined acreage of the four major federal land-holding agencies, the National Park Service, the Fish and Wildlife Service, the Forest Service, and the Bureau of Land Management.

By the 1980s the construction of new dams was coming to a halt. The application of such thinking has come later to forest fire. It was only in the 1990s that control over forest fire came to be seen as yet another failure of scientific management. Like other such failures, forest fire management was both an economic boondoggle and an environmental disaster. Beyond that, the very goal of controlling forest fire as an element of controlling nature is now widely disavowed. A forest fire is also a part of nature, and like a wilderness, in the ideal should be left free of human hand.

Of course, a forest fire is also potentially a large threat to human life and property. There are other such threats. Wolves and grizzly bears were eliminated from most of the West as part of scientific wildlife management. There is now an effort to reverse this history as well, restoring these animals to the forests of the West. This also encounters the objection that human lives may be put at risk. However, the degree of hazard to human welfare from a forest fire transcends any other element of forest management. It will never be possible as a general management principle to let forest fires run wild.

The shifting value foundations in American life and the failure of the original scientific management ideals have yielded a crisis of purpose for the Forest Service. Its employees no longer have the high morale of professionals confident that they possess the requisite expert skills to serve important goals of the nation. In the natural resource area there is a wide perception today of a "declining availability of highly trained Federal agency personnel at the local level."[35] Experiencing a loss of trust, Forest Service professionals no longer expect that politicians and judges will give them much autonomy to pursue an efficient and effective administrative course of action. Political leaders themselves are unable to articulate comprehensible values and goals for the management of the national forests. The Forest Service has been left without any vision to guide its actions and is today simply floundering without direction.

As a study commissioned by the Western Water Policy Review Advisory Commission indicated in 1997, the old model involved federal agencies that "retained a high level of discretionary authority (as defined by law), political clout, and respect as impartial scientific resource managers." Today, however, "most [federal] natural resource agencies no longer possess those qualities in the same magnitude." As a result, "it has become increasingly difficult for agencies to unilaterally exercise authority in an area where they have been unable to build supportive constituencies." Because existing federal agencies for land and resource management are grounded in outmoded assumptions, and the confused governance structure of federal and state authority is ill suited to fill the gap, the overall result, seen throughout natural resource management in the West, has been political stalemate and inaction—in short, policy and management "gridlock."[36]

THE PLAN OF THE BOOK

This book concludes that the Forest Service is incapable of solving its problems. The loss of the scientific management ethos that guided the agency in the twentieth century is fatal. It is possible to stumble along making incremental changes but this merely delays the inevitable and increases the costs. Instead, the current functions of the Forest Service should be reassigned to other new and existing federal agencies, to states, and to the private sector. The opportunity to remake the system of management for the national forests will make it possible to achieve necessary changes in the near term that otherwise could take decades if left to Forest Service leadership.

The leading policy issues today on the national forest system—issues that demonstrate the inability of the current Forest Service to deal with the basic problems of the national forests—revolve around forest fire and its ecological consequences. Chapter 1 shows how a century of fire suppression by the Forest Service has ended up shaping the current ecological condition of the interior national forests of the western United States for the worse. These suppression policies are no longer tenable, economically or environmentally, raising fundamental policy choices that the Forest Service seems incapable of adequately formulating or resolving.

Chapter 2 examines how the new ideas of "ecosystem management" and "sustainability" are being applied to the interconnected problems of excessive fuels buildups, large forest fire hazards, and "unnatural" ecological outcomes. These fire-related problems pose the leading current test of the practical viability of ecosystem management. The two main policy instruments available to the Forest Service for putting ecosystem management into practice on the national forests are prescribed burning and mechanical removal of timber (involving some form of timber harvesting). Yet, there are fundamental obstacles in the way of either approach, making it unlikely that the Forest Service will succeed in taking any effective action, despite the urgency of the problems it now faces.

Chapter 3 shows how the likely failure of ecosystem management also reflects fundamental conceptual failings in current Forest Service thinking. The policy issues being raised today by the management of forest fire raise deep value questions for American society, in part questions of a "theological" character. However, the Forest Service, as an agency grounded in the doctrines of "scientific management," is ill suited to lead a process of value debate and resolution in American society.

As a result, as explored in chapter 4, the agency lacks legitimacy in the eyes of the outside groups most concerned with the national forests. The Forest Service must operate in an environment of pervasive distrust of its motives and capabilities. Even though the Forest Service sought to put ecosystem management into practice in the 1990s, its environmental critics continued to challenge agency actions at every opportunity, contributing to the condition of gridlock on these lands. Other potential supporters of the agency were equally skeptical.

Chapter 5 examines how, as policy-making and management institutions fail at the national level, the beginnings of a movement to shift decision making to local levels are emerging in the West. As claims to scientific skills no longer bestow social legitimacy, the approval of those people directly affected locally becomes more important. As scientists are more humble in their claims to expert knowledge, and trial and error assumes greater importance, it becomes more necessary to have local flexibility to respond quickly to changing circumstances. The pervasive lack of trust in Forest Service motives and capabilities means that it is unlikely any time soon to have this necessary flexibility.

Chapter 6 shows how the current funding arrangements for the national forests create significant disincentives for decentralization of management authority. At present, the federal government sends many billions of dollars per year to western states to fund management of the national forests as well as other federally owned lands. Any viable proposal for decentralization of national forest management will have to address the political and economic realities of the large financial benefits to the West of the status quo on the public lands.

Finally, chapter 7 proposes the transfer of management authority for the national forests to local decision-making venues, where local citizens can directly resolve the critical value choices. In the short run, significant movement toward decentralization could be achieved by giving assemblies of local groups in essence the role of a corporate board of directors for individual national forests. In the long run, as the case of fire policy helps to make clear, brand-new institutions for decentralized management of lands now in the national forest system will be necessary. These institutions will be better suited to the problems and the social and economic circumstances of the twenty-first century than is the existing Forest Service.

NOTES

1. For histories of the Forest Service, see Harold K. Steen, *The U.S. Forest Service: A History* (Seattle: University of Washington Press, 1976); and Glen O. Robinson, *The Forest Service: A Study of Public Land Management* (Baltimore: Johns Hopkins University Press, 1975). The classic study of the history of the public lands is Paul W. Gates, *History of Public Land Law Development* (Washington, D.C.: Government Printing Office, 1968).

2. See Samuel Trask Dana and Sally K. Fairfax, *Forest and Range Policy: Its Development in the United States* (New York: McGraw-Hill, 1980).

3. Jeanne Nienaber Clarke and Daniel C. McCool, *Staking Out the Terrain: Power and Performance Among Natural Resource Agencies* (Albany: State University of New York Press, 1996), p. 49.

4. Gifford Pinchot, *Breaking New Ground* (New York: Harcourt, Brace, 1947), p. 261.

5. See Robert H. Nelson, *Reaching for Heaven on Earth: The Theological Meaning of Economics* (Lanham, Md.: Rowman & Littlefield, 1991).

6. Samuel P. Hays, *Conservation and the Gospel of Efficiency: The Progressive Conservation Movement, 1890–1920* (Cambridge: Harvard University Press, 1959).

7. Dorothy Ross, *The Origins of American Social Science* (New York: Cambridge University Press, 1991).

8. Eliza Wing-yee Lee, "Political Science, Public Administration, and the Rise of the American Administrative State," *Public Administration Review* (November/December 1995).

9. Ibid., pp. 539, 541.

10. Ibid., p. 543.

11. Ibid., pp. 541, 542.

12. Nancy Langston, *Forest Dreams, Forest Nightmares* (Seattle: University of Washington Press, 1995), pp. 5, 8, 10.

13. Quoted in Stephen J. Pyne, *World Fire: The Culture of Fire on Earth* (New York: Holt, 1995), p. 185.

14. David A. Clary, *Timber and the Forest Service* (Lawrence: University Press of Kansas, 1986), pp. 76, 95.

15. Jenks Cameron, *The Development of Governmental Forest Control in the United States* (Baltimore: Johns Hopkins Press, 1928), pp. 326–27, 378–81.

16. Langston, *Forest Dreams, Forest Nightmares*, pp. 249, 250, 252.

17. Ibid., pp. 250, 251, 253.

18. Pyne, *World Fire*, pp. 185, 192.

19. Charles E. Lindblom and David K. Cohen, *Usable Knowledge: Social Science and Social Problem Solving* (New Haven: Yale University Press, 1979), p. 35.

20. Charles E. Lindblom, "The Science of 'Muddling Through,'" *Public Administration Review* (Spring 1959).

21. Lindblom and Cohen, *Usable Knowledge*, ch. 4.

22. See Robert H. Nelson, *Rethinking Scientific Management*, Resources for the Future Discussion Paper 99-07 (Washington, D.C.: November 1998).

23. For the story of another failure of public land management, based on similar causes, see Robert H. Nelson, *The Making of Federal Coal Policy* (Durham: Duke University Press, 1983); see also A. Dan Tarlock, "The Making of Federal Coal Policy: Lessons for Public Land Management from a Failed Program, an Essay and Review," *Natural Resources Journal* (April 1985).

24. Pyne, *World Fire*, p. 253.

25. General Accounting Office, Western National Forests: Catastrophic Wildfires Threaten Resources and Communities, testimony by Associate Director Barry T. Hill before the Subcommittee on Forests and Forest Health, Committee on Resources, U.S. House of Representatives, September 28, 1998, pp. 1–2.

26. See Robert H. Nelson, *Public Lands and Private Rights: The Failure of Scientific Management* (Lanham, Md.: Rowman & Littlefield, 1995).

27. Hays, *Conservation and the Gospel of Efficiency*, ch. 2.

28. Marc Reisner, *Cadillac Desert: The American West and Its Disappearing Water* (New York: Penguin Books, 1993), pp. 160–61.

29. Terry L. Anderson, *Water Crisis: Ending the Policy Drought* (Washington, D.C.: Cato Institute, 1983).

30. See Richard W. Wahl, *Markets for Federal Water: Subsidies, Property Rights and the Bureau of Reclamation* (Washington, D.C.: Resources for the Future, 1989).

31. See Roderick Frazier Nash, *The Rights of Nature: A History of Environmental Ethics* (Madison: University of Wisconsin Press, 1989); also Stephen Fox, *John Muir and His Legacy: The American Conservation Movement* (Boston: Little, Brown, 1981).

32. Quoted in John McPhee, *Conversations with the Archdruid* (New York: Farrar, Straus and Giroux, 1971), p. 159.

33. See Roderick Nash, *Wilderness and the American Mind* (New Haven: Yale University Press, 1967).

34. General Accounting Office, *Federal Lands: Information on Land Owned and on Acreage with Conservation Restrictions*, GAO/RCED-95-73FS (January 1995), p. 3.

35. Douglas S. Kenney, *Resource Management at the Watershed Level: An Assessment of the Changing Federal Role in the Emerging Era of Community-Based Watershed Management*, Report prepared for the Western Water Policy Review Advisory Commission (October 1997), p. 68.

36. Ibid., p. 55.

1

Scientific Management of Fire

Before European settlement, we now know that fire was a pervasive presence in the forests of the West.[1] Many fires were started by lightning. Perhaps even more were set by Native Americans, who actively used fire as a way of manipulating the landscape for hunting, transportation, farming, and other purposes.[2] As the leading student of the history of fire, Stephen Pyne, has commented, "it is often assumed that the American Indian was incapable of modifying his environment and that he would not have been much interested in doing so if he did have the capabilities." The truth is much different, that "he possessed both the tool and the will to use it. That tool was fire." Indeed, fire for American Indians was "a wonderful instrument without which most Indian economies would have collapsed."[3]

Owing to both natural and human causes, fire historically visited most western forests on a frequent basis, in many places as often as every ten or fifteen years. For example, recent research on the history of Sierra Nevada ecosystems finds the following frequency of fire before the twentieth century: red fir—fire could be expected to burn over stands every twenty-six years; mixed conifer–pine—every fifteen years; mixed conifer–fir—every twelve years; ponderosa pine—every eleven years; and blue oak—every eight years.[4]

The arrival of European settlement in the West, however, greatly reduced the frequency of fire. The new settlers displaced the existing native Indian populations from most areas, concentrating the few surviving Indians on reservations, and ending Indian burning practices. Europeans introduced cattle and other domestic livestock, which in yet another "tragedy of the commons" rapidly exhausted the supplies of many native grasses. These grasses had served as combustible fuel to sustain natural

15

and Indian fires and to carry fire easily from one place to another. Then, early in the twentieth century, the federal government introduced a policy of active suppression of fire, rejecting as "primitive" and "unscientific" the idea that fire should be used as a basic tool of forest management. As the U.S. Forest Service believed, the timber supplies of the federal forests should be efficiently used for lumber to build the homes of the nation, not "wasted" in uncontrolled forest fires.

As a result, over the course of the twentieth century, fire was largely eliminated from most western forests. On the same Sierra Nevada ecosystems noted above, it is estimated that the frequency of fire exhibited in this century has been as follows: red fir—at current rates, a fire would be expected to burn through any given stand every 1,644 years; mixed conifer–fir—every 644 years; mixed conifer–pine—every 185 years; ponderosa pine—every 192 years; and blue oak—every 78 years. For each tree species, the expected incidence of fire has been 10 percent or less what it would have been in the period before European settlement.

FIRE AND FOREST ECOLOGY

With fire removed from its historic role in many forests throughout the West, the ecological workings of these forests were drastically altered.[5] The character of the marvelous ponderosa pine forests, for example, which covered large parts of the Northern and Southern Rocky Mountains and of the Sierra Nevada mountain range in the nineteenth century, has been drastically altered by the absence of fire.[6] In the Deschutes National Forest of Oregon, fire suppression has led to the replacement of ponderosa pine by Douglas fir and mixed conifers over 67 percent of the former pine acreage.[7] Large ponderosa pines, like redwoods and certain other tree species, have thick bark and in other ways are resistant to fire. In a typical ponderosa pine stand of the presettlement era, fire would sweep through the forest on a regular basis, perhaps every decade or two. Such fires would clear the forest floor of shrubbery and smaller trees of various invading species but would leave the large pines—often five feet or more in diameter—unharmed. The settlers arriving in the West commented frequently about the beautiful "parklike" conditions of the ponderosa pine forests; they could drive their wagons easily among the large trees spaced well apart. Or, as one early arriving settler in the Blue Mountains of northeast Oregon remarked of the pine forests there, "I do not know as I was ever so much affected with any scenery in my life."[8]

Forest fire played a similar role in sustaining the wonderful giant sequoia forests of the western range of the Sierra Nevada in California.

Historically, frequent low-intensity fires swept through these forests every four to thirteen years, killing much of the understory of white fir, sugarpine, incense cedar, and other "mixed conifers," but leaving the large sequoia unharmed. Studies of five giant sequoia groves, going back three millennia, revealed 3,200 fire scars and evidence of an additional 2,400 fire dates. Native American burning in the Sierra Nevadas for agricultural and basket making purposes played an important role in sustaining this frequent occurrence of fire. However, in the twentieth century a regime of fire suppression has led to a sharp reduction in the high-frequency but low-intensity fires and instead allowed an increase in the lower frequency but much more intense fires—fires that are often "stand replacing crown fires" and thus pose a new threat to the giant sequoia as well.[9]

In the past, shade-intolerant species such as sequoia also depended on localized intense forest fire to open clear areas where regeneration of new trees could occur. Partly because such fires are now largely suppressed, foresters have been finding that Sierra Nevada forests are experiencing "decreased or absent giant sequoia recruitment." As the National Park Service gradually came to a recognition of the harmful consequences of its own past fire suppression efforts, it ended the policy of suppression in Sequoia and Kings Canyon National Parks in 1968, and for Yosemite National Park in 1972, and instituted instead a program of prescribed burning (the Forest Service did not follow suit in its nearby sequoia forests until the 1990s). Yet, the new policies have merely slowed the decline of these forests; the effects of a century of National Park Service and Forest Service fire and other policies have left a continuing major "problem of giant sequoia regeneration" today, and a current "unsustainable" condition of these forests.[10]

Lodgepole pine, another important species found throughout much of the inland West, has also been significantly affected by fire, but in a different way from the ponderosa pine and sequoia forests.[11] As a shade-intolerant species, lodgepole pine historically depended on more intense fire to open up new areas where brand-new lodgepole pine forests could spring up. In some cases, where a fire had burned over wide areas, a large stand of even-aged lodgepole pine would result. In other cases, where fires were smaller and had created patches of open forest at different times, the lodgepole pine forest would be uneven-aged. In the absence of fire, firs and other shade-tolerate species would invade the lodgepole forest and eventually displace it. Indeed, as policies of fire suppression have been pursued in the West, there has been a considerable expansion of such shade-tolerant species, relative to shade-intolerant species such as lodgepole pine and aspen.

Today, partly as a result of a century of fire suppression, by some estimates stands of aspen have been reduced by more than 50 percent of their former range throughout the forests of Colorado, Idaho, Utah, and other states of the inland West. Aspens typically depend on fire to remove the existing forest vegetation and to open the ground for the development of new aspen stands. Stated another way, aspen is a "disturbance" species, which thrives in disequilibrium circumstances and fares poorly as a forest moves toward a "climax state." Without fire, as other more shade-tolerant trees gradually move into an area, the aspens will eventually lose out.

At higher elevations, the suppression of forest fire has had a significant impact, but not to the same degree as in most lower and mid-elevation forests. In the Sierra Nevada, for example, high-elevation forests of red fir typically experienced fire regimes that were "far less intense" than the mixed conifer and other forests lower down. Fire suppression has led to some increases in the density of the Sierra Nevada red fir forests but, on the whole, suppression measures "are thought to have had less effect . . . both because suppression activities began later (1920s to 1930s) . . . and because fewer fires would have burned there without suppression anyway."[12] With the trees less valuable for wood and many fewer second homes and other structures located at the higher elevations, and with the costs of fire suppression often higher in remote and difficult mountain terrain, the Forest Service has also been under less pressure to act as rapidly to put out fires at high elevations.

Yet, on broad areas of forests across the West, smaller trees and shrubs that formerly had been kept down by frequent fire now survive and grew prolifically. In one study of the Cococino National Forest in Arizona, two researchers estimated that the number of trees had increased from 23 per acre in presettlement times to a present level of 851 trees per acre. In the Kaibab National Forest in Arizona, the increase was from 56 trees per acre many years ago to 276 at present.[13] In southwestern Montana, Douglas firs have encroached into areas that formerly had been grasslands, because frequent past rangeland fires that would have burned the Douglas firs instead are now suppressed.[14]

In one Research Natural Area on the Boise National Forest, forest fire had been entirely suppressed since 1911, as part of a scientific experiment. Due to this long-standing suppression effort, the density of Douglas firs in this study area had now reached three times the expected number of trees that had been found under forest fire patterns as they had historically been experienced. The thinner, shorter, and tightly packed firs now posed a major fire hazard, not only because of the much increased volume and density of wood but also because the fierce competition for survival had left most of the trees in a weakened condition. Indeed, fully 60 percent of the Douglas firs at this scientific research site were now dead.

Jay O'Laughlin comments that it is not possible "to overemphasize the role of wildfire in creating and maintaining forests in Idaho."[15] On the Panhandle National Forest in Idaho, the absence of fire has led to a displacement of the historically prominent western larch by other species of trees on 69 percent of the former larch acreage.[16] Throughout Idaho, many decades of prior Forest Service policies, suppressing historic patterns of fire, have meant that "Idaho's national forests are in decline." Throughout much of the state, they are filled with "dense stands" that pose a major risk of "catastrophic wildfire."[17] The damage to Idaho would be both economic and environmental, including loss of wildlife habitat, declines in water quality, and the straining of public treasuries to pay for emergency fire control measures.

Not all the forests in Idaho have these problems. Indeed, they are largely confined to the national forest system. O'Laughlin observes that Idaho national forests have 33 percent greater wood volume per acre than state and private forests. The state and private forests have in general been more intensively managed, involving higher timber harvest levels per acre and greater application of labor and capital for thinning, disease control, reforestation, and other purposes. Yet, contrary to a common public impression, the more intensively managed state and private forests "appear to be healthier than [the] unmanaged forests," mostly in the national forest system. Paradoxical as it may seem, "intensive care" may be necessary not only to reduce fire hazards but also to bring Idaho national forests back to the conditions that prevailed a century and more ago—before Forest Service fire suppression drastically altered the workings of the natural forest environment.[18]

The total land area of the national forest system is 192 million acres; excluding wilderness areas, there are 152 million acres. The Forest Service estimates that 57 million of these acres involve ecological systems where periodic fire should be a normal part of the ecosystem workings. However, at present an estimated 39 million acres contain excess fuels buildups or other problems that make their current forest condition unsustainable.[19]

TINDER BOX FORESTS

Such forests in the typical case have become economically less productive, subject to disease and insect infestation, aesthetically unattractive, and ironically now also prone to new and much greater fire hazards. The severe fire seasons of 1994 and 1996—coming after the Yellowstone and other large fires across the West in 1988—were no accident. They were partly a result of a century of federal fire policy that has sought to eliminate fire from the western landscape but instead has merely changed its time and place. In 1994, more than 500,000 acres in the national forests of Idaho burned. At this rate, and recognizing that 1994 was a bad fire season throughout the West, it would take only forty years to burn over the entire national forest system of Idaho.

Figure 1-1 shows the overall trend of forest fire on the national forest system over the course of the twentieth century. Fire suppression was having a major effect by the 1920s. In 1926, the Forest Service introduced a policy goal that all forest fires should be controlled to be kept below 10 acres in size. In 1935 the Forest Service adopted its "10:00 A.M. policy," setting an agency-wide target that every reported forest fire should be controlled by 10:00 A.M. of the next day. All these efforts succeeded in sharply reducing the number of acres burned on the national forests each year. After World War II, the Forest Service escalated its fire suppression efforts, including the Smokey Bear campaign.[20] The low point in terms of national forest acreage burned was reached by the mid-1960s and stayed at that level through the mid-1980s. Since then, the number of national forest acres burned each year has climbed rapidly upward, reaching levels not seen since the 1920s.

Figure 1-1   Number of National Forest Acres Burned by Fire, Fiscal Years 1910–97

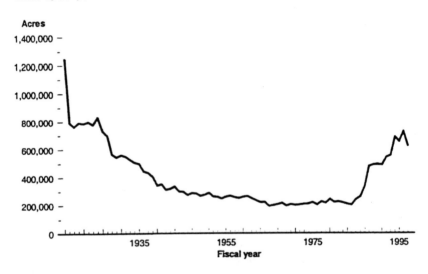

Note: The number of acres represents the ten-year rolling average at each point. Since 1990, 90 percent of national forest acres burned by fire were in the interior West.

Source: General Accounting Office, Western National Forests: Catastrophic Wildfires Threaten Resources and Communities. GAO-RCED-99-79 (September 28, 1998), p. 18.

Like failing to balance the budget, the suppression of fire in the past did not mean that the threat of fire was eliminated but instead it could be deferred into the future (and to the watch of some later politician). One might say that federal fire policies have been "unsustainable." And when the fire debt eventually is fully repaid, as with money debt, the repayment will likely come with interest. Indeed, Pyne labels federal fire policies in the interior West as "the environmental equivalent of the S&L scandal."[21]

DESTRUCTIVE FIRES

Following the widespread forest fires of 1994 and 1996, the many more such fires expected in the future will be more intense, more difficult to control, and more ecologically harmful than the forest fires of the past. That is partly because if a fire breaks out now, existing forests are like torches waiting to be lit. The new dense stands of thinner trees burn rapidly and with greater heat than the more frequent but lower intensity ground fires of earlier times. Also, fire often breaks out now in trees either weakened, dying, or dead, and thus all the more flammable. The intense competition for survival among large numbers of small trees leaves them exposed to insects, microbes, and other agents of disease.

In the dense forests of the West resulting from a century of fire suppression, advancing fires can now often reach up into the lower branches, and from them spread to the "crown" of the ponderosa pines and other large old trees. Thus, instead of leaving the larger trees undamaged, as in the forest fires of the past, the entire forest is today more likely to burn, and sometimes at intensities and temperatures previously unknown to these areas. Indeed, the temperatures can be so hot that—rather than replenishing the soil, as fires historically did—they now may destroy the biotic community altogether or fuse the soil, leaving an ugly and sterilized forest environment in which any regeneration will be much delayed. As one ecologist warns, "the trend of increasing intensity of fires may have adverse consequences on soil nutrients" because it can "volatilize large amounts of nitrogen and other volatile nutrients, disrupt soil structure, and induce water repellency and erosion."[22]

The high-intensity fires are less frequent, but when they do occur, they are likely to burn the entire forest. In the Upper Columbia River Basin (including lands in parts of Idaho, Montana, Nevada, Utah, and Wyoming), 58 percent of the acres burned on Forest Service and Bureau of Land Management lands now involve "stand-replacing" fires in which the entire forest goes up in flames. Historically, before the current fuels buildups in these forests, only 19 percent of total acres burned involved such high-intensity fires. On the other hand, historically more frequent "low-severity fires" used to cover 31 percent of the forest acreage burned, but this figure today has declined to 11 percent.[23]

Some species such as the lodgepole pine and the giant sequoia depend on fire even to regenerate; the cones of these species lie dormant on the forest floor until the seeds can be released by the heat of a forest fire. With the introduction of policies to suppress fire, however, a new Darwinian process of natural selection has been created, more favorable initially to species formerly selected out by fire, which have proliferated in many areas. Yet the condition of these forests is often unhealthy, suggesting that they will be temporary as well. As the outcome of the new evolutionary process was described in one recent report:

> There are twenty times as many trees crowded onto sites as there were less than 100 years ago. Idaho's Boise National Forest is a good example. A survey conducted in 1906 found there were twenty-eight Douglas-fir trees per acre, and another six western white pines. Today, there are 533 Douglas-fir crowded onto each acre, and another 155 pines. Shouldered together in tight quarters, these trees have little chance of survival. When the dying is done the dead fall across one another like giant pick-up sticks. In some places, the piles are knee deep.[24]

Fully 98 percent of forest fires today are rapidly and effectively controlled under current policies. However, if a fire is not quickly controlled today in the fire-prone forests of the West, there may be no stopping it—especially in periods of drought and wind when the fire hazard in a dry forest escalates. Indeed, the 2 percent of fires that are not successfully controlled account for 94 percent of burned acres and 60 percent of forest–fire-fighting expenditures. The very large fires in the West today, even larger than they used to be, are the ones that do the real damage to homes and other property. They are the ones that endanger the lives of firefighters and frighten the public, creating virtually irresistible political pressures for massive government expenditures for (often ineffective) emergency fire suppression.

BURNING DOLLARS

As forest fires were fewer, and as the Forest Service began to recognize that much of its previous fire suppression efforts had been counterproductive, fire expenditures were generally declining from the mid-1970s to the mid-1980s. However, since the mid-1980s, as large fires have become more intense and destructive, and as acreage burned has increased, Forest Service expenditures for fire protection and fire fighting have climbed rapidly. As shown in table 1-1, as compared with $226 million for emergency fire suppression in 1985, that number would seem small in the 1990s. The Forest Service devoted a record $762 million in 1994 to emergency fire suppression. Combined Forest Service spending on fire for all purposes in 1994 equaled about one-third of the agency's total budget.[25] With Interior Department (DOI) and other federal spending added in, total federal forest fire emergency expenditures reached $925 million in 1994. Large state and local spending occurred on top of that. Including also routine presuppression and other fire protection expenditures budgeted in advance, total federal spending on forest fire management in 1994 was well in excess of $1 billion. In addition to the large financial costs, a total of thirty-four firefighter lives were lost in that year.

Table 1-1. Forest Service Fire Protection and Fire-fighting Expenditures (1994 Dollars in Millions), Fiscal Years 1970–94 by Major Class of Expenditure

Fiscal year	Protecting forest fires (presuppression)	Fighting forest fires (suppression)	Total
1970	120.6	105.1	225.7
1971	120.9	297.9	418.8
1972	112.7	211.8	324.5
1973	110.1	201.0	311.1
1974	114.2	331.2	445.4
1975	142.3	312.7	455.0
1976	113.2	378.4	491.6
1977	333.7	238.9	572.6
1978	309.9	66.9	376.8
1979	260.9	169.3	430.2
1980	291.5	125.2	416.7
1981	284.9	174.8	459.7
1982	219.1	45.7	264.8
1983	227.8	52.0	279.8
1984	222.5	93.4	315.9
1985	215.0	226.4	441.4
1986	199.2	152.1	351.3
1987	200.9	334.1	535.0
1988	202.7	547.4	750.1
1989	188.4	402.1	590.5
1990	201.0	288.4	489.4
1991	197.9	147.7	345.6
1992	199.5	307.7	507.2
1993	194.8	185.7	380.5
1994	188.6	762.5	951.1

Source: U.S. Forest Service, *Fire Economics Assessment Report* (September 1, 1995), p. 6.

When forest fires again raged across the West in 1996, this time they covered 6.1 million acres, compared with 4.7 million acres in 1994. The federal government now was forced to spend $721 million, and state governments to spend another $325 million for emergency suppression purposes. Forest Service fire management absorbed $835 million in all, or about a quarter of the total national forest system spending for all purposes in 1996.[26] As seen in figure 1-2, this high 1996 federal spending for forest fire emergency suppression represented a continuation of a strong trend apparent since the mid-1980s.

Timber harvests have been falling rapidly over the same period as the trend of expenditures for fire fighting has been moving rapidly upward. In 1989 the harvest of timber on the national forests was 12 billion board feet, about 20 percent of the U.S. softwood timber supply. By 1994, the national forest timber harvest was only 5 billion board feet. In 1994 the total costs of fire fighting exceeded the total revenues from the timber harvested by about 10 percent. Under current trends, that gap will only grow. In 1996, another bad fire season, total spending for forest fires exceeded total timber revenues by $202 million.

Figure 1-2.   Forest Service's Expenditures for Wildfire Suppression, Fiscal Years 1986–94

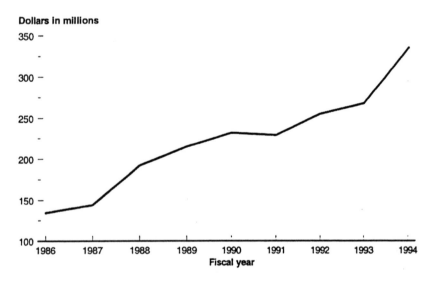

Note: The expenditures for each year represent the ten year rolling average in constant 1994 dollars. Since 1990, 95 percent of these expenditures have been in the interior West.

Source: General Accounting Office, *Western National Forests: Catastrophic Wildfires Threaten Resources and Communities.* GAO-RCED-99-79 (September 28, 1998), p. 22.

These developments point toward a new economics of timber policy and management for the Forest Service. The fire-fighting activities of the Forest Service could be justified economically in the past as necessary to protect the commercially valuable timber stored on the national forests. For many years revenues from timber sales in fact substantially exceeded the costs of fire fighting. However, this is no longer the case. If saving the timber for harvest is no longer a top priority, new justifications for spending hundreds of millions of dollars per year on forest fire control will be necessary.

Protection of human life and property will of course always be important. The greater intensity of fires in the current conditions of western national forests, and the greater ecological damage caused, are partial explanations for the rise in fire spending. However, another important factor is the spread of human populations and housing development into forested areas. By some Forest Service estimates, as much as 60 to 70 percent of current agency expenditures for fire fighting is devoted to protecting lives and physical structures in the "wildland/urban interface."[27] With many western forests having reached an incendiary condition, and with populations having moved outward into forested areas surrounding many urban areas of the West, large fires often pose significant risks to human well-being. To be sure, in many cases the Forest Service levels of spending for fire protection are economically questionable; much more is often spent to protect a piece of private property than the market value of this property.

RETHINKING FIRE POLICY

Serious questions were first raised concerning federal fire policies in the 1960s and 1970s among a circle of ecologists and fire experts. In part, this resulted from the creation of the national wilderness system, following the enactment of the Wilderness Act in 1964. Management of newly established wilderness areas posed fire policy conundrums that were difficult to answer within the existing fire-fighting paradigm.

Under the existing fire policy in place when the Wilderness Act passed, the Forest Service tried to put out any fire, anywhere in the national forest system, including a wilderness area. However, this was clearly at odds with the basic concept of wilderness, which meant letting nature run its course free of human interference. However, fire cannot be easily contained in any one area, so letting wilderness fires burn free ran a large risk of having a forest fire get out of control and also burn over large areas of adjacent nonwilderness.

Moreover, the goal of "nature," on close inspection, proves difficult to pin down in wilderness (and other) areas. The character of many wilderness areas prior to European settlement was actually shaped by Indian manipulation of fire. Thus, in one interpretation a "natural" wilderness might be one that had never before existed at any time in history. It might be suggested that natural is pre–Native American as well as pre-European, but to go back at least 10,000 years, before Indians arrived in the Americas, would be to move close to the Ice Age and an altogether different set of climatic and other environmental circumstances than the present. Besides Indian fire, the forests in existing wilderness areas had often been extensively manipulated by the Forest Service itself, prior to wilderness designation. Hence, letting natural fires now burn again would often achieve a result never seen before in history.

Despite such problems of determining an appropriate fire policy for wilderness areas, the Forest Service in 1971 did modify its policies. It now allowed fires set by lightning to continue to burn in wilderness areas. In 1985, the Forest Service went further to allow the deliberate human setting of fires in wilderness areas under controlled conditions. Since the mid-1960s, the National Park Service had already come to regard fire in the national parks as a natural and acceptable—perhaps desirable—occurrence (a policy that had to be reassessed and in part rescinded following the massive Yellowstone fires of 1988).[28]

Then, in the 1990s, fire policy became a central element in the broader debate over the future management of the national forests (the Bureau of Land Management in the Interior Department also manages valuable federal forests in Oregon and northern California). This greater attention has reflected in part the new emphasis being placed on ecological management and the recognition that fire policy can play a critical role in shaping the character of many forest ecologies.[29] It has also reflected a concern over the rapidly rising costs for fire suppression and the growing incidence of large, destructive fires in the West. Still, while these matters have been increasingly discussed in the forest policy community, the broader public, for the most part, has remained unaware of these developments. Many Americans still hold to the Smokey Bear attitudes so effectively promoted for many decades by the Forest Service—that forest fire is an evil, a waste of good resources as well as a hazard to human life and property, to be defeated at all costs as part of the scientific advance of progress in the world.[30]

THE NEW CONSENSUS

If thus far with only modest success, in the mid-1990s a number of leaders in the American forestry profession commenced an active campaign to change public attitudes. The difficulty of the task is all the greater because those now telling the members of the public that they must fundamentally rethink forest fire come from the very same professional groups that—it must be admitted—spread much of the bad information in the past. But whatever the awkwardness in this regard, a host of professional forestry panels and commissions in the past few years have sought to make up for the mistakes of earlier years. Expert study after expert study has explained how the federal fire policies of this century have now reached an economic and environmental dead end.[31]

Neil Sampson, until recently executive director of American Forests, one of the oldest and most respected organizations giving voice to the views of the American forestry profession, has been a particularly influential voice in directing professional attention to conditions on western forests. Sampson helped to bring together a group of thirty-five leading public and private foresters in 1993 to examine the condition of the forests of the inland West. The group's report found that matters had often reached a crisis state:

> In many forested areas of the inland western United States, trees across wide landscapes are dying faster than they are growing or being replaced. In other areas, conditions exist that virtually guarantee an onset of serious forest health problems, which may lead to large wildfires, reburning, erosion, and loss of habitat and property. In those areas, it is not just trees and their values that are at risk. Where terrestrial ecosystems are adversely impacted, the entire range of aquatic resources, wildlife and other values are affected as well.

> The forests at greatest risk are composed of an unsustainable combination of tree species, densities, and age structures that are susceptible to the fire and drought regimes common to the region. Although the situation differs significantly from place to place, the forest areas under the most stress contain too many trees, or too many of the wrong kind of trees, to continue to thrive. As the trees get older and larger, the competition intensifies, stress increases, and the likelihood of catastrophic change goes up accordingly.

> Wildfires in these ecosystems have gone from a high-frequency, low-intensity regime which sustained the system, to numerous high-intensity fires that require costly suppression attempts, which often prove futile in the face of overpowering fire intensity. High fuel loads resulting from the long-time absence of fire, and the abundance of dead and dying trees, result in fire intensities that cause enormous damage to soils, watersheds, fisheries, and other ecosystem components.[32]

In 1994 the National Commission on Wildfire Disasters, chaired by Sampson, spread this message to a wider public. The commission declared that "millions of acres of forest in the western United States pose an extreme fire hazard from the extensive build-up of dry, highly flammable forest fuels." In many forests, for example, shade-tolerant tree species such as firs—which formerly were contained by periodic fires—now crowd around the larger and older trees of the forest. In such circumstances, "every fire ignition, unless suppressed immediately, has a very high chance of climbing into the tree crowns on the readily-available dry fuels." Such fires tend to "become so hot and fast-moving that control by human means is impossible and only large breaks in the type of forest/fuel condition or the arrival of cooler, wetter weather will stop it." The overall result is that we now face a greatly expanded danger in the forests of the West of "large, intense, unmanageable, and highly destructive [fire] events."[33]

Existing federal fire policies, the commission reported, were having negative impacts on timber supplies, watershed conditions, wildlife habitat, air quality (from the smoke of large fires), and the protection of homes and other physical property located in forest areas. These policies were also harmful to the basic ecological functioning of the forest. "As we learn more about ecosystems and their essential components, we realize that wildland fires are one of the natural processes that may be essential to the maintenance of a healthy ecosystem." Forest managers therefore faced a challenge of "determining how to manage fire at an acceptable scale and intensity, given today's conditions and demands."[34]

Two main options for limiting future damage from large fires were identified. Excessive fuels buildup might be removed by prescribed burning—allowing certain natural fires to continue to burn and deliberately setting other fires in appropriate times and places. However, in many cases the commission recognized that fire would be "too risky to be used as a management tool."[35] Fires allowed to burn anywhere near urban areas might, for example, pose a large risk of destroying valuable homes and other properties, if they got out of control. In other places a forest fire might create unacceptable air pollution; it might become a "crown" fire, destroying the entire forest; or it might burn at too high a temperature and thus do major ecological damage to the soils and other forest components.

Hence, if any action were to be taken at all, it might have to be something other than prescribed burning. The main alternative would be mechanical removal of unwanted trees and shrubs. Commercial thinning and other forms of timber harvesting might have to serve, at least in the first round of removal of excess trees and other vegetation from western forests, as a modern substitute for the historic workings of fire. If the timber is worth anything economically (in some cases it is not), the value of the timber can also help to cover the costs of excess fuels removal. It might help to justify taking removal actions in the eyes of skeptical budget examiners.

Yet another influential 1995 report by Sampson (together with Lance Clark) indicated that it was on the national forests and other federal forests where the greatest problems existed and that private industry forests were in better shape. As they stated, "the majority of forest health problems in the region exist on the public lands. Most privately held forests in the Inland West are owned by timber companies that intensively manage their lands. Managed forests are not the same as the pre-European forests, but that [timber industry] management generally meant some sort of stocking control, avoiding the fuel buildup from fire exclusion that has become such a hazard on federal forests."[36]

SHIFTING GOVERNMENT POLICY

By 1994, the need for major changes in fire policy had become a top concern of Forest Service leadership. As it moved to reverse an agency policy direction that dated all the way back to 1910, the Forest Service now publicly acknowledged in a number of documents that its past fire suppression had had many harmful consequences. A 1995 Forest Service publication, *Course to the Future: Repositioning Fire and Aviation Management,* stated that "we need to make a course correction." The central problem was that "paradoxically, if we remain on a course of fire exclusion—it will directly conflict with our ecosystem goals." As a result of past policies, "the potential for large, catastrophic wildfires continues to increase." Basic changes in fire policy were also needed to "improve our firefighter safety" and at the same time to "increase our cost efficiencies."[37]

The Draft 1995 RPA Program of the Forest Service now recognized that in the current condition of the national forests, large fires could have "catastrophic" consequences for forest ecologies, including "devastating effects on soil, water, and air."[38] Yet, the Forest Service recognized that a new policy to integrate fire into normal forest management operations would be difficult because "the public's expectation for wildfire protection is growing." This reflected the growth of recreational and other demands for the use of public forests, along with the continuing movement of homes and other buildings into forest environments. As the Forest Service commented, even while strong public pressures were demanding greater ecological sensitivity in its management practices, there was "little public understanding—or tolerance—for the [fire-based] ecological processes necessary for the health and sustainability of forests over the long term."[39]

The emerging new consensus on the harmful effects of past fire suppression received an official blessing at the highest levels in 1995 when the Secretary of Agriculture and the Secretary of the Interior jointly released a report on Federal Wildland Fire Management. The report reiterated the conclusions of previous studies, describing a "growing recognition that past land-use practices, combined with the effects of fire exclusion, can result in heavy accumulations of dead vegetation, altered fuel arrangement, and changes in vegetative structure and composition." Such circumstances posed the risk of "more rapid, extensive ecological changes beyond any we have experienced in the past," partly because, paradoxically in light of past federal efforts to eliminate fire, "today's fires tend to be larger and more severe." In short, the effects of "one hundred years of fire suppression" had left "millions of acres of forests and rangelands at extremely high risk for devastating fires to occur."[40]

Indeed, as a result of the buildup of "hazardous fuel accumulations," the report found that "many areas are in need of immediate treatment of both live and dead vegetation to prevent large-scale, high intensity fires and to maintain their sustainability as healthy ecosystems." The necessary treatments could "be achieved by mechanical, chemical, biological, and manual methods, including the use of fire."[41]

In April 1997 a panel of leading professional foresters, convened at the request of Representative Charles Taylor of North Carolina, presented its final report at a congressional hearing. The panel clarified that forest health problems were not limited to the interior West (lands east of the summits of the Cascade and Sierra Nevada mountains) but were also serious—if somewhat different in character—in the much wetter forests on the western slopes of these mountains and the coastal ranges near the Pacific Ocean.

> Federal lands and National Parks on the Pacific Coast from California to Washington also contain buildups of fuel caused by protection from ground fires and by windstorms. Fires in the Pacific Northwest occur less frequently than in the Inland West, but can be even more catastrophic because of the high fuel volumes (dead trees). The limited road system and infrastructure make federal lands in this region especially susceptible to catastrophic fires. The trend is toward increasing fires in [both] the Inland West and Pacific Coast.[42]

UNSCIENTIFIC FORESTRY

Historically, fire policy in the Forest Service has always closely reflected broader currents of thinking concerning the role of professional forestry in land management. Indeed, in the progressive era at the beginning of the twentieth century, Forest Service fire policy took shape as part of the agency's grand design for the "scientific management" of the national forests. Although in many ways outmoded, the ideas of scientific management still serve in important ways to give legitimacy to the activities of the Forest Service and to define the culture and ethos of the agency.[43]

The conservation movement of early in this century has been described by Samuel Hays as being grounded in a "gospel of efficiency."[44] What could be less efficient, it seemed to the early members of the Forest Service, than to let valuable timber burn in large amounts, a result of the spread of forest fires that were preventable? Following the devastating fires of 1910, when around 5 million acres of national forests burned, including 3 million in Idaho and Montana alone, the course of Forest Service policy was set for most of the rest of the century. In *The Training of a Forester*, Gifford Pinchot would write in 1917 that "the work of a Forest Ranger is, first of all, to protect the District committed to his charge against fire. That comes before all else."[45]

The main subjects of historical writing once were kings, merchants, and a few other leading figures of wealth and power in their time. Later, reflecting the spread of egalitarian values, historians would devote much more attention to the lives of ordinary people. In recent years, pioneered by William Cronon's *Changes in the Land,* yet another perspective on history has emerged—environmental history, or the story of the environment past of an area. A recent example of this new genre of historical writing is *Forest Dreams, Forest Nightmares*, by the ecologist Nancy Langston, examining the environmental history of the Blue Mountains of northeast Oregon and southeast Washington.

The "dream" of Langston's title is the scientific management of the national forests to maximize the benefits to the multiple users of the nation; the "nightmare" is the actual result in the Blue Mountains (and, Langston suggests, many other forest areas of the West). At the end of the nineteenth century the Blue Mountain area was a "land of lovely open forests full of yellow-bellied ponderosa pines five feet across." By the end of the twentieth century, "in their place were thickets of fir trees" that served as the "favored food for numerous pests." Indeed, on the 5.5 million acres of national forests in the Blue Mountains, half were under insect attack, in some stands affecting nearly 70 percent of the trees. The result was not only ugly in a visual way but posed a major threat of "infernos" that would kill entire stands of trees and do far-ranging environmental damage. Indeed, in many other areas as well, "the inland West has witnessed a massive set of errors, tragedies, and follies."[46]

How had this modern environmental nightmare come about? Langston in her research found that "in an unusual admission of guilt and confusion, the Forest Service stated that this crisis was caused by its own forest management practices." The problem traced back to earlier "American visions of the proper human relationship to nature."[47] As Langston writes:

> Landscape changes were the result of human attempts to manage, perfect, and simplify the forests: to transform what one forester called in 1915 "the general riot of natural forest" . . . into a regulated, productive, sustained-yield forest. . . . It is a story about the complex metaphors people use to mediate their relationship to nature—and the ways those metaphors have led to millions of acres of dying trees.[48]

The thinking of scientific management in the early twentieth century suggested that the powers of scientific knowledge had given human beings the power to put nature to human use for whatever purposes might be selected. The goal would be selected to maximize net human benefits ("the greatest good of the greatest number in the long run," as Pinchot once had famously said), and then science would reveal how to achieve this goal in the most efficient manner possible. On the national forests, however, all this turned out to be illusion. In the end, as Langston writes, the great irony was that "in trying to make the land green and productive, they ended up making it sterile," setting into "motion exactly the forces they were trying to guard against." It was "a tragedy in which decent people with the best of intentions destroyed what they cared for most."[49]

Such a history was perhaps on his mind when Jack Ward Thomas, then chief of the Forest Service, said in a 1995 speech that the agency had learned from painful experience that "the responses to management action are not as predictable or as reliable as once thought." Indeed, the reality is that "ecological processes are too complex to ever be fully understood."[50] Forest management strategies that assumed otherwise, as was characteristic of the plans derived in the twentieth century through the application of scientific management, are likely to prove fatally flawed. However, for many decades the Forest Service believed otherwise.

Failing to understand the fragility of its own methods, the Forest Service plowed ahead as though it were actually possible to manage and control nature through scientific processes. Operating under such a grand illusion, it should not be surprising that the real world outcomes were often most unhappy. The Forest Service disdained other less formal and abstract means of obtaining knowledge as backward and outmoded ("premodern"). Greater acceptance of these forms of knowledge would also have challenged the basic legitmacy of the centralization of power that the Forest Service sought.

Applied in the specific area of forest fire policy, as Stephen Pyne writes, this meant that:

> Against folk wisdom, [professional foresters] proposed science; against laissez-faire folk practices, they argued for systematic regulation of burning that would support, not confront, professional forestry; against the self-evident waste of fire—not only what it directly destroyed but those benevolent "forest influences" that it indirectly laid to waste—they conjured up a vision of conservation, the rational, industrially efficient exploitation of natural resources. . . . Fire fighting was the pragmatic merger of idealism with reality by means of applied science.[51]

At the end of the twentieth century, to be sure, the old claims to scientific management are no longer persuasive. Langston comments that, lacking another source of legitimacy and authority, we now find an "increasing chaos of federal land management—fires, lawsuits, insect epidemics and the collapse of faith in government policies." If scientific management implied that there would be one correct answer to most forest management questions, Langston argues that perhaps we should "focus more on the specific places—a task that would mean giving up our absolute ideas, and allowing for variability and uncertainty." The attempts in the past to find guidance in "efficiency and productivity" for the national forests have proven "very poor guides for management."[52]

Newer attempts to recast scientific management, such as the pursuit of biodiversity, may also be problematic, Langston says, because "science is never impartial; conservation biology cannot give us a set of laws to live by, much as we wish it could." On close examination, even "biodiversity means whatever ecologists want it to mean." In the end, perhaps the essential ingredient is "to be humble," because the record of the sorry history of the Blue Mountains shows that "everyone who has ever tried to fix the forests has ended up making them worse."[53]

THE FEDERAL MONEY TREE

In 1995, following the expenditure by federal agencies of almost $1 billion in the 1994 fire season for emergency suppression purposes, Forest Service Chief Jack Ward Thomas sent a message to his troops that "we must dispel the myth that emergency fire costs are 'free.' This is a completely unacceptable attitude—especially in terms of its tremendous impacts on taxpayers and to other Forest Service programs."[54] Chief Thomas elaborated in a 1995 speech at the University of Montana on the perverse incentives facing federal fire prevention efforts:

> It is essential to begin a process of producing situations in managed forests wherein fire can play an appropriate role. This will require not only a shift in management policy but a shift in focus and in funding priorities. It is well past time to face up to the costs of fire management. "Funding games" with the federal land agency budgets should cease. These games make it appear that budgets for fire management are much lower than is actually the case. Fire management is funded at too low a level to make proactive, effective management possible. And, then, agencies are afforded an "open check-book" to fight fires of adequate size and intensity to provide adequate political impact. Such an approach is misleading both in terms of the actual budget allocated to fire management over the long term and in terms of making the best and most effective use of those funds.[55]

Thomas was alluding in part to the specific workings of the federal budget process for fire fighting. Each year funds for fire suppression are initially appropriated based on the average expenditure for the previous ten years—for example, for the years from 1986 to 1995 an average of $296 million per year. However, when appropriated funds are exhausted, as is sure to happen early in any bad fire season, the agency then turns to other sources. The fire-fighting Emergency Contingency Fund, which in 1996 had a balance of $100 million, can be used. When this fund is exhausted (which it was), moneys can be borrowed from various other Forest Service accounts such as the Knutson-Vandenberg (K-V) Fund. Moreover, there is an implicit understanding with the Congress that emergency fire-fighting money drawn from K-V or other such sources will later be replenished with supplementary appropriations. For example, the 1996 Forest Service budget approved by Congress included $420 million to pay back the K-V Fund for moneys withdrawn in earlier years in support of fire suppression. The net effect is to create a "blank check" for fire-fighting expenditures.

Forest Service spending for various fire protection and suppression purposes set a new record in 1988, equal to $750 million (in 1994 dollars). More than $500 million was spent in 1989 and 1992 on fire. Then, 1994 yielded another all-time record, $951 million in total fire spending, followed by another bad fire season and very high costs in 1996 (although less than 1994). Figure 1-2 above shows this trend of ever-rising costs in the budget of the Forest Service for forest fire emergency suppression. In the past ten years, the expected fire costs for the Forest Service in an average year have approximately doubled.

On the basis of the rising trend over the past twenty years, the Forest Service projects that on average its total fire expenditures will increase every year into the future by $19 million per year.[56] If that were to continue, billion dollar federal fire seasons might well become routine in the near future.

Since 1990, the Interior Department has worked from a combined fire budget for all of the DOI agencies with fire-fighting responsibilities—the Park Service, Bureau of Land Management, Fish and Wildlife Service, and Bureau of Indian Affairs. The fire accounts are handled in much the same way as the Forest Service. When initially appropriated funds for the year are used up, the DOI can continue spending as needed by drawing on other accounts. In 1994 and 1996, emergency fire efforts of the various Interior agencies involved total suppression costs of $167 million and $173 million, respectively. Combined with routinely budgeted fire protection and other fire management activities, the Interior total expenditures for forest fire typically exceed $300 million per year.

As with the Forest Service, in the heat of a fire emergency, the actual practice is that the money is spent and then the Interior Department figures out where it will come from. Thus, unlike a normal government program, there is no fixed budget for emergency fire suppression that cannot be exceeded without the approval of higher level executive authorities or the Congress. Many Forest Service and Interior employees are conscientious about economizing on fire spending but inevitably this will not be a universal attitude. As the Forest Service states, the reality is that "there is a powerful disincentive . . . to reduce spending," in part because "the line officer is not required to make up [emergency fire fighting] deficits from the unit's budget."[57]

The National Commission on Wildfire Disasters found that "if a wildfire breaks out, the agencies can adopt any strategies, spend any amount of money, and tolerate any kind of outcome (including, at times, some very bad outcomes), while retaining a high level of support from both Congress and the public. In general, that support recognizes that the agencies are doing their best against a commonly recognized enemy, and if they fail, they have still done what they could against insurmountable odds."[58] Criticizing high levels of emergency fire-fighting expenditures is like trying to criticize the amount of money supporting the troops in a time of war.

FIRE BOONDOGGLES

When "free" money is available, it is a normal human propensity to make use of it. Murray Taylor, a current federal firefighter and veteran of thirty years, commented recently that "a growing number of line officers, smokejumpers, hotshots, and other fire specialists are becoming increasingly disturbed, if not outright disgusted, by what they see as blatant overstaffing and wasteful spending on many of the large fires in the Lower 48." He observed that in 1988 "I came off of a fire I fought . . . in the Bitterroots just west of Hamilton, Montana. When we left it, it was twenty acres, had a small bulldozer on it, and could have been handled by two 20-person crews." Yet he found at the site 400 people and "what looked a lot like a government-sponsored jamboree. People running around in red plastic vests, rented Ryder trucks, generators, computers, a kitchen being set up."[59]

In other instances, Taylor saw "expensive helicopter modules being moved all over the country . . . by high-salaried management personnel." The government contracted for heavy lift helicopters at $28,000 per day, part of the reason why total Forest Service fire-fighting costs for such helicopters in 1994 were $58 million.[60] Yet, helicopters and other expensive equipment often sit idle for days at a time. Although a certain amount of down time is inevitable as insurance against the unpredictable outbreak of fire, Taylor was skeptical that much of this spending "is really buying us anything." If nothing was done to improve the situation, federal fire fighting would "descend further and further into a black hole of inefficiency, excessive waste, mediocrity, and declining morale."[61]

Jack Ward Thomas commented recently that, once a forest fire "reaches a large size, putting it out is a joke."[62] Or, as a 1995 Forest Service study commented:

> Conventional wisdom for fires that have escaped initial attack suggests that increases in expenditures tied to massive mobilizations lead to increases in suppression effectiveness. We suspect this is not true. The cost of suppressing these large fires is increasing, yet we do not see a corresponding decrease in acres burned. We are becoming more aware, especially in fire-adapted ecosystems, that we are operating past the point of diminishing returns during large fire suppression activities.[63]

Or, as the saying has it, the Forest Services rains dollars from the treasury on forest fires, and then waits for rain from the skies to put the fires out.

Federal fire fighting, as a product of the scientific management philosophy, reflects an outcome regrettably familiar to other government programs founded in similar thinking. Rather than the dictates of science, as in the original concept, it is actually ordinary politics that typically motivates government decision making. Rather than efficiency, it is the subsidization of various beneficiary groups that frequently becomes a driving force.

Today, the Forest Service spends hundreds of millions of dollars in many years to bail home and other property owners out of the threat of advancing fires. Yet many homeowners continue to build cabins and other structures in places where fire poses a large hazard and protection is difficult.

They often fail to undertake even the most minimal steps—such as cutting down trees near the house or using fireproof roofing and siding materials—to reduce the degree of fire risk. As noted above, a large portion of federal fire-fighting expenditures are now devoted to protecting physical structures, many of them in the urban-forest intermix.

The federal government today often finds itself spending $1 million (or potentially any amount—the legal obligation is almost whatever it will take) to protect, say, a $100,000 home. As the Forest Service reports, "the current perception by both the public and many fire suppression personnel is that the Forest Service will utilize whatever resources are available to prevent the loss of property without regard to its value, ownership or jurisdiction." In effect, "by assuming this responsibility and cost, the Forest Service is acting as a surrogate for the Federal Emergency Management Agency."[64]

Scientific management could never reconcile the tension between its technocratic ideals and the workings of American democracy. Inevitably, democracy won, with the result that efficiency and effectiveness lost out in government. In the case of the fire-fighting program of the Forest Service, the agency acknowledges that "large-fire decisions are usually driven by non-economic factors—such as political and social pressure."[65] As in the case of the many pork barrel water projects in the West, such programs not only waste money on a grand scale but also can inflict large environmental damages. As with fighting forest fires, free money often turns out in the end not to be so free.

Today, it is possible to spend nearly $1 billion on forest fire fighting in a single year, much of it wasted, because a politician can never afford to say no when voter lives and property are at stake in a forest fire. In Yellowstone in 1988, according to Stephen Pyne, the federal government spent more than $130 million in "nominal suppression," a heroic effort that did not have "any significant effect on the fires or improvement of the ecosystem."[66]

But there is more to it than that. An unspoken purpose of fire fighting is to create jobs and boost local economies in the West. The Forest Service contracts with many private groups for labor and equipment in a bad fire season. Inside the agency, fire-fighting money also helps to pay the salaries of Forest Service and other federal agency personnel at a time when money is scarce and these agencies have been facing major cutbacks. About 50 percent of Forest Service personnel are qualified for fire fighting, and more than half of these saw duty in the 1994 fire season. Fire fighting brings time-and-a-half pay, an important supplement for many employees. Beyond that, fire-fighting money in general helps to cover costs of administrative overhead of the Forest Service, helping to sustain higher total funding levels for the agency as a whole.

Many temporary people are also hired during a bad fire season. In 1994, seasonal or short-term employment by the Forest Service for fire-fighting duties amounted to work for 20,777 people. Another 38,872 were employed from the private sector as "casuals" on fire suppression activities.[67] Following the bad fire years of 1994 and 1996, the 1997 fire season was mild because of a wet summer. In Utah, fewer than 30,000 acres burned in 1997, compared with 470,000 in 1996. All this meant economic trouble for many people in the West. The Lolo National Forest in Montana spent less than $1 million on fire suppression in 1997, compared with $9.1 million in 1994. Indian tribes, with their high unemployment rates, have a ready supply of workers available for fire fighting on short notice. The *High Country News* reported that a slow fire season like 1997 "devastates Indian reservations."[68] Firefighters from the Blackfoot tribe in 1994 and 1996 took home $7 million and $3 million, respectively, but in 1997 there were 400 people still waiting for the phone to ring.

University of Montana economist Thomas Power comments that fire-fighting jobs "are some of the best-paying jobs in Montana. They are heavily sought after," not only by Indians but also by many others.[69] Besides paying good regular wages, the jobs offer large amounts of overtime at 50 percent additional pay and 25 percent more for hazard pay when actually fighting a fire. A smokejumper can make more than $15,000 in just a few months in an intense fire season. The economic benefits of fire fighting extend beyond jobs to service and equipment contracts throughout the West for food, lodging, dry cleaning, and many other items in high demand in a bad fire year.

In short, whatever harmful impacts fire fighting may have on local forest ecologies, whatever tendencies current suppression may have toward creating still greater fire hazards in the future, any significant change will have to address the fact that there are also significant economic incentives for important groups to maintain the forest fire status quo. The problem is compounded by the fact that some of the important economic beneficiaries are the very same people who are charged with making the resource allocation decisions with respect to fire-fighting strategy.

CONCLUSION

Fighting forest fire was for many years advertised by the Forest Service as a great advance in the scientific management of the national forests. Forestry professionals would put expert management techniques to work to suppress forest fire, bringing wild nature under human control and preserving the timber inventories of the forests for future human use.

It turns out, as the same forestry professionals now tell us, that all this effort was a great mistake. Suppressing forest fire has changed the ecological condition of the national forests for the worse. It has made the forests aesthetically less attractive. It has filled the forests with dense stands of low-quality trees. Finally, in the long run it has not even succeeded in reducing fire risks and the incidence of forest fire because increasingly these tinder box stands of trees are capable of breaking out into a fire inferno at any moment.

If a private firm made such large mistakes and failed so entirely to achieve its goals, the firm would go bankrupt, the management would be fired, and the remaining assets would be distributed through some reorganization plan. Perhaps the Forest Service today should be held to a similar standard of accountability.

NOTES

1. For a general bibliography of fire impacts on forests, see R. J. Matrogiuseppe, M. E. Alexander, and W. H. Romme, *Forest and Rangeland Fire History Bibliography* (Missoula, Mont.: U.S. Forest Service, Intermountain Forest and Ranger Experiment Station, November 1983).

2. Stephen W. Barrett, "Indians and Fire," *Western Wildlands* (Spring 1980); Stephen W. Barrett and Stephen F. Arno, "Indian Fires as an Ecological Influence in the Northern Rockies," *Journal of Forestry* (October 1982).

3. See Stephen J. Pyne, *Fire in America: A Cultural History of Wildland and Rural Fire* (Princeton: Princeton University Press, 1982), p. 71. See also Stephen J. Pyne, *World Fire: The Culture of Fire on Earth* (New York: Holt, 1995), pp. 183–218; and Stephen J. Pyne, *An Introduction to Wildland Fire: Fire Management in the United States* (New York: Wiley, 1984).

4. Kevin S. McKelvey et al., "An Overview of Fire in the Sierra Nevada," in *Status of the Sierra Nevada, Volume II: Assessments and Scientific Basis for Management Options*, Sierra Nevada Ecosystem Project, Final Report to Congress (Davis: University of California, Wildland Resources Center Report No. 37, July 1996), p. 1034.

5. Stephen F. Arno, "Forest Fire History in the Northern Rockies," *Journal of Forestry* (August 1980); Stephen W. Barrett, "Fire Suppression's Effects on Forest Succession within a Central Idaho Wilderness," *Western Journal of Applied Forestry* vol. 3, no. 3 (1988).

6. R. Steele, S. F. Arno, and K. Geier-Hayes, "Wildfire Patterns Change in Central Idaho's Ponderosa Pine–Douglas Fir Forest," *Western Journal of Applied Forestry* vol. 1, no. 1 (1986).

7. General Accounting Office, *Western National Forests: A Cohesive Strategy Is Needed to Address Catastrophic Wildfire Threats*, GAO/RCED-99-65 (April 1999), p. 24.

8. Nancy Langston, *Forest Dreams, Forest Nightmares: The Paradox of Old Growth in the Inland West* (Seattle: University of Washington Press, 1995), p. 21.

9. Deborah L. Elliot-Fisk et al., "Mediated Settlement Agreement for Sequoia National Forest, Section B. Giant Sequoia Groves: An Evaluation," in *Status of the Sierra Nevada, Addendum,* Sierra Nevada Ecosystem Project, Final Report to Congress (Davis: University of California, Wildland Resources Center Report No. 40, March 1997), p. 290.

10. Ibid., pp. 291–92.

11. James K. Brown, "Fire Cycles and Community Dynamics in Lodgepole Pine Forests," in *Management of Lodgepole Pine Ecosystems Symposium Proceedings,* ed. David M. Baumgartner (Pullman: Washington State University Cooperative Extension Service, 1975).

12. Chi-Ru Chang, "Ecosystem Responses to Fire and Variations in Fire Regimes," in *Status of the Sierra Nevada, Volume II,* p. 1088.

13. Study results given in R. Neil Sampson et al., *Assessing Forest Ecosystem Health in the Inland West* (Washington, D.C.: Forest Policy Center, American Forests, 1995), p. 7.

14. Stephen F. Arno and George E. Gruell, "Douglas-Fir Encroachment into Mountain Grasslands in Southwestern Montana," *Journal of Range Management* (May 1986). See also Stephen F. Arno and George E. Gruell, "Fire History at the Forest–Grassland Ecotone in Southwestern Montana," *Journal of Range Management* (May 1983).

15. Jay O'Laughlin, "Forest Ecosystem Health Assessment Issues: Definition, Measurement, and Management Implications," *Ecosystem Health* vol. 2, no. 1 (March 1996), p. 32. See also, Jay O'Laughlin et al., *Forest Health Conditions in Idaho,* Idaho Forest Wildlife and Range Policy Analysis Group, University of Idaho (Moscow, Idaho: December 1993).

16. General Accounting Office, *Western National Forests,* p. 24.

17. O'Laughlin, "Forest Ecosystem Health Assessment Issues," pp. 28, 29.

18. Ibid., pp. 28, 29.

19. Enoch Bell et al., *The Economics Assessment Report,* A Report Submitted to Fire and Aviation Management, U.S.D.A. Forest Service, September 1, 1995, p. 15.

20. Susan J. Husari and Kevin S. McKelvey, "Fire-Management Policies and Programs," in *Status of the Sierra Nevada, Volume II,* p. 1102.

21. Stephen J. Pyne, "Flame and Fortune," *Evergreen* (Winter 1994–1995), p. 7.

22. Chang, "Ecosystem Responses to Fire and Variations in Fire Regimes," p. 1078.

23. U.S. Forest Service and U.S. Bureau of Land Management, *Upper Columbia River Basin Draft Environmental Impact Statement, Volume 1,* Interior Columbia Basin Ecosystem Management Project (Boise, Idaho: May 1997), p. 2–20.

24. "A Season of Fire," *Evergreen* (Winter 1994–1995), p. 50.

25. U.S. Forest Service, *Course to the Future: Positioning Fire and Aviation Management* (Washington, D.C.: May 1995), p. 2.

26. U.S. Forest Service, Department of Agriculture, *Report of the Forest Service, Fiscal Year 1996* (Washington, D.C.: July 1997), p. 152.

27. The Forest Service reports that "Most knowledgeable people believe that the protection of private property consumed a disproportionate share of fire-fighting re-

sources—an estimated 60 percent of resources on all of the fires in 1994." See U.S. Forest Service, Department of Agriculture, *Fire Suppression Costs on Large Fires: A Review of the 1994 Fire Season* (Washington, D.C.: August 1, 1995), p. 13.

28. For one account of the Yellowstone fires, see Micah Morrison, *Fire in Paradise: The Yellowstone Fires and the Politics of Environmentalism* (New York: HarperCollins, 1993).

29. See Stephen F. Arno and James K. Brown, "Managing Fire in Our Forests: Time for a New Initiative," *Journal of Forestry* vol. 86 (1989), pp. 44–46; Stephen R. Arno and James K Brown, "Overcoming the Paradox in Managing Wildland Fire," *Western Wildlands* (Spring 1991).

30. There have been a number of popular articles emphasizing the ecological importance of forest fire. See, for example, Jim Motavalli, "The Forest Primeval: In the Pitched Battle Between Loggers and Environmentalists, A Timber Tinderbox Waits for a Match," *E Magazine* (September/October 1997); John G. Mitchell, "In the Line of Fire: Our National Forests," *National Geographic* (March 1997); Michael Parfit, "The Essential Elements of Fire," *National Geographic* (September 1996); Michael Paterniti, "Torched," *Outside* (September 1995); Tom Knudson, "How the West's Asbestos Forests Were Turned into Tinderboxes," *High Country News* (March 6, 1995), p. 8; William K. Stevens, "Fire Seen as Vital for Nature, Igniting Ecological Debate," *New York Times* (October 25, 1994), p. C1; and Jennifer Ackerman, "Carrying the Torch," *Nature Conservancy* (September/October 1993). However, given the long-standing view that fire is a menace, these articles have thus far had only a limited impact on public opinion.

31. See U.S. Department of Agriculture and U.S. Department of the Interior, *Final Report on Fire Management Policy* (Washington, D.C.: May 1989); National Association of State Foresters, *Fire Protection in Rural America: A Challenge for the Future*, A Report to the Congress and Other Policy Makers (Washington, D.C.: January 1994); *Report of the National Commission on Wildfire Disasters* (Washington, D.C.: 1994); U.S. Forest Service, *Western Forest Health Initiative Report* (Washington, D.C.: 1994); U.S. Forest Service, *Fire Management Strategic Assessment Report* (Washington, D.C.: 1994); U.S. Department of the Interior, U.S. Department of Agriculture, *Federal Wildland Fire Management: Policy and Program Review* (Washington, D.C.: December 18, 1995); and Forest Health Science Panel, *Report on Forest Health of the United States* (Washington, D.C.: April 4, 1997).

32. R. Neil Sampson et al., *Assessing Forest Ecosystem Health in the Inland West*, report of a workshop at Sun Valley, Idaho, November 14–19, 1993 (Washington, D.C.: Forest Policy Center, American Forests, n.d.), p. 5–7.

33. *Report of the National Commission on Wildfire Disasters* (Washington, D.C.: 1994), pp. 9–10.

34. Ibid., p. 11.

35. Ibid.

36. Lance R. Clark and R. Neil Sampson, *Forest Ecosystem Health in the Inland West: A Science and Policy Reader* (Washington, D.C.: Forest Policy Center, American Forests, 1995), p. 2.

37. See, for example, U.S. Forest Service, *Course to the Future*, p. 1.

38. U.S. Forest Service, Department of Agriculture, *The Forest Service Program for Forest and Rangeland Resources, A Long-Term Strategic Plan, Draft 1995 RPA Report* (Washington, D.C.: October 1995), p. III-3.

39. U.S. Forest Service, *Course to the Future*, p. 2.

40. Department of the Interior, Department of Agriculture, *Federal Wildland Fire Management*, pp. 7, 8, 17.

41. Ibid., p. 13.

42. Forest Health Science Panel, *Report on Forest Health of the United States*, A Panel Chartered by Charles Taylor, Member, United States Congress, 11th District, North Carolina (Washington, D.C.: April 4, 1997), Part 3, p. 6.

43. See Robert H. Nelson, "Mythology Instead of Analysis: The Story of Public Forest Management," in *Forestlands: Public and Private*, ed. Robert T. Deacon and M. Bruce Johnson (Cambridge, Mass.: Ballinger Publishing Co., 1985).

44. Samuel P. Hays, *Conservation and the Gospel of Efficiency: The Progressive Conservation Movement, 1890–1920* (Cambridge, Mass.: Harvard University Press, 1959).

45. Gifford Pinchot, *The Training of a Forester* (Philadelphia: J.B. Lippincott Co., 1917), p. 32.

46. Langston, *Forest Dreams, Forest Nightmares*, pp. 3, 10.

47. Ibid., pp. 4, 5.

48. Ibid., p. 5.

49. Ibid., pp. 5, 6, 7, 8, 10.

50. Jack Ward Thomas, "The Instability of Stability," speech delivered at the University of Montana, Missoula, Montana, October 16, 1995, pp. 5, 11.

51. Pyne, *World Fire*, p. 187.

52. Ibid., pp. 270, 280, 284.

53. Ibid., pp. 284, 285, 295.

54. U.S. Forest Service, *Course to the Future*, transmittal letter from the chief.

55. Thomas, "The Instability of Stability," p. 13.

56. U.S. Forest Service, Department of Agriculture, *Fire Suppression Costs on Large Fires*, p. A-3.

57. Ibid., p. C-1.

58. *Report of the National Commission on Wildfire Disasters*, p. 22.

59. Murray Taylor, "Dousing the Fiscal Flames," *Inner Voice*, published by the Forest Service Employees for Environmental Ethics (January/February 1997), p. 17.

60. U.S. Forest Service, Department of Agriculture, *Fire Suppression Costs on Large Fires*, p. 16.

61. Ibid.

62. March 1997 interview with Jack Ward Thomas, *Wildland Firefighter* (May 1997), p. 32.

63. U.S. Forest Service, *Course to the Future*, p. 1.

64. U.S. Forest Service, Department of Agriculture, *Fire Suppression on Large Fires*, p. 13.

65. U.S. Forest Service, *Course to the Future*, p. 11.

66. Pyne, *World Fire*, p. 232.

67. See U.S. Forest Service, Department of Agriculture, *National Forest Fire Report 1994*, prepared by Fire and Aviation Management Staff (Washington, D.C.: August 1966), p. 11.

68. Mark Matthews, "Wet Summer a Bust for Fire Fighters," *High Country News* (September 15, 1997), p. 3.

69. Quoted in Matthews, "Wet Summer a Bust for Fire Fighters," p. 3.

2

Ecosystem Management as Fire Management

In June 1995, the Interagency Ecosystem Management Task Force, including participants from the Departments of Agriculture and Interior, as well as the Environmental Protection Agency (EPA), Department of Energy, and a number of other federal agencies, issued its final report. Reflecting the broader position of the Clinton administration, the task force stated that "as a matter of policy, the federal government should provide leadership in and cooperate with activities that foster the ecosystem approach to natural resources management, regulation, and assistance."[1] Indeed, one key testing ground for ecological management will be the inland national forests of the West.

The task force defined an ecosystem in broad terms as "an interconnected community of living things, including humans, and the physical environment in which they interact." The practice of ecosystem management would mean first setting a "goal" that represented a "vision of desired future conditions." This vision would have to be given specific content in light of the circumstances of each area and its particular ecological system, but in general terms it would mean efforts "to restore and sustain the health, productivity, and biological diversity of ecosystems." The means of achieving this goal should include a combination of "ecological, economic, and social" policy instruments, designed to work together in such a way that they "sustained the overall quality of life through a natural resource management approach that is fully integrated with social and economic goals."[2]

Such broad language in this and other discussions of ecosystem management has generated considerable cynicism that ecosystem management is so vague a concept that almost anything can fit within its scope. Throughout the federal government, as the General Accounting Office

45

(GAO) has observed, "ecosystem management has come to represent different things to different people." Or, as the GAO found one person putting it more sarcastically, "there is not enough agreement on the concept to hinder its popularity."[3]

Nevertheless, ecosystem management offers a significant departure from past management practices in important ways.[4] It shifts the focus of management from the human uses of the forest to the ecological conditions. In the past, foresters aimed to maximize human well being through producing timber, livestock forage, recreation days, and other outputs; Gifford Pinchot famously said that the goal of national forest management was to promote "the greatest good of the greatest number [of people] in the long run."[5] The condition of the forest was highly relevant to and functioned as a constraint on this effort, but was not in itself a main object of policy. Under ecological management, however, the very goal becomes to achieve an environmental vision for the forest, subject to the pragmatic constraint that the social and economic consequences are acceptable to society—that is to say, the management steps required are politically feasible.

To be sure, the environmental vision does not define itself; that task must be assumed by human beings, even if they do not perceive their efforts as designed to promote human welfare in the first place.[6] The three criteria described by the Interagency Ecosystem Management Task Force for an environmentally desirable vision of the future were the "health," the "productivity," and the "biological diversity" of an ecological system.[7] Again, while these are somewhat vague terms, they are potentially capable of being given more concrete understandings.

For example, the ecological condition of the inland national forests of the West would seem to fail in each respect. It would be difficult to describe diseased forests, often infested with insects, suffering high tree mortality, as "healthy." On the Lincoln National Forest in New Mexico, 57 percent of the ponderosa pine acreage is infected with round-headed beetles; and 50 percent of the Douglas fir acreage is infected with dwarf mistletoe disease. On the Panhandle National Forest in Idaho, white pine blister rust caused the loss of 90 percent of the white pine forests and 64 percent of the whitebark pine forests.[8] As Ross Gorte of the Congressional Research Service has commented, it is widely believed that "the extent and severity of the fires [of 1994] was largely due to the poor health of the national forests of the West."[9] The stunted rates of growth of low-quality wood in these densely packed forests, wood now often not worth the cost of harvesting it, all this resulting from a century of fire suppression, also would seem to fail the test that the forests should be "productive."

Finally, because fire suppression has eliminated the main natural source of disturbance in western forests, and as timber harvests (another main source of disturbance) have declined rapidly in recent years, there is today a growing tendency toward the dominance of shade-tolerant climax species over shade-intolerant forest species. Therefore, there is a failing to meet the third "biodiversity" criterion for ecosystem management. In the sequoia forests of the Sierra Nevadas, for example, the "fire suppression in the past century has resulted in drastically reduced pyrodiversity," resulting in a corresponding decline in the biological diversity associated with the former wide variation in "ecosystem effects."[10]

RESTORING PRESETTLEMENT FORESTS

To be sure, any effort to implement ecosystem management will require more than a negative verdict on existing management.[11] There are in fact many goals for the national forests that might be consistent with the language of ecosystem management. However, in practice, one theme runs through many environmental writings and government policies with respect to the definition of an ecological goal. As a 1994 National Park Service document, offering official policy guidance for fire management, states:

> Natural resources will be managed with a concern for fundamental ecological processes as well as for individual species. . . . Managers . . . will try to maintain all the components and processes of natural evolving park ecosystems, including the natural abundance, diversity, and ecological integrity of the plants and animals.

> A healthy ecosystem is one whose components, such as species diversity and forest stand structure, are fluctuating within the range of variability that existed prior to European settlement. A healthy ecosystem is sustained by the free and unobstructed interaction of natural processes that influenced the formation of the ecosystem. These processes include climatic cycles, animal population dynamics, pathogens and fire.[12]

The Forest Service, under its new 1990s policy directives to practice ecosystem management, has in essence a similar goal for ecosystem outcomes. In a 1993 Forest Service analysis of *Fire Related Considerations and Strategies in Support of Ecosystem Management*, the agency states that it is important to consider "the historic and natural role of fire within the forest ecosystem." The closer a forest goal ("Desired Future Condition") is "to the natural condition," the more "sustainable" that goal is likely to be. Given the fact that "sustainability is a key element of Ecosystem Management," the movement of forest conditions toward a "natural" forest state must be a central objective of ecological management on the national forests.[13]

The Committee of Scientists in its 1999 report to the Secretary of Agriculture and Chief of the Forest Service found that the proper goal for the management of the national forests was to maintain the "ecological integrity" of the "ecological systems" found on these forests. The committee recognized, however, that "the concept of ecological integrity is relatively new and the scientific foundations underlying it are not fully developed." The basic approach, however, would be to develop a concept and associated measures of a "reference condition" and then to judge "ecological integrity" by reference to this baseline.[14]

Consistent with evolving Forest Service practice, the Committee of Scientists proposed that the "historic range of variability" should serve as the reference baseline. It would have to be established by analysis of the "ecological history of a landscape" that would determine the historic "rate and change in selected physical and biological variables." The committee recognized that, given the dynamic character of most forest ecological systems, this approach would require the specification of a particular historic "time interval" as the baseline. It was admittedly difficult to say exactly which "time interval" was most relevant but the committee did offer the suggestion that it "might be a time period characterized by climate, species composition, and disturbance similar to those of today."[15] The problem with this proposal, however, is that it might easily become a defense of the status quo.

Indeed, pressed to give an example of an appropriate use of the concept of "range of historic variability," the Committee of Scientists suggested following the model of the Interior Columbia Basin Ecosystem Management Project, a recent multiagency federal study. This project, the committee reported, had usefully "simulated the HRV [historic range of variability] by developing pre–Euro-American settlement succession/disturbance models for each vegetation type in the Interior Columbia Basin." These simulations provided the reference baseline needed to obtain an operational measure of "ecological integrity." This measure was justified by the fact that "human disturbances of a post–Euro-American settlement . . . were of a type, size, and rate that were not typical of disturbances under which the endemic plant and animal species and ecosystems had developed."[16]

Yet, as the Committee of Scientists recognized, and unlike the National Park Service, the Forest Service faces a much broader range of social and economic constraints. Its forests must, to some extent at least, meet society's needs for timber, forage, recreation days, and other economic outputs. Hence, as current Forest Service policy guidance says, many management alternatives that would advance ecosystem health and sustainability may be "infeasible (socially, legally, or economically)." It is nevertheless important that, while the social and political constraints may properly "shape" the formulation of forest alternatives, they must not "displace" legitimate ecosystem objectives.[17]

In making this determination, Forest Service planners, based on historical and ecological analysis, are instructed to first determine the "normal ecological amplitude" of a forest area—the "natural" range of conditions of the forest, historically speaking. While social and economic considerations may preclude replicating the exact natural conditions of the past, the Forest Service states that achieving a policy alternative that remains "within the site's [historic] ecological amplitude" is essential. On the national forests such a policy close to the historic norm will have "a higher probability of remaining sustainable"—and as noted, will therefore meet one of the basic requirements of ecosystem management.[18] Or, as a team of five ecologists recently defined it, and similar to the views of the Committee of Scientists, "ecosystem management is an attempt to maintain the historical structural complexity and suite of processes that occurred in these ecosystems before Euro-American influence."[19]

In short, "natural" and "historic" conditions of the national forests must in practice be translated to mean "pre-European"—and in the formerly Spanish southwest probably to mean "pre–English-speaking European." On the inland forests of the West it appears that ecosystem management in actual practice means pursuit of the goal of the restoration of forest conditions as they existed in about the mid-nineteenth century. This was prior to the banishment of Indians to reservations, the introduction of cattle and sheep grazing, and the active Forest Service efforts to suppress forest fires.

This goal is to be pursued on the national forests, subject to a constraint that any negative impacts on affected social and economic groups must not be politically unacceptable. Because political feasibility often shifts over time and may depend significantly on the political and communications skills of ecosystem management advocates, it will never be possible to specify precisely the goal of ecosystem management. However, federal planners can generally specify a set of bounds of forest outcomes within which the results of ecosystem management should fall.

FIRE AS A POLICY TOOL

Because the forest fire policies of the Forest Service have done more than any other management actions to create the current "unnatural" conditions on many national forests, it follows that the implementation of ecosystem management will in many cases have to begin with a basic reconsideration of fire policy. Two researchers at the Pacific Southwest Research Station of the Forest Service observed recently that "strategic fuel management is an integral component of ecosystem management."[20] Or, as William Moore (formerly the chief of fire management for the Northern Region of the Forest Service) put it, the agency in recent years has faced the necessity "to organize fire programs to help managers attain the objectives they wanted to achieve on each unique ecosystem, large or small, under their jurisdiction."[21]

Two of the more astute observers of national forest management, Douglas MacCleery of the Forest Service and Dennis Le Master of Purdue University, recently explained that, if answers to the current diseased and fire-prone conditions of many federal forests in the West were not found, there would be:

(1) increasing risks to federal and non-federal ecosystems from insects, disease, and conflagration events, (2) a rising toll of loss and degradation of watershed values and wildlife habitats from abnormally intense wildfires, as well as continued losses in the biological diversity of vegetation types that were historically characterized by frequent, low intensity fires, (3) increased risks to the human communities located in forested areas and to the fire fighters sent in to protect them, and (4) significant and increasing losses to taxpayers in fire suppression costs and resource values.[22]

Finding the necessary policy answers, they argue, will provide "a clear test for the operational application of ecosystem management principles." Indeed, resolving these problems of western national forests, attributable in major part to past fire suppression policies, will be a "litmus test" as to whether the ecosystem management concept can move beyond current shibboleths to assume any kind of concrete and practical meaning.[23]

Although Congress has not officially ratified the goal of ecosystem management, speaking in 1995 as then chief of the Forest Service, Jack Ward Thomas stated that "it is increasingly obvious that the overriding de facto policy for the management of Federal lands is the protection of biodiversity. That de facto policy has simply evolved through the interaction of laws, regulations, court cases, and expedient administrative direction."[24] Chief Thomas was acknowledging the evolving reality that the goals of national forest management increasingly were divorced from specific uses such as timber harvesting and recreation and were now defined by the ecosystem conditions to be sought for their own sake.[25]

This new world of forest management was symbolized most visibly by forest developments in the Pacific Northwest, following the designation in

1990 of the northern spotted owl as a threatened species under the Endangered Species Act of 1973.[26] In the development of the recovery plan for the spotted owl, the maintenance of owl habitat took clear priority over any timber harvest or other traditional utilitarian considerations relating to human welfare. If occurring in less conspicuous and nationally publicized ways, other similar events have been occurring throughout the national forest system in other parts of the West.

PRESCRIBED BURNING

Fire was not the only part of nature that federal managers had sought to banish in the twentieth century from the national forests and other public lands of the West. They had sought to extinguish wolves, grizzly bears, prairie dogs, mountain lions, coyotes, and other species—with varying degrees of success. Now, also like fire, federal managers are trying to reverse the consequences of a century of their own policies. Wolves are being reintroduced into Yellowstone National Park and several national forests in Idaho. Heroic efforts are being made to revive grizzly bears from the current small and scattered remnant populations. Also like fire, these efforts were in some cases complicated by potential risks to human life and property, causing some Westerners to oppose the whole effort.

Yet, Interior Secretary Bruce Babbitt was determined to move forward with wolf reintroduction and other plans to revive the pre-European patterns of wildlife distribution in western forests and other lands. He also saw fire policy in much the same light. In an April 1997 speech in Boise, Idaho, Babbitt described the unfortunate consequences of a century of federal attempts to reverse the natural course of forest fire. "Two decades ago we spent an average of $100 million each year to put out fires; today, we spend $1 billion, yet the crisis only grows worse." The environment often suffered most of all. For example, the large 1992 Foothills fire in Idaho "wiped out an entire population of native bull trout. It vaporized soil elements critical to forest recovery; then when the rains come, floods and mudslides will pour down hardpan slopes, threatening lives and property a second time."[27]

Consistent with the goals of ecosystem management, Babbitt considered that the forests must be returned to a more natural condition. Like wolves, forest fire must be brought back. Or, as he put it in his Boise speech, "to restore health, character, and structure to our forests, then, the obvious first step is to bring back their own ancient predator, wildland fire."[28]

An absolute and literal application of Babbitt's policy recommendation would allow all natural fires (as set by lightning) to continue to burn without any hindrance. All human-caused fires would have to be put out as fast as possible. In addition, reversing existing policy, no new fires would be deliberately set as part of efforts to manipulate future forest vegetative and other conditions.

To be sure, however much this might in some ways represent an ideal of a true "natural" forest ecology, Babbitt was realistic enough to know that it was unworkable in the current day and age. Wolves might eventually be allowed to run free through many forests in the West, but fire could never be allowed the same degree of freedom. Similarly, the Committee of Scientists observed, "some dimensions of HRV are difficult to reestablish within some landscapes. As an example, the forests of the western Cascades in Oregon and Washington will not be managed for the large, infrequent, high-intensity burns that created them. It is just not socially acceptable," however ecologically desirable. The committee did note that "such burns may occur," but it could not be "through purposeful public policy."[29] Babbitt also acknowledged that many forests are "choked with fuel," owing to past policy actions, so that in their current condition a new small fire might be "a drip torch [that] could set off an uncontrollable inferno."[30] It might not only cause widespread loss of human life and property but also far-reaching ecological damage to the forest.

Hence, there would have to be a limit to being "natural"; it would apparently be necessary to treat new fires with considerable caution. Moreover, there were many forests that posed an immediate threat of a conflagration, if a fire should break out in a dry period of the year. It would be necessary to deal with this threat immediately through measures to reduce wood volume in the forests, to clear strips that would be free of any trees and thus offer a barrier to fire movement, and to take other preventive actions. Therefore, even though it was hardly a "natural" solution, Babbitt endorsed the existing policy of setting controlled fires to clear forests of fire-prone and otherwise unwanted trees and vegetation. In some cases, natural fires set by lightning could also be allowed to continue to burn for this purpose. Indeed, in the past few years, under its policy of conducting such various forms of "prescribed burning," the Forest Service has raised its goal of acreage to be burned in a controlled fashion—involving both naturally occurring and human-set fires—from several hundred thousand acres per year to several million acres.[31]

It may often be worth spending this money, as a few economic calculations can show. In the Sierra Nevadas, about 50,000 acres per year have been burned in prescribed burns in recent years, with annual costs of about $5 million. In 1994, twenty-six large fires burned in these areas that involved total fire suppression costs of about $75 million. However, in order to have much chance of preventing these large fires, it is estimated that the scope of the current prescribed burning program in the Sierra Nevadas would have to be escalated by a factor of at least 5 to 10—thus raising costs to $25 million to $50 million per year.[32] Then, if this annual spending did succeed in eliminating most of the potential need for high future suppression costs for several large and destructive fires, the prescribed burning program might well pass a simple benefit-cost test. To be sure, further analysis of this issue is needed in the Sierra Nevada forests—and similar studies in other forest areas around the West—partly because it is unlikely that any prescribed burning program would altogether eliminate the occurrence of large fires.

If the precepts of ecological management are followed, the long run goal will be a return to the fire patterns of pre-European times—frequent smaller fires instead of a few large intense burns spaced far apart. The current program of prescribed burning thus ideally should be only an interim step toward the goal of a forest ecosystem eventually functioning naturally on its own. It might be at least 50 or 100 years, however, before any such state of strictly natural fire would be attainable in many national forests across the West.

PRACTICAL PROBLEMS

Indeed, the practical feasibility of many current plans for prescribed burning is in considerable doubt. For one thing, it would release large amounts of smoke, which in some areas would pose a major conflict with air quality laws. The EPA in 1997 extended regulation of particulate matter to particles of smaller than 2.5 microns. If they are eventually upheld (implementation is now being blocked by the federal courts), and without an exception from these rules, prescribed burning may well have to be excluded over large parts of the West. Forest fires release large volumes of these tiny particles that EPA now argues are more dangerous to health because they can penetrate deep into the lungs. According to the GAO, "prescribed burning to restore the forest's health and to sustain diverse plant and animal communities may be appropriate under the Forest Service's planning statutes but may be difficult to reconcile in the short term with air and water quality standards under the Clean Air and Clean Water Acts."[33] In a more recent 1999 report, GAO indicated that "many agency officials told GAO they do not believe it is possible to set controlled fires to reduce fuels on a scale replicating that of natural fires and still meet air quality standards under the Clean Air Act."[34]

Prescribed burning can also create major risks to human life and property. Given funding and other resource constraints, it is not possible to reduce to zero the risk that a fire will get out of control; unexpected weather or other unplanned events can cause the best made fire plans to go seriously awry. For example, in the Okanogan Valley of British Columbia, a forest fire occurred in the summer of 1994 near the rural town of Penticton. With light winds blowing away from the town, forest managers decide to let the fire continue to burn, as a way of removing excess fuels and improving grazing conditions for wild mountain sheep. After a few days, however, a strong wind arose in the opposite direction, which caused the pine forest to erupt in a sheet of flame, moving rapidly toward the town. With heroic efforts, most of the town was eventually spared, but with a loss of 18 homes and large costs incurred for emergency fire controls.[35] Again, the GAO considered that over much of the national forest system the threat of such an event meant that "the danger of fire's escaping from such controlled burning is often too high in many areas for this method to be used."[36]

Prescribed burning may be incapable of attaining the natural forest condition sought by ecological management. In the forest fire patterns of the past, the frequent fires kept the amount of invading trees and other ground vegetation at low volumes. Fire removed this vegetation from the forest floor but did not damage the larger and older trees. However, today, following years of fire suppression, a newly set fire might well erupt from the dense understory into the crowns of the older trees, causing their destruction as well. The much more intense heat of such a fire—creating a fire condition that would never have occurred before the twentieth century—could also cause further major ecological damage to soils and other forest elements.

Prescribed burning is also expensive. Typical costs, depending on the precautions required to ensure that the fire does not get out of control, and other local circumstances, can range widely, running from $25 per acre to more than $300 per acre. If perhaps 50 million acres of federal forest in the West today would benefit from prescribed fire, the total costs for burning all this acreage might well approach $5 billion. Meeting a target of 2 to 3 million acres per year is likely to require $200 million to $300 million annually. Funding thus far has never come close to these levels, and many observers doubt that anything like this amount of money will actually ever be made available by the Congress.

There are other nonmonetary costs as well, including the loss of hiking, fishing, bird watching, and other recreational opportunities, at least in the short run following a fire. The residue of a forest fire is aesthetically objectionable to many national forest users. Until it begins to grow back, there will be a complete loss of forest functions and the forms of recreational use associated with these functions in the area of the fire. The new resident of a second-home cabin adjacent to a national forest is likely to oppose strenuously any plan to burn over the lands near his property and in his viewing area. Backpackers simply do not want to hike through charred wood residues.

For all these reasons, prescribed fire is likely to be an option for only a rather limited part of the national forests of the interior West—generally most feasible on the more remote areas with more wild characteristics. As urban populations move further into and make more use of the forests, the area where prescribed burning will be acceptable is likely to shrink still further. In 1993 the Forest Service's own Office of Fire and Aviation Management stated that it was skeptical concerning the prospects for any widespread use of prescribed fire on the national forests of the West:

> Although Forest Service policy recognizes the ecological importance of fire, a serious dilemma precludes the agency's ability to effectively manage fire-adapted ecosystems. The adverse effects and occasional damage that results from prescribed fire failures are poorly tolerated by the public and frequently embarrass the agency. . . .
>
> In the absence of fire, forest insect and disease problems periodically become epidemic, causing mortality that disrupts sustained-yield rotations and other resource management objectives. Fire exclusion has contributed to an accumulation of fuels and changes in stand structure that make many fire-adapted stands more flammable and highly susceptible to severe, stand-replacement burning. Both the control of wildfire and use of prescribed fire have become considerably more difficult as a result of these changes.
>
> The costs and risks involved in an extensive reintroduction of fire will be high. The use and enjoyment of National Forest System lands has grown tremendously over the past several decades. These rising values, combined with unnaturally flammable fuel conditions and the enormous uncertainties surrounding wildland burning, severely constrain prescribed fire applications that can be managed within acceptable limits of risk.[37]

To be sure, the major existing constraints on the use of prescribed fire do not mean that the forest will not be burned. However, unless other steps are taken, the fires that do occur are likely to be unplanned, large, and difficult to control. In the Pacific Northwest, for example, a leading forester, Professor Chadwick Oliver of the University of Washington, comments that "our region's forests have a history of frequent, violent, large scale disturbance." Under the existing policies being driven by the spotted owl recovery plan, the end result is that "we walk away and leave these [old growth] forests to nature." In light of the fuels buildup and other conditions in these forests, however, "we have no assurance that forests set aside will actually grow older." Indeed, as Oliver says, "there is a greater probability they will burn up or blow down first."[38]

TIMBER HARVESTING AS ECOSYSTEM MANAGEMENT

If prescribed burning is impractical for many forest areas, the choice may be as follows: Find an alternative means of reducing fire hazards, or accept that large, difficult-to-control, and destructive fires will periodically break out to cut a large swath through the national forests of the West. At present, the main alternative possibility for reducing excess fuels in the national forests is simply to remove the timber by mechanical means. The Forest Service might cut down the dense thickets of immature trees that pose such a large fire hazard. If the wood is worth anything, it could be physically removed and used for timber or pulp. In that case, it would make sense to have the same company do the cutting and the harvesting of the timber. That is to say, ecosystem management by mechanical means would in many cases amount to a new Forest Service timber sale program, now justified by ecological objectives, rather than traditional timber harvest targets or other economic goals.

Even in circumstances where prescribed burning would be technically and politically feasible, timber sales might better be employed to clean up the forest floor. As an economist would describe the situation, there is an "opportunity cost" to burning up good wood in prescribed fires. The average sale value of the commercially valuable trees available for harvest on the national forests of the interior West is perhaps $500 per acre. Rather than burn the wood, where positive net revenues from timber sales are possible, such revenues can be used to cover at least in part the costs for removal of excess fuels.

Some sales may not fully cover their costs but nevertheless offer sufficient revenues that, in combination with reductions in future fire risks (and resulting reductions in expected future costs of fire control measures), along with the expected ecosystem benefits, the sales will be socially justifiable. Given the current federal spending for emergency fire suppression of $500 million to $1 billion per year in bad fire seasons, there is a potential for large direct economic benefits, if any significant reductions in the probability of future large fires and the associated necessity of expensive fire suppression measures can be achieved.

Nevertheless, if excess fuels removal by mechanical means now turns out to be essential for ecosystem management over much of the inland West, the Forest Service may, in some cases, find that it has to pay to have certain trees removed. This could prove to be very expensive. At the upper end of estimates, the GAO recently suggested that excess fuels removal needed on as much as 39 million acres of national forest in the interior West could ultimately involve total long-run costs of $12 billion between now and the year 2015. This would require average federal expenditures of $725 million per year.[39]

It is hard to imagine where funding of this magnitude would be found. Two Forest Service researchers thus recently asked, "How will we pay for all the silviculture and fuel management that will be necessary?" Given the budget pressures on the Forest Service of recent years, it seemed "highly unlikely that federal appropriated funds—even from multiple functions—will be adequate."[40] The only solution they could see, if excess fuels removal from fire-prone forests was going to occur on any widespread basis, was as follows:

> Large-scale fuel treatments will have to be the result of economically self-sustaining activities. Yet much of the needed treatment involves removal of small trees that often have marginal or negative market value. Part of the solution may come from multiproduct sales, in which sawtimber and other high-value products subsidize the removal of lower value material. One of the challenges for managers will be to locate and design multiproduct or other sales in ways that make them economically viable. In addition, however, it probably will be important to support the establishment of particleboard or other plants capable of generating value from small trees. Public land managers and private entrepreneurs need to discuss whether and how it may be possible to provide sufficient assurances of a continuing supply of biomass from public lands (e.g., for several decades) to warrant the capital investment in such plants.[41]

Achieving such timber harvest goals will also mean major changes in procedures historically followed by the Forest Service in the planning of future timber harvests and the conduct of sales. As MacCleery and Le Master explain, "forest management practices designed to maintain forest health will be different than those used to produce timber as a primary objective." Some of the differences will include the fact that "there will be more use of thinnings, salvage, and other treatments that involve only a portion of the trees on a site." The costs per unit of timber volume will likely be higher and the quality of the timber harvested in many cases will be lower. The overall goal will be to employ "silvicultural operations in support of forest health objectives," in this manner seeking to generate "win-win situations" in ecological and economic terms alike for the national forest system.[42] In a recent study, GAO concluded that the Forest Service was moving slowly to make the necessary changes in its timber sale rules and regulations to achieve such a reorientation in the purpose of many of its timber sales.[43]

In 1993, the Forest Service began to distinguish between timber sales having a "forest stewardship" as opposed to a "timber commodity" purpose. From 1993 to 1997, the forest stewardship sales rose from 23 percent to 40 percent of timber sales. In 1997, stewardship sales earned $211 million in gross timber revenues in the process of pursuing their nontimber goals.[44] This may well have been the difference for the Forest Service between being able to carry out such forest improve..._nt activities and having to forego them for budgetary reasons.

In his 1997 Boise speech, Secretary Babbitt stated that, although his preference was for "fighting fire with fire," there would also be circumstances where it would be necessary for the Forest Service, Bureau of Land Management, and other federal agencies to engage in the practice of "carefully thinning excess young trees" with mechanical means.[45] In some circumstances, there was simply no other feasible way to get from the current forest condition to the goal of a naturally functioning forest ecology, as found in pre-European settlement times. In the Sierra Nevadas, for example, the most populated forest areas "lie within the [same] elevation zone most frequently burned during the twentieth century." Hence, in this intermix area, "it may be desirable to focus more on nonfire silvicultural treatment methods in order to minimize concerns about smoke and potential escapes" of fire.[46]

INCREASING FUELS INVENTORIES

In the interior West the volume of wood that could be harvested in an effort to clear the forests of the debris of a century of fire suppression is very large. Since 1952, with fire largely excluded, the total biomass of the national forests of the parts of the West located east of the summits of the Sierra Nevada and Cascade Mountains has increased by more than 40 percent. Most of this increase is in smaller trees of less than 17 inches in diameter, which have themselves increased by more than 50 percent in biomass volume. Thus, contrary to a popular impression of a dwindling supply of timber today on the national forests, the total wood volume—if often of low quality—in this region has increased significantly.

Moreover, this increase has occurred despite large increases in timber harvests in the post–World War II era in the interior West. From 1960 to 1990, timber harvests on the national forests in this region were typically around 2 billion board feet per year. It is only in the 1990s that harvest levels in the interior West have fallen precipitously to around 300 million board feet per year. These sharp cutbacks in federal timber harvests are not the result of any shortage of wood supply but of changing environmental values and shifting government policies with respect to the role of timber harvesting on the federal forests.

Indeed, if excess fuels removal and other ecological rehabilitative actions were undertaken for, say, 1.5 million acres per year in the interior West, the resulting volume of wood removals could be as much as 3 billion board feet or more per year in this region alone—more than the old timber harvest level under now discredited "even flow" policies. This basic circumstance holds for the entire national forest system. The Committee of Scientists reported in 1999 that, if timber harvesting were not sharply increased—and the constraints on prescribed fire effectively prevented the wide adoption of this alternative method of fuels reduction—there would be further rapid buildups of wood fuels on the national forests.

Softwoods such as Douglas fir and lodgepole pine are the main wood output of the national forests. Despite the sharp increases in softwood timber harvests in the decades following World War II, the Committee of Scientists found that "growth in softwoods on the national forests has exceeded removals for the period of reporting (1952 to 1991) and will increasingly exceed removals during the next 40 years (2000 to 2040)." In fact, without significant increases in removal of softwoods, by timber harvesting or any other method of wood removal feasible, the volumes of softwood trees on the national forests nationwide would be expected to increase by 50 percent by 2040. It would require annual increases of timber harvests of around 4 to 5 billion board feet for all the national forest system, the committee reported (without itself drawing any policy conclusion), merely to hold current volumes of softwood inventories—the potential fuels supply for future forest fires, if not harvested otherwise—at their current board feet levels.[47]

At present, however, timber harvests have been declining rapidly, not increasing, on the national forests of the interior West. The trend in the interior West mirrors harvest trends nationwide on the national forests. Following World War II, as shown in figure 2-1, the harvesting of timber climbed rapidly. Timber sales became the principal revenue-generating activity of the Forest Service and by most accounts the highest priority of the agency. As recently as 1989, almost 12 billion board feet of timber were harvested from national forest lands, about 20 percent of the total national supply of softwood timber.

Yet by 1995, largely as a result of the spotted owl recovery plan and other environmental conflicts in other national forest areas, total Forest Service timber harvests had plummeted nationwide to 3.9 billion board feet. Timber sales (not harvests) in 1994 were 3.1 billion board feet and fell still further in 1995 to 2.9 billion board feet, indicating that future harvests would be even lower. It is only a rising volume of "stewardship" timber sales that has sustained harvests at their current low levels. Often the trees now being offered in sales designed for removing forest fire hazards are dead or diseased, offering buyers a wood quality much inferior to that of the past. Unless future timber harvests in some form rise sharply in the future, the fire hazards from excess fuels on western national forests will continue to escalate.

Figure 2-1.   Forest Service Timber Sales 1905-95

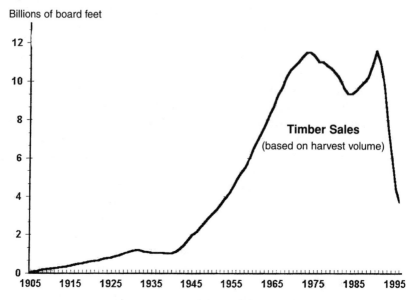

Billions of board feet

Source: USDA Forest Service *Cut & Sold Reports.*

THE END OF TIMBER PLANNING

As timber harvests in the future increasingly are designed to meet excess fuels removal, wildlife habitat, ecosystem management, and other non-commodity objectives, this will mean the end of the even flow and other decision-making apparatus of the old Forest Service timber program. It will no longer make any sense to have a plan for harvesting (or selling) so much total timber nationwide, or regionwide, every year. The central planning apparatus of the Forest and Rangelands Renewable Resources Planning Act of 1974 (RPA) will be irrelevant. Indeed, the Forest Service has now declared that timber harvesting is a "secondary goal" that should be pursued only where it is "needed to meet the [forest] structure goals," or "to the degree it is cost-efficient and does not compromise attainment of the primary (forest structure) goal."[48]

To be sure, abandoning the old timber planning apparatus associated with the even flow policy will be good riddance for more than ecological reasons. It never made much economic sense, either.[49] The even flow policy has been largely mythical in any case, even while it has been the official Forest Service standard for many decades for setting timber harvest levels in national forests throughout the United States. The fictional qualities have been revealed for all to see by the events of the 1990s with their sharp harvest declines—which the even flow policy was supposed to guarantee would never happen. Calculations of even flow levels—for which the Forest Service typically used large complex computer models (all to show how "scientific" the results were)—were intended to be the technical mechanism for translating the statutory goal of "sustained yield" forest management into an operational outcome. Thus, for the dozens of Resource Management Plans developed by the Forest Service under the requirements of the National Forest Management Act of 1976, these plans set the timber harvest level at the maximum harvest that would never require a future timber harvest reduction—the technical definition of an "even flow" level.

In the end, all this turned out to be pure fiction. It is one more example illustrating why comprehensive long-run planning for forests—or for virtually any other large social and economic system—has almost always been a misguided and utopian ideal. Even flow calculations were long portrayed by the Forest Service as the "scientific forestry" standard for calculating timber harvest levels. The demise of the even flow policy is one more powerful example of the failure of scientific management on the national forests, one more nail in the scientific management coffin.

Instead of the even flow mythology, total timber harvests will instead be the cumulative product of individual forest plans, developed on a site-specific basis, that determine timber harvests in their new role of a tool of broader forest management policy, including ecosystem considerations as a main factor. Bruce Lippke and Chadwick Oliver argue that the best way to achieve both the goals of biodiversity and ecosystem management is through an active process of "landscape management." By adopting an active management regime for a range of landscape goals simultaneously on the same lands, "the total cost of producing timber, wildlife habitat, biodiversity and other ecological values together . . . will generally be lower than producing them separately"—the mistaken approach now typically followed by federal managers.[50]

The ultimate outcome, as many people may be surprised to discover, may be a significant level of timber harvesting, perhaps even a level considerably higher than the much-reduced harvests of recent years. Many millions of acres of western interior forests are in dire need of remedial fuels reduction actions, and in many cases mechanical harvesting of the existing trees will be the only realistic way of reducing the large fire hazards associated with fuels buildups from the past. The only alternative may be massive unplanned outbreaks of forest fires—"catastrophic" fires, as the GAO considers them—across the West, the last resort if policy gridlock on the national forests continues to undermine every other possibility.

CONCLUSION

The Forest Service has entered into a new era in which the costs of fire fighting in average years will be exceeding gross revenues from timber sales and will greatly exceed these revenues in some bad fire years. If there were no other environmental or social considerations, the economic solution—the way to maximize the "net present value" of the national forest—would now simply be to let the fires burn. In the aggregate, it now costs more to try to suppress fires on the national forests than the timber saved is worth.

Some environmentalists might prefer such a course of action as well. The National Park Service has argued that the widespread outbreaks of fires covering significant portions of Yellowstone National Park in 1988 were ecologically beneficial. Letting the fires burn might be the quickest way to return to "natural" conditions in some national forest areas. Of course, rural communities that are still dependent on federal timber—subsidized timber in many cases—would lose access to traditional sources of wood supply. The hazards to human life and property, and other major obstacles described above to widespread prescribed burning, would also come into play. Nevertheless, it is a brand new era when, economically and environmentally, the best course of action for the national forests themselves may simply be to let the fires burn, and it is only practical constraints that limit the adoption of such a policy.

In this new era, to the extent that timber harvesting will be justified economically, it will not be principally for the value of the timber, but at least as much as a means of limiting exposure to future forest fire hazards and associated potential large fire suppression costs. As timber harvesting is justified as an instrument of ecosystem management, economic analysis of the direct benefits of timber harvesting will also have to focus on the economic values of alternative ecological—and fire hazard—outcomes.[51]

Yet as noted above, timber sales may pay in the long run even in a narrow economic sense, if they reduce fire risks and thus avert large future fire control expenditures. As also discussed above, society seems willing in addition to spend at least a certain amount of money to achieve ecosystem outcomes for their own sake. The problem is that it will be difficult if not impossible to calculate the fire savings or to assess the public preferences in any precise way. As will be examined below, the only answer may be to require that the main beneficiaries of national forest management actions also be required to pay for them. If subjective judgments must be made, those making the judgments should be required to do a balancing that confronts the same party with both the benefit and the cost sides. The balancing should also be done by the ones who will bear the impacts. In short, decentralization of national forest management will offer the best path to effective management in the future.

NOTES

1. *The Ecosystem Approach: Healthy Ecosystems and Sustainable Economies,* Report of the Interagency Ecosystem Management Task Force (Washington, D.C.: National Technical Information Service, June 1995), p. 8.
2. Ibid., p. 1.
3. General Accounting Office, *Ecosystem Management: Additional Actions Needed to Adequately Test a Promising Approach* (Washington, D.C.: August 1994), p. 38.
4. See Robert B. Keiter, "An Introduction to the Ecosystem Management Debate," in *The Greater Yellowstone Ecosystem: Redefining America's Wilderness Heritage,* ed. Robert B. Keiter and Mark S. Boyce (New Haven: Yale University Press, 1991); Robert B. Keiter, "NEPA and the Emerging Concept of Ecosystem Management on the Public Lands," *Land and Water Law Review* vol. 25, no. 1 (1990); and Robert B. Keiter, "Taking Account of the Ecosystem on the Public Domain: Law and Ecology in the Greater Yellowstone Region," *University of Colorado Law Review* vol. 60, no. 4 (1989).
5. Gifford Pinchot, *Breaking New Ground* (New York: Harcourt, Brace, 1947), p. 261.
6. See Sarah Bates, *Discussion Paper: Managing for Ecosystems on the Public Lands,* Western Lands Report No. 4 (Boulder: Natural Resources Law Center, University of Colorado School of Law, 1993); also Wayne A. Morrissey, Jeffrey A. Zinn, and M. Lynne Corn, *Ecosystem Management: Federal Agency Activities,* Congressional Research Service Report No. 94-339 ENR (April 19, 1994).
7. *The Ecosystem Approach,* p. 1.
8. General Accounting Office, *Western National Forests: A Cohesive Strategy is Needed to Address Catastrophic Wildfire Threats* GAO/RCED-99-65 (April 1999), p. 25.
9. Ross W. Gorte, "Forest Fires and Forest Health," Congressional Research Service Report for Congress, 95-511 ENR (Washington, D.C.: July 14, 1995), p. 1.
10. Deborah Elliot-Fisk et al., "Mediated Settlement Agreement for Sequoia National Forest, Section B. Giant Sequoia Groves: An Evaluation," in *Status of the Sierra Nevada, Addendum,* Sierra Nevada Ecosystem Project, Final Report to Congress (Davis: University of California, Wildland Resources Center Report No. 40, March 1997), p. 290.
11. See Kathryn A Kohm and Jerry R. Franklin, eds., *Creating a Forestry for the 21st Century: The Science of Ecosystem Management* (Washington, D.C.: Island Press, 1997).
12. National Park Service, Branch of Fire and Aviation Management, U.S. Department of the Interior, *Fire Management and Ecosystem Health in the National Park System* (Washington, D.C.: September 22, 1994), p. 2.

13. U.S. Forest Service, Office of Fire and Aviation Management, Department of Agriculture, *Fire Related Considerations and Strategies in Support of Ecosystem Management* (Washington, D.C.: January 1993), pp. 18–19.

14. Committee of Scientists, *Sustaining the People's Lands: Recommendations for Stewardship of the National Forests and Grasslands in the Next Century,* a report to the Secretary of Agriculture and to the Chief of the Forest Service (Washington, D.C.: U.S. Department of Agriculture, March 15, 1999), pp. 34–35.

15. Ibid., pp. 35–36.

16. Ibid., p. 32.

17. Ibid.

18. Ibid., pp. 22–23.

19. Elliot-Fisk et al., "Mediated Settlement Agreement for Sequoia National Forest," p. 307.

20. C. Phillip Weatherspoon and Carl N. Skinner, "Landscape-Level Strategies for Forest Fuel Management," in *Status of the Sierra Nevada, Volume II,* p. 1483.

21. "A Conversation with Dr. William 'Bud' Moore," *Evergreen* (Winter 1994–1995), p. 34.

22. Douglas W. MacCleery and Dennis C. Le Master, *Producing and Consuming Natural Resources Within an Ecosystem Management Framework: What Is the Proper Context,* unpublished paper (January 2, 1996), p. 47.

23. Ibid., pp. 46, 47.

24. Jack Ward Thomas, "The Instability of Stability," speech delivered at the University of Montana, Missoula, Montana, October 16, 1995.

25. See H. Michael Anderson, "Reforming National-Forest Policy," *Issues in Science and Technology* (Winter 1993–1994).

26. See Alston Chase, *In a Dark Wood* (New York: Houghton Mifflin, 1995).

27. Bruce Babbitt, "A Coordinated Campaign: Fight Fire with Fire," speech at Boise State University, Boise, Idaho, February 11, 1997.

28. Ibid.

29. Committee of Scientists, *Sustaining the People's Lands,* pp. 36–37.

30. Ibid.

31. U.S. Forest Service, *Fire Economics Assessment Report,* p. 16.

32. Susan J. Husari and Kevin S. McKelvey, "Fire-Management Policies and Programs," in *Status of the Sierra Nevada, Volume II,* p. 1113.

33. General Accounting Office, *Forest Service Decision-Making: A Framework for Improving Performance,* GAO/RCED-97-71 (Washington, D.C.: April 1997), p. 11.

34. General Accounting Office, *Western National Forests,* p. 7.

35. Patrick Moore, *Pacific Spirit: The Forest Reborn* (West Vancouver, B.C., Canada: Terra Bella Publishers, 1995), pp. 63–64.

36. General Accounting Office, *Western National Forests,* p. 7.

37. U.S. Forest Service, *Fire Related Considerations and Strategies in Support of Ecosystem Management,* p. 28.

38. Quoted in "A Season of Fire," Evergreen (Winter 1994–1995), p. 50. See also James K. Agee, *Fire Ecology of Pacific Northwest Forests* (Washington, D.C.: Island Press, 1993).

39. General Accounting Office, *Western National Forests,* p. 41.

40. Weatherspoon and Skinner, "Landscape-Level Strategies for Forest Fuel Management," p. 1486.

41. Ibid.

42. MacCleery and Le Master, *Producing and Consuming Natural Resources Within an Ecosystem Management Framework,* p. 47.

43. General Accounting Office, *Western National Forests.*

44. U.S. Forest Service, U.S. Department of Agriculture, *Forest Management Program Annual Report, Fiscal Year 1977* (July 1998), p. 48.

45. Babbitt, "A Coordinated Campaign: Fight Fire with Fire."

46. Weatherspoon and Skinner, "Landscape-Level Strategies for Forest Fuel Management," p. 1484.

47. Ibid., pp. 8–9.

48. Discussed in K. Norman Johnson, John Sessions, and Jerry K. Franklin, "Initial Results from Simulation of Alternative Forest Management Strategies for Two National Forests of the Sierra Nevada," in *Status of the Sierra Nevada, Addendum,* p. 180.

49. See Robert H. Nelson and Lucian Pugliaresi, "Timber Harvest Policy Issues on the O&C Lands," in *Forestlands: Public and Private,* ed. Robert T. Deacon and M. Bruce Johnson (San Francisco: Pacific Institute for Public Policy Research, 1995).

50. Bruce Lippke and Chadwick D. Oliver, "Managing for Multiple Values: A Proposal for the Pacific Northwest," *Journal of Forestry* (December 1993), pp. 15–16.

51. This is not to suggest that the Forest Service should begin to use the economic method of "existence value" in its benefit-cost calculations. See Donald H. Rosenthal and Robert H. Nelson, "Why Existence Value Should Not Be Used in Benefit-Cost Analysis," *Journal of Policy Analysis and Management* (Winter 1992); and Robert H. Nelson, "Does 'Existence Value' Exist: Economics Encroaches on Religion," *The Independent Review* (Spring 1997).

3

A Theology of Timber Harvesting

Many environmentalists are fearful that proposals for increased fuels removal will represent an attempt to revive the old Forest Service timber program in a new dress. Warning against any such efforts, Interior Secretary Bruce Babbitt declared on one occasion that "we need not sacrifice the integrity of God's creation at the altar of commercial timber production."[1] Bringing up the subject of God and religion in the context of management of the nation's lands and resources might seem surprising in the normally secular policy world of Washington. However, it was not the first time Babbitt had done so. In an April 1996 speech he stated that the Endangered Species Act should be defended "for spiritual reasons"; it was "the Noah's ark of our day." As the Bible instructs, and is still relevant today, "the whole of creation," not just the limited number of species of practical value to human beings, must be preserved as part of complying with "God's covenant to protect life."[2]

Further mention of religion in the context of natural resource policy came recently from an even more surprising quarter, the Committee of Scientists. The committee avoided explicit reference to biblical texts but incorporated religious purposes into its concept of the proper goals of the national forest system. The committee defined "effective management of National Forest System lands" as management that "provides important material, aesthetic and spiritual contributions to society." The committee similarly stated that the national forests are "places where people work, live, worship, and play."[3] Little further was said about the specific content here of the "spiritual" purposes or of the manner of "worship" expected on the national forests. Yet the mere mention of such religious subjects by a scientific group was a sign of changing times.

In some ways, this new willingness to bring up religious considerations may be regarded as a constructive development. It recognizes that social values are at the heart of much of current environmental policy making, that values are traditionally derived from religious teachings, and that perhaps it might be beneficial to have a value discussion with respect to the best future policies for the national forests—and other federally owned lands and resources. Policies for these resources, the traditional views of the Forest Service and other federal agencies notwithstanding, are often not a matter of finding a "scientific" resolution.

Indeed, the environmental movement, as many leading environmental thinkers have themselves said, often seeks to change core American values.[4] Joseph Sax, University of California law professor and also a past staff assistant to Secretary Babbitt, once wrote that the members of the American preservation movement are "secular prophets, preaching a message of secular salvation."[5] American environmentalism might best be understood as in its essence a new religious movement in a nation famous for its religious crusades.[6]

To be sure, Babbitt's new approach—and the broader efforts of American environmentalists—open up the possibility of a new kind of inquiry. To the extent they are interested in values at all, social scientists have tended to take the values as given and then to treat them as casual factors in some broader model for explaining social and economic behavior. However, if the central policy issues now often rest on the appropriateness of a certain set of values to be applied, this form of social science research will have little or nothing of use to say. Ordinary people, however, are less hesitant to make judgments about values. They may well spend much of their time thinking about proper values for themselves and trying to inculcate them in their children. Given any set of values raised for their consideration, they might, for example, decide that these values are shallow, are based on defective ethical reasoning, are based on core assumptions that are factually incorrect, or in other ways are ethically flawed.

Hence, while it is not a traditional social science form of inquiry, when Secretary Babbitt, as the leading spokesman for the Clinton administration on western land and resource matters, proposes a certain set of values based on God's plan for the world, it may be time to engage in a theological examination of such a value position—understanding the field of theological and value inquiry in a broad sense.

THE GOSPEL OF CONSERVATIONISM

To be sure, Babbitt and the Committee of Scientists were not the first to bring up the subject of religion in connection with national forest management. Gifford Pinchot declared in *The Fight for Conservation* that his efforts in founding the Forest Service and other actions for the cause of conservation had been intended "to help in bringing the Kingdom of God on earth."[7] This is not one of Pinchot's better known statements, partly because in a secular age the Forest Service has not done much to publicize it. Yet Pinchot's thinking in this regard was very much in tune with many other progressive intellectuals of the late nineteenth and early twentieth century. The social gospel movement of the time has been characterized as seeking the "social salvation" of mankind, as having the overall objective to achieve "the coming to earth of the kingdom of heaven."[8]

The culture of the Forest Service from its early days exhibited a strong conviction of doing God's work in the world. One student of the Forest Service, Ashley Schiff, found that the agency had a culture of "moral righteousness" that was only "embroidered with scientific technology."[9] Pinchot said that Forest Service employees were not to be motivated by "the desire to earn good money;" rather, they were doing "good work in a good cause." He and his fellow professional foresters were busy fending off the "vast power, pecuniary and political, . . . [of the] . . . railroads, the stock interests, mining interests, water power interests, and most of the big timber interests." The basic reason the Forest Service would win, Pinchot stated, was that "in the long run our purpose was too obviously right to be defeated."[10] Another former chief of the Forest Service would declare that the agency had been "born in controversy and baptized with the holy water of reform."[11]

Indeed, American progressivism and its conservationist offshoot were not only concerned with providing more goods and services, but also were involved in a grand undertaking of spiritual renewal. If the details of achieving economic progress might differ among them, American progressivism shared with a host of "religions of progress" of the early twentieth century the core conviction that the end to material scarcity would mean an end to ancient conflicts among people over resources, and a broad solution to long-standing problems of the human condition.

Progressive "theology" had its own economic interpretation of original sin.[12] People had been driven throughout previous human history to steal, cheat, and lie—to behave in evil ways—merely as a matter of obtaining the material means to survive. In the future, as a general condition of material abundance came to prevail, human beings would finally be freed from such harsh competition for resources, enabling them instead to perfect their better natures. Progress based on science and economics would become the secular religion, not only of the Forest Service and professional forestry, but also for the American welfare and regulatory state of the twentieth century.[13]

The preoccupation with material advance explains why, as Samuel Hays has written of conservationism more broadly, the creed of the Forest Service was a "gospel of efficiency."[14] The test of efficiency became for the Forest Service and other agencies in American government a new measure of good and evil, a new superior morality. All this followed logically enough from the precepts of progressive religion. If material progress were the correct route to the end of scarcity and to heaven on earth, the achievement of such progress would require ever-higher levels of efficiency in the use of resources. To become more efficient was thus to move closer to a secular salvation here on earth. In traditional religion, the distinction between good and evil has reflected a view that a good action must bring a person closer to salvation and the kingdom of heaven (in the hereafter). If a good action meant coming closer to God, evil actions were those that separated human beings further from God. The progressive gospel of efficiency merely secularized these long-standing beliefs of Western religion.

If the new route to salvation followed along a path of economic progress, it followed that a new priesthood of experts in efficiency would now have greater social authority than the old Catholic and Protestant clergy. The distinguished American historian of the progressive era, Robert Wiebe, has commented that the new expert professionals of the progressive era found that "the shared mysteries of a specialty allowed intimate communion." The self-concept of being a professional offered a sense of "prestige through exclusiveness," a brotherhood of men brought together by their common "desire to remake the world," and a "deep satisfaction" that accompanied a "revolution in identity" that followed initiation into a select class of fellow professionals. The rites of professional life were designed to ensure that "the process of becoming an expert, of immersing oneself in the scientific method, eradicated petty passions and narrow ambitions."[15] The professional culture that Pinchot sought to instill in the Forest Service followed this model closely.

Another leading historian of the political values of the progressive era would also note the close connections between the belief in efficiency of the professional classes and the beliefs of earlier priesthoods of traditional religion. As Dwight Waldo has noted, in the progressive era "it is yet amazing what a position of dominance 'efficiency' assumed, how it waxed until it had assimilated or over-shadowed other values, how men and events came to be degraded or exalted according to what was assumed to be its dictate." Looking back over many centuries, Waldo found that "every era has a few words that epitomize its world-view and that are fixed points by which all else can be measured. In the Middle Ages they were such words as faith, grace, and God; in the eighteenth century they were such words as reason, nature, and rights; during the past 50 years in America they have been such words as cause, reaction, scientific, expert, progress—and efficiency."[16] The historian Samuel Haber declared that in the progressive era the United States seemed to be possessed by "an efficiency craze" that amounted to "a secular Great Awakening."[17]

If the conservation movement represented the application of progressive principles to the field of natural resources, one might say that the Forest Service in the twentieth century has been in some sense part of a modern form of "church."[18] Its mission was to transform the resources of the natural world (as found on the national forests) into the material outputs of an ever-growing national economy. In so doing, the Forest Service would be playing its part in the grand crusade to save the world by abolishing material scarcity, ending the desperate struggle for access to the resources to survive that had been the bane of past human existence.

The contemporary environmental movement can be seen in part as a reaction against these ideas. It is true that material progress has greatly improved the quality of life for the people living in the developed parts of the world (and most of us are extremely grateful for it). Yet economic advance has not yielded the improvement in human character and the sense of well being for all that had been expected. Despite all the high hopes of the early twentieth century, no "new man" (or woman) emerged from the enormous material progress of the century. And science proved to be a double-edged sword, capable of providing great benefits to humanity but also of creating major threats to the environment and even to future human survival.

Contemporary environmentalism goes beyond these generally shared expressions of doubts about the religion of scientific management and progress. As Sax indicated, it offers a new form of secular salvation of its own. Here, the fact that many environmental advocates are well meaning, that they have a great strength of ethical conviction—an appealing feature in an age of moral and religious uncertainty—does not mean that they deserve any suspension of critical judgment. The history of Western religion is filled with human and other victims of various well-intentioned crusades to save the world. It is thus important to examine closely the tenets and the logic of environmental theology—the value foundation for the current policies of ecosystem management.

NONHUMAN INDIANS

The manner of the treatment of American Indians in the prevailing interpretations of ecosystem management, for example, is unfortunately reminiscent of earlier thinking about American Indians. As Stephen Pyne keeps reminding us, many Indians pervasively manipulated the forests and other lands of North America through the deliberate setting of fires. It was often essential to their very manner of feeding and clothing themselves. Yet in defining "natural" forest conditions as an ideal, ecosystem management for good practical reasons must set the goal at achieving "pre-European" conditions.

However, any such way of thinking depends on an almost willfully maintained ignorance of the historic Indian use of fire and other impacts on nature. To continue to assert that pre–European settlement forests are "natural," and current forests are not, as Pyne has commented, amounts to "stripping American Indians of the power to shape their environment"; it is an act that "is tantamount to dismissing their humanity."[19]

In other words, to suggest that Indian actions are "natural" is to put Indians in the same environmental category as wolves, grizzly bears, and other nonhumans. In effect, if unintentionally, it would revert to the most blatant of anti-Indian prejudices of the past—when Indians could actually be treated as virtually nonhuman because they did not worship the right God, because they were not rationally responsible for their actions, or for other such theological reasons. Cotton Mather, as Roderick Nash reminds us, believed in his deep Puritan convictions that "the natives were not merely heathens but active disciples of the devil"—and the Puritan settlers had been brought by God to the new world to reclaim its territories for His greater glory.[20] Such grounds were in fact then and for many years to come offered for slaughtering Indian populations, cheating on treaty obligations, moving Indians around from one place to another, and other actions now greatly regretted.

Surely, a return to such old ways of thinking about Indians is not what Secretary Babbitt, or other environmentalists, wish to advocate. Yet in value and philosophical terms—theological terms, broadly speaking— that is what they are implicitly saying. In this newest incarnation of the old Indian prejudices, Indians once again do not count. Before European settlement, many environmentalists have in effect been telling us, there really was only wild nature.

VIRTUAL NATURE

There are other fundamental problems with the goal of achieving forest conditions as they existed prior to European settlement. Large amounts of money would be spent in effect to recreate the forest environment of the West as it existed before European civilization made basic changes in the ecological workings of these forests. Yet the only way to restore the forests of the past is by applying the current scientific instruments of that same European civilization. Given all that has happened in the past 150 years, "letting nature run its course" simply will not do the trick. If the Forest Service were to adopt a policy of nonmanagement, the result today would be a forest condition without any natural or historical precedents and much different from the environmental conditions prior to the arrival of Europeans.

However, if human beings have to design and create the forest, what is created may not be "nature" at all but "virtual nature"—as William Cronon describes it, a vision of "nature as Eden" that amounts to "nature as artifice, nature as self-conscious cultural construction." The study of environmental history has "demonstrated that human beings have been manipulating ecosystems for as long as we have records of their passage." When the pervasive historical impacts of human actions on all aspects of the environment are considered, "all of this calls into question the familiar modern habit of appealing to nonhuman nature as the objective measure against which human uses of nature should be judged."[21]

If an old Rembrandt masterpiece is burned in a fire, recreating it, no matter how exactly, will never restore the original. Indeed, if people were to try to fool themselves into thinking that they had really found the original, this self-deception, if not outright hypocrisy, would in itself for many people be objectionable. Environmentalists today may risk putting themselves in the position of the priests of the Catholic Church who once claimed to have found relics of Jesus himself—only to have carbon dating in recent years show these claims to have been gross deceptions (however well intended initially).

The much prized "old-growth" forests—the traditional forester term of art for these mature forests of Douglas fir and other tree species in Oregon, Washington, northern California, and other western states—are believed by most Americans to be the original forests. Recognizing that language can be a critical factor in modern soundbite politics, environmental groups promptly relabeled these Pacific Northwest forests in their writings and speeches as "ancient forests." In the fierce struggle over the future use of the federal forests in the Pacific Northwest, centered around the preservation of habitat for the northern spotted owl under the Endangered Species Act, the remaining uncut forests were regularly described by environmentalists as "cathedrals," "sacred places," and other religious terms.

It was as though the "ancient forest" was like the original condition in the Garden of Eden; indeed, many people seemed to feel that the struggles over the spotted owl, and over the future of these forests, involved virtually the same old struggle of good versus evil in the world. The temptations of the devil—now taking the form of corporate timber profits and other ill begotten earnings from the national forests—are once again threatening to undermine the innocent harmony of an original nature.

Yet all this was more poetry than fact. In analyzing the policy options for the Sierra Nevada forests in California, three leading American foresters, Jerry Franklin, Norman Johnson, and John Sessions, proposed five broad objectives. One of the objectives was "rebuilding late-successional forests" and a second separate and distinct objective was "reintroducing historical ecosystem processes." By late-successional forests, the foresters meant the existence of forest conditions representing the later stages of forest evolution toward a climax forest species composition. In other words, in a Douglas fir forest in the Pacific Northwest, this would be an old-growth or ancient forest. Yet achievement of late-successional forests was not the same goal as restoring the operation of historical ecological processes.

Indeed, the definitions of an old-growth forest, as worked out in the Pacific Northwest, have been based on conditions at forest sites that had not been significantly affected by fire for many years. Thus, the conditions found in these current old-growth forests are, as foresters Carl Skinner and Chi-Ru Chang report, "at least in part the result of years of fire suppression." Because fire suppression has significantly affected even existing old-growth forests—encouraging greater understory growth, for example—"current conditions of old growth . . . are not necessarily representative of stands dominated by large, old trees that existed under a functioning presettlement fire regime." Indeed, it is likely that "large-scale prescribed fire programs" would have to be developed and implemented in order to move from current old-growth forests to "sustainable old growth forests" on the presettlement model.[22]

Old-growth forest objectives thus also require an active human intervention for their achievement; letting nature "do its thing" will not get the forests to the desired end state. As the regional forester for the Southwest Region of the Forest Service testified to Congress, "the more we attempt to maintain an ecosystem, particularly a forested ecosystem, in a fixed or an unchanging condition when its natural condition is subject to considerable change, the less likely we are going to be able to do what we intended."[23] The Working Group on Late-Successional Conservation Strategies reported that "all the strategies would require significant investments to produce and maintain LS/OG [late-successional and old-growth] forests ecosystems in the Sierra Nevada" forests. Another fact much at odds with the conventional public view is that "plans which provide for habitat needs of the California spotted owl may not provide for maintenance of significant amounts of intact undisturbed LS/OG forest."[24]

That is to say, the spotted owl does not necessarily work well as a surrogate, as is often claimed, for the preservation of sustainable old-growth forests. Indeed, timber harvesting in an appropriate fashion, to some extent substituting by thinning and other fuels reduction for the past workings of forest fire, may in some cases serve old-growth protective purposes better than spotted owl protection. As Franklin and coauthor Jo Ann Fites-Kaufmann of the Forest Service explain, recent forestry thinking points toward "the practicality of prescriptions which maintain a high level of late-successional forest function [with large diameter trees, snags, and logs] while providing for significant timber harvest."[25] In those old-growth forests where risks associated with prescribed forest fire are simply too great (or the economic costs are simply too high), timber harvesting might have to substitute for the historical ecological role of fire in sustaining the old—the "ancient"—trees.

It is true, to be sure, that late-successional and old-growth forests, if not necessarily corresponding precisely to their current old-growth versions, did occupy about two-thirds of the Sierra Nevada forests prior to settlement times. For high-quality sites, timber harvesting and other human-caused disturbances have now reduced these types of forests to about 16 percent of their former Sierra Nevada range. So there has been a great human impact on the condition of the forest over the past 150 years. However, whether the goal is an old-growth forest or a presettlement forest (owing to fire and other natural disturbances, fully one-third of the presettlement forest was not in a late-successional old-growth stage), given all that has happened in the past, this outcome will now have to be manufactured by human actions.

DISNEYLAND FORESTS

The idea of "nature" in such circumstances loses all real meaning. Professional foresters are today simply being asked to create the illusion of nature, and environmental organizations seem to be volunteering to market this illusion to the American public. They are all seemingly the heirs to Walt Disney, who found that "frontierland" (along with "fantasyland" and "tomorrowland") were also highly marketable images. Television programming in the 1950s and 1960s was filled with "westerns" that purported to portray the western United States as the early pioneers first found it.

To think of "nature" prior to Europeans as somehow "real nature" is, as Stephen Pyne writes, historically "absurd."[26] Or, as Alston Chase observes of Yellowstone Park, it has "become all symbol and no substance, a Potemkin Village constructed to impress visitors where the illusion of biodiversity is sustained by myth."[27] To be sure, however mythical, environmentalists are today appealing to the deepest values in Western civilization, the great hope that "original nature," as once found in the Garden of Eden, can be recovered again, a place free of sin and corruption. That is why their message resonates so powerfully in American life.

In that sense, Billy Graham may be a closer parallel than Walt Disney. Indeed, John McPhee once said of David Brower, the former executive director of the Sierra Club in the 1960s and widely considered the leading environmentalist of the past fifty years, that "his approach is in some ways analogous to the Reverend Dr. Billy Graham's exhortations to sinners to come forward and be saved now. . . . Brower's crusade, like Graham's, began many years ago, and Brower's may have been more effective."[28]

ENVIRONMENTAL CALVINISM

There is a still more fundamental philosophical issue relating to the goal of achieving pre-European settlement conditions. Assuming that this goal were somehow achievable, why should this be the goal? Why should the highest value—the driving policy priority—in forest management be to achieve a condition of the forest before human (or at least European) impacts began to change the forest ecology? The same set of values, to be sure, is found in the definition of a wilderness area, as set out in the Wilderness Act of 1964.[29] A wilderness, the act says, is "an area where the earth and its community of life are untrammeled by man, where man himself is a visitor who does not remain."

A wilderness is, in short, a place where roads, buildings, motorized vehicles, and other signs of human impact are minimized to the extent possible. If a wilderness is a cathedral of environmentalism, the place where its highest values are expressed, there is a strong suggestion here that human actions are unworthy, if not corrupting. In the most profound symbolic statement of the environmental belief system—the environmental "theology"—the role of human beings is a negative one. It is as if the Garden of Eden should be defined by the fact that human beings were not present in the original condition. This is, it might be noted, the mirror opposite of the value system of professional economists, where something can have value only by its direct consumption, necessarily involving a direct human presence.[30]

But in the environmental belief system a significant human presence in nature in effect becomes an act of contamination. We are getting close here to the idea of original sin; humans have been corrupted since they destroyed the original natural harmony of the Garden of Eden. They are still living in sin, and for many Christian believers we can hope to escape this condition only when God brings on a whole new world. As environmental historian Donald Worster has commented, environmentalism has inherited from old-style American Protestantism its Calvinist legacy of "ascetic discipline." Environmentalism today offers a secularization of the "deep suspicion in the Protestant mind of unrestrained play, extravagant consumption, and self-indulgence, a suspicion that tended to be very skeptical of human nature, to fear that humans were born depraved and were in need of strict management." In short, as Worster writes, in the past quarter century "the antidote for environmental destruction has been a movement called environmentalism and that movement has, in the United States, owed much of its program, temperament, and drive to the influence of Protestantism" and especially the Calvinism of the early Puritans in American history.[31]

For a secular environmentalist, to be sure, there is no God who can be counted on to bring on a new world.[32] For nonbelievers, the closest that human beings on this corrupted earth can get to experiencing a true harmony with nature is to visit a wilderness area—an area minimally corrupted by contact with sinful human beings. In other words, to the degree that human salvation can be conceived without the intervention of one or another god, wilderness is the effective path of salvation in the secular religion of environmentalism. As the motto of the Wilderness Society says, borrowing from Henry David Thoreau, "in Wildness is the preservation of the world."

This all has, as Worster suggested, a deeply Calvinist flavor.[33] Calvin once said that most human beings, deeply infected by sin, must live a depraved existence in this world. In extreme cases, leading environmentalists such as David Brower and Dave Foreman have labeled the very human presence on the earth as a "cancer."[34] In recently recanting the mistaken "misanthropic" attitudes of her youth, a current (and still radical, but now seeking radical human solutions as well) environmentalist Anne Petermann described that former outlook on the world:

> When I was a teenager, I was deeply misanthropic. I loved nature and spent as much time as possible out of doors. But at night, I would look out the window at the Burger King across the street, at the gas stations on all sides, at the noisy stinking stream of traffic, and I would loathe humanity, dreaming of its demise. When I found Earth First!, the campfire chants of "Billions are living that should be dead" or "fuck the human race" appealed to me. Yes, I thought, humans are a cancer on the Earth.[35]

For those despairing for the fate of the earth, a wilderness area is perhaps all that can be saved from the cancerous growth of human civilization over the rest of the world. Having turned away from Earth First! at the

end of the 1980s, Foreman has taken on an another environmental crusade. Through his wildlands project, he now hopes—seemingly unrealis-
tically—that perhaps as much as 40 percent of the United States might
eventually be saved in a wild condition.

Thus, when Interior Secretary Babbitt says that more widespread mechanical removal of excess fuels would represent a direct assault on
"God's creation," he is putting on the table some of the underlying theological roots of the environmental belief system. Human beings are sinful.
The world of the Americas was free of sin until European settlers arrived.
As Stephen Pyne puts it, "environmentalists have told the story of the Garden of Eden and the fall from grace over and over again."[36] Today, however, Americans have a chance to reassert the forces of good in the world
against the forces of evil. This act of salvation means restoring at least
some parts of nature to its original uncorrupted and pre-
European condition—recovering in at least some parts of the world the
innocent harmony with nature of the Garden of Eden.

Or, as John Muir believed, "the clearest way into the Universe is
through a forest wilderness." He liked to spend "a month's worship with
Nature in the high temples of the great Sierra Crown." This was the path
of discovery for Muir, as Roderick Nash explains, of "life's inner har-
monies, fundamental truths of existence"—that is, for Muir, of the existence and meaning of God.[37] A wilderness in the environmental belief
system has been a cathedral in the same sense as Notre Dame in Paris for
a member of the Catholic Church—a place to be uplifted and spiritually
inspired by the closer presence of God.

For many years, this religious belief system of environmentalism—
sometimes made explicit as by Muir, more often left implicit—did not attract much critical scrutiny. It fit comfortably for many American environmentalists whose heritage was in fact a strict Protestantism and whose
value system was in many ways a secular Calvinism. If Thomas Huxley
once said that European socialism was "Catholicism, minus God," it might
be appropriate to describe American environmentalism as "Calvinism,
minus God."[38] Given the enormous impact of Puritanism throughout
American history, originally in traditional Calvinist forms and more recently in secular dress, the strong Calvinist element of environmentalism
goes far to explain the obvious deep resonance of environmental thinking with large parts of American culture today.[39]

THE PROBLEM WITH WILDERNESS VALUES

Recently, however, some leading environmental thinkers have begun to
express doubts about the Calvinist sense of sinfulness and the doom and

gloom of the environmental counsel of despair at the human presence in the world. They argue that it is not only theologically misconceived, but also can do real damage by preventing the adoption of government policies that would in fact be more genuinely beneficial to the environment. The modern age was shaped as well by the optimism of the Enlightenment, which pushed the old Puritan pessimism into the background. The environmental movement includes many diverse views and values within its broad umbrella. There are also many leading environmentalists today who think that contemporary environmentalism should focus on improving this world, rather than lamenting its sins, or seeking to escape it into the wilderness.

Their views were given voice in the 1990s by the distinguished environmental historian William Cronon, earlier well known as the author of *Changes in the Land*.[40] In 1995 Cronon published an article, "The Trouble with Wilderness, or Getting Back to the Wrong Nature," that stirred up a hornet's nest of controversy within the environmental movement.[41] Cronon believes that for the environmental movement—and Cronon considers himself an environmentalist—intellectual honesty requires that "the time has come to rethink wilderness." The environmental movement in general has mythologized the idea of "Nature," much to its own detriment. The very concept of wilderness is very much a "product of [our] civilization." Investing wilderness with a deep moral significance, Cronon argues, "we too easily imagine that what we behold is Nature when in fact we see the reflection of our own unexamined longings and desires." It has been for some people living harried urban lives an outlet for their "nostalgia for a passing frontier way of life," a refuge from a fear that modern life has become "confining, false, and artificial." It has been for other people a place of spiritual inspiration; in the wilderness one might even hope to "meet God."[42]

Yet as Cronon also suggests, such thinking about wilderness has little more objective reality than the belief that Disneyland is the real world. The meaning of a church does not lie in the collection of bricks; it lies in the symbolic significance given the church by a religious belief system. So it is with wilderness churches and American environmentalism.[43] Moreover, Cronon is not happy with the symbolic message of the wilderness church. The idea of "wilderness serves as the unexamined foundation on which so many of the quasi-religious values of modern environmentalism rest." Unfortunately, the "specific habits of thinking that flow from this complex cultural construction called wilderness" exert a "pervasive" but "insidious" influence throughout government policy making for the environment—including national forest policy. The emphasis on areas free of human impact as the closest possible places to perfection, as expressed powerfully in the very idea of wilderness, diverts the attention of the environmental movement from the fundamental question of "what an ethical, sustainable, *honorable* human place in nature might actually look like."[44] Under ecosystem management, the Forest Service now proposes to extend such wilderness values much more broadly, to most of the national forest system.

The wilderness value system also involves, in truth, a large degree of hypocrisy for most people. As Cronon explains all this:

> To the extent that we live in an urban-industrial civilization but at the same time pretend to ourselves that our *real* home is in the wilderness, to just that extent we give ourselves permission to evade responsibility for the lives we actually lead. We inhabit civilization while holding some part of ourselves—what we imagine to be the most precious part—aloof from its entanglements. We work our nine-to-five jobs in its institutions, we eat its food, we drive its cars (not least to reach the wilderness), we benefit from the intricate and all too invisible networks with which it shelters us, all the while pretending that these things are not an essential part of who we are. By imagining that our true home is in the wilderness, we forgive ourselves the homes we actually inhabit. In its flight from history, in its siren song of escape, in its reproduction of the dangerous dualism that sets human beings outside of nature—in all of these ways, wilderness poses a serious threat to responsible environmentalism at the end of the twentieth century.[45]

> [Instead], we need an environmental ethic that will tell us as much about *using* nature as about *not* using it. The wilderness dualism tends to cast any use as *ab*-use, and thereby denies us a middle ground in which responsible use and non-use might attain some kind of balanced, sustainable relationship. My own belief is that only by exploring this middle ground will we learn ways of imagining a better world for all of us: humans and non-humans, rich people and poor, women and men, First Worlders and Third Worlders, white folks and people of color, consumers and producers—a world better for humanity in all of its diversity and for all the rest of nature too.[46]

If scientific management—part of the secular religion of progress—was one grand scheme imposed across all the western national forests to their ultimate detriment in the twentieth century, modern environmentalism with its new religion of antiprogress and skepticism about human capacities to improve the world could be promoting yet another sorry episode in the history of these lands. As Karl Hess has written, it is a history lasting now for 200 years in which one after another grand "vision" is imposed by people far removed from the landscape, who often know little of the actual requirements of particular places, in the name of one or another utopian hope or grand messianic dream.[47]

THE MORAL SIGNIFICANCE OF A CHAOTIC UNIVERSE

Yet another basic problem with the pre-European vision of ecosystem management for the national forests is more a matter of the assumed scientific facts of the situation, as opposed to deficiencies of ethical philosophy, as described by Cronon. Yet if theology begins with bad facts, the result can hardly be anything but bad theology.

In the thinking of many environmentalists, the idea of restoring the forest to a pre-European settlement condition assumes implicitly that there was some equilibrium state of the forest that long existed, until disrupted by industrial civilization. If the forest ecology were constantly changing in basic ways—if the essential forest workings in 1750 were much different from 1800, which were much different from 1850, and so on and so on—there would not be much point to restoring the conditions of any one point in time. If the forest evolved rapidly through a succession of ecological conditions, as new major influences entered to disturb the prior equilibrium, the human disturbances of the past 150 years could well be seen in much the same light—just another in a long-running series of new disturbance factors, like a new foraging animal in a forest or a new insect pest, that causes the very character of the forest ecology to be altered rapidly in some basic way. Such changes, it seems, are happening all the time in the real world of nature.

Another of America's leading environmental historians, Donald Worster, has addressed this issue in a well-known essay, "The Ecology of Order and Chaos." In the older and original ecological understanding, as Worster writes, expert students of the ecology of a forest or other natural area could offer what amounted to a program of "moral enlightenment." The study of ecology was considered to be a process of identifying natural conditions of "equilibrium, harmony, and order"—the secular equivalent of the Garden of Eden. Having done this, the management objective for forests and other natural environments could then easily be spelled out; it consisted of the pursuit of "a restored equilibrium between humans and nature"—as in restoring the national forests to their pre-European conditions, the current goal of the Forest Service.[48]

The problem was that the continuing field investigations of working ecologists were simply not sustaining this vision. What ecologists were finding, as Worster explains, was instead a world of "disturbance, disharmony, and chaos."[49] All this was bound to be subversive of the prevailing vision of ecological management, as it is today still offered in the official policy guidance of government agencies such as the National Park Service and Forest Service. Their former clear vision to restore forests and other ecologies to conditions of pre-European settlement now becomes much

cloudier. It now becomes necessary to specify one time among many periods in the past that may have involved different natural conditions. Such
a choice, moreover, may simply be arbitrary. As a management goal, it
may have about as much objective validity as picking a number from a lot-
tery.[50]

In short, there may be any number of possible natural ecological states
of the forest; there is no clear reason, at least within the framework of ecological science alone, why any one is any better than any other. The term
ecological "health," as commonly employed in forest management discussions today, glosses over rather than resolves this problem. Forest
"health" is like beauty; it is in the eyes of the beholder. Or, as Worster
writes:

> John Muir once declared, "When we try to pick out anything by itself, we
> find it hitched to everything else in the universe." For him, that was a man-
> ifestation of an infinitely wise plan in which everything functioned with
> perfect harmony. The new ecology of chaos, though impressed like Muir
> with interdependency, does not share his view of "an infinitely wise plan"
> that controls and shapes everything into order. There is no plan, today's
> scientists say, no harmony apparent in the events of nature. If there is order
> in the universe—and there will no longer be any science at all if order van-
> ishes—it is going to be much more difficult to locate and describe than we
> thought.
>
> For Muir, the clear lesson of cosmic complexity was that humans ought to
> love and preserve nature just as it is. The lessons of the new ecology, in con-
> trast, are not at all clear. . . . What is there to love or preserve in a universe
> of chaos? How are people supposed to behave in such a universe? If that is
> the kind of place we inhabit, why not go ahead with all our private ambi-
> tions, free of any fear that we may be doing special damage? What, after all,
> does the phrase "environmental damage" mean in a world of so much natu-
> ral chaos? Does the tradition of environmentalism to which Muir belonged,
> along with so many other nature writers and ecologists of the past, people
> like Paul Sears, Eugene Odum, Aldo Leopold, and Rachel Carson, make
> sense any longer?[51]

Worster does not answer his own questions in any definitive way. He
seems to wish very much that the old Muir (and Aldo Leopold) way of
thinking could be maintained—it is, after all, essentially his own religion—but he also seems to doubt that he can in good conscience any
more stoutly defend it. Worster is like a Christian preacher of the second
half of the nineteenth century, finding that Darwin has now undermined
much of his old message, but honest enough to concede that Darwin's
facts and science must be respected.

As an intellectual, Worster is properly exposing his fears and doubts to
public view. The Forest Service, however, cannot afford this luxury; it is,

after all, by its actions making some American citizens big winners and others big losers. Thousands of people lost their jobs in the Pacific Northwest as the Forest Service and other federal agencies, driven by the litigation over the spotted owl, put a new vision of ecosystem management into practice. If this vision is simply one aesthetic (or spiritual) choice among many possible such choices, if the choice of forest goals must in the end be somewhat arbitrary—a random and subjective result in a chaotic world of constant disturbance—these people who lost their jobs may have sacrificed for no necessary reason.[52]

If they should come to think that they have been merely the accidental pawns in a government process that is itself more a matter of chaos than order, their anger might be difficult to contain.[53] The Forest Service—and other federal land agencies—would in any case be deprived of future legitimacy in their actions. National forest management would have to look to some other institutional arrangements, and other belief systems, for its future social legitimacy.

CONCLUSION

If Bruce Babbitt is correct, if land management requires a religious vision, it will require some rethinking of the basic organizational framework for the national forests. Americans typically regard religion as a personal matter, but the management of the national forests cannot be merely personal. If moral principles based on religious beliefs are to guide national forest management, and these principles are to be grounded in religion, it is also true that Americans are likely to be uncomfortable acknowledging the religious roots of the necessary land ethic. If the Forest Service is to function as a part of a "church" of a particular faith, how can that be squared with traditional American ideas about separation of church and state? How does the government justify using public funds to promote a particular form of religious expression?

Seeking to avoid such dilemmas, the awkward compromise in the twentieth century was to make simultaneously a claim for a moral imperative in forest management and a claim that the resulting necessary management actions had a valid scientific justification. The result, however, was all too often a corruption of both moral discourse and scientific inquiry. Discussion of ethical issues relating to the forests had to take place under a superficial camouflage of scientific terminology. Genuine scientific inquiry was frustrated because the results of forest research was already determined by prior ethical convictions.

Scientific management has so often proven to be a failure, among other reasons, because it has really been ethically driven management—seeking to recover the Garden of Eden or to enact some other implicit religious theme. The Forest Service finds it difficult, however, to abandon scientific pretenses because so much of its social legitimacy depends on a claim to scientific status. It was the idea of the one scientific answer (the "objective" answer) that originally justified the centralization of final authority for all the national forests, encompassing fully 10 percent of the land area of the United States, at the federal level in Washington, D.C.

If the old beliefs about the role of science and scientific management of national forest lands have to be abandoned, the most fundamental assumptions about the institutional arrangements for the management of national forest lands will be up for grabs. It could even mean—as subsequent chapters will argue, it should mean—the abolition of the U.S. Forest Service.

NOTES

1. Quoted in Stephen Stuebner, "Government Plans More Fires to Prevent Fires," *The New York Times* (February 9, 1997), p. 30.

2. Bruce Babbitt, "Leading America Closer to the Promise of God's Covenant," Keynote Address to Associated Church Press 1996 Annual Convention, Mesa, Arizona, April 11, 1996. See also Bruce Babbitt, "Our Covenant: To Protect the *Whole of Creation*," circulated to top staff of the Interior Department through the e-mail system, December 14, 1995. This speech was delivered on several occasions, including to the League of Conservation Voters in New York City in early December 1995. See also Robert H. Nelson, "Bruce Babbitt, Pipeline to the Almighty," *The Weekly Standard* (June 24, 1996).

3. Committee of Scientists, *Sustaining the People's Lands: Recommendations for Stewardship of the National Forests and Grasslands into the Next Century,* a report to the Secretary of Agriculture and the Chief of the Forest Service (Washington, D.C.: Department of Agriculture, March 15, 1999), p. 44.

4. See Bill Devall and George Sessions, *Deep Ecology* (Salt Lake City: Peregrine Press Books, 1985) and Theodore Roszak, *The Voice of the Earth* (New York: Simon and Schuster, 1992).

5. Joseph L. Sax, *Mountains Without Handrails: Reflections on the National Parks* (Ann Arbor: University of Michigan Press, 1980), p. 104.

6. See Robert H. Nelson, "Unoriginal Sin: The Judeo-Christian Roots of Ecotheology," *Policy Review* (Summer 1990).

7. Gifford Pinchot, *The Fight for Conservation* (Seattle: University of Washington Press, 1967), p. 95.

8. Charles Howard Hopkins, *The Rise of the Social Gospel in American Protestantism, 1865–1915* (New Haven: Yale University Press, 1940), pp. 320–21.

9. Ashley L. Schiff, *Fire and Water: Scientific Heresy in the Forest Service* (Cambridge: Harvard University Press, 1962), p. 5.

10. Gifford Pinchot, *Breaking New Ground* (New York: Harcourt, Brace, 1947), pp. 258–60.

11. Cited in Schiff, *Fire and Water,* p. 5.

12. For further discussion of the religious character of American progressivism, see Robert H. Nelson, *Reaching for Heaven on Earth: The Theological Meaning of Economics* (Lanham, Md.: Rowman & Littlefield, 1991), Chapter 5.

13. See James. C. Scott, *Seeing Like a State: How Certain Schemes to Improve the Human Condition Have Failed* (New Haven: Yale University Press, 1998), pp. 87–102.

14. Samuel P. Hays, *Conservation and the Gospel of Efficiency, The Progressive Conservation Movement, 1890–1920* (Cambridge: Harvard University Press, 1959).

15. Robert H. Wiebe, *The Search for Order, 1877–1920* (New York: Hill and Wang, 1967), pp. 113, 161.

16. Dwight Waldo, *The Administrative State: A Study of the Political Theory of American Public Administration* (1948; reprint, New York: Holmes and Meier, 1984), pp. 19–20.

17. Samuel Haber, *Efficiency and Uplift: Scientific Management in the Progressive Era, 1890–1920* (Chicago: University of Chicago Press, 1964), p. ix.

18. Robert H. Nelson, "The Forest Service as a Church," paper presented at a conference on "A Vision for the Forest Service: Where Should the Forest Service Be in 2009 and How Might It Get There?", sponsored by Resources for the Future and the Pinchot Institute for Conservation, April 29, 1999, Washington, D.C.

19. Stephen J. Pyne, *World Fire: The Culture of Fire on Earth* (New York: Holt, 1995), p. 244.

20. Roderick Nash, *Wilderness and the American Mind* (New Haven: Yale University Press, 1973), p. 36.

21. William Cronon, "Introduction: In Search of Nature," in *Uncommon Ground: Toward Reinventing Nature,* ed. William Cronon (New York: Norton, 1995), pp. 22–23, 32, 35.

22. Carl N. Skinner and Chi-Ru Chang, "Fire Regimes, Past and Present," in *Status of the Sierra Nevada, Volume II,* Sierra Nevada Ecosystem Project, Final Report to Congress, (Davis: University of California, Wildland Resources Center Report No. 40, March 1997), p. 1061.

23. U.S. Senate Subcommittee on Forests and Public Land Management, Committee on Energy and Natural Resources, statement by Charles W. Cartwright, Regional Forester for the Southwest Region of the Forest Service, *Hearings on Federal Forest Management,* August 29, 1995, S. Hrg. 104–182 (Pt. 2) (Washington, D.C.: Government Printing Office, 1996), p. 210.

24. Working Group on Late-Successional Conservation Strategies, "Alternative Approaches to Conservation of Late-Successional Forests in the Sierra Nevada and Their Evaluation," in *Status of the Sierra Nevada, Addendum,* pp. 55, 67.

25. Jerry F. Franklin and Jo Ann Fites-Kaufmann, "Assessment of Late-Successional Forests of the Sierra Nevada," in *Status of the Sierra Nevada, Volume II,* p. 655.

26. Pyne, *World Fire,* p. 242.

27. Alston Chase, "Vanishing Species of Conservationists," *Washington Times* (September 5, 1997), p. A20.

28. John McPhee, *Conversations with the Archdruid* (New York: Farrar, Straus and Giroux, 1971), p. 83.

29. See Nash, *Wilderness and the American Mind.*

30. See Robert H. Nelson, "Sustainability, Efficiency, and God: Economic Values and the Sustainability Debate," *Annual Review of Ecology and Systematics* vol. 25 (1995).

31. Donald Worster, "John Muir and the Roots of American Environmentalism," in *The Wealth of Nature,* ed. Donald Worster (New York: Oxford University Press, 1993), pp. 185, 197.

32. See Interview with Robert H. Nelson, "Judeo-Christian Tradition Best Basis for Environmentalism," *Religion and Liberty* (March/April 1999).

33. See also Nelson, "Unoriginal Sin"; Robert H. Nelson, "Environmental Calvinism: The Judeo-Christian Roots of Eco-Theology," in *Taking the Environment Seriously,* ed. Roger E. Meiners and Bruce Yandle (Lanham, Md.: Rowman & Littlefield, 1993); and Robert H. Nelson, "Calvinism Minus God," in *Saving the Seas: Values, Scientists and International Governance,* ed. L. Anathea Brooks and Stacy D. VanDeever (College Park, Md.: A Maryland Sea Grant Book, 1997).

34. Foreman is quoted in Douglas S. Looney, "Protection or Provocateur," *Sports Illustrated* (May 27, 1991).

35. Anne Petermann, "Tales of a Recovering Misanthrope," *Earth First!: The Radical Environmental Journal* vol. 19, no. 6 (June–July 1999), p. 3.

36. Quoted in Ed Marston, "Experts Line up on All Sides of the Tree-Grass Debate," *High Country News* (April 15, 1996), p. 13.

37. Nash, *Wilderness and the American Mind,* p. 126.

38. See Nelson, "Calvinism Minus God."

39. The central role of the Puritan heritage in American life is described in Kevin Phillips, *The Cousins' Wars: Religion, Politics, and the Triumph of Anglo-America* (New York: Basic Books, 1999).

40. William Cronon, *Changes in the Land: Indians, Colonists, and the Ecology of New England* (New York: Hill and Wang, 1983).

41. William Cronon, "The Trouble with Wilderness, or Getting Back to the Wrong Nature," in *Uncommon Ground: Toward Reinventing Nature,* ed. William Cronon (New York: Norton, 1995). For various responses to Cronon, see articles in a symposium on "Opposing Wilderness Deconstruction," *Wild Earth* (Winter 1996–97).

42. Cronon, "The Trouble with Wilderness," pp. 51, 54, 58.

43. For a general discussion of the way in which history is frequently shaped by strong preconceptions brought by the historian, see William Cronon, "A Place for Stories: Nature, History and Narrative," *Journal of American History* (March 1992).

44. Cronon, "The Trouble with Wilderness," pp. 54, 61, 62.

45. Ibid., pp. 61–62.

46. Ibid., p. 66.

47. Karl Hess, Jr., *Visions Upon the Land: Man and Nature on the Western Range* (Washington, D.C.: Island Press, 1992).

48. Donald Worster, "The Ecology of Order and Chaos," in *The Wealth of Nature,* ed. Donald Worster (New York: Oxford University Press, 1993), pp. 156, 158.

49. Ibid., p. 158.

50. Worster's influence reached well beyond academic circles into popular discussions. See Dennis Farney, "Chaos Theory Seeps into Ecology Debate, Stirring Up a Tempest," *Wall Street Journal* (July 11, 1994), p. 1.

51. Worster, "The Ecology of Order and Chaos," pp. 169–70.

52. See Robert H. Nelson, "Urban Environmentalism vs. Rural America," *Range* (Fall 1997).

53. See R. McGreggor Cawley, *Federal Land, Western Anger* (Lawrence: University of Kansas Press, 1993); and Phillip D. Brick and R. McGreggor Cawley, eds., *A Wolf in The Garden: The Land Rights Movement and The New Enviornmental Debate* (Lanham, Md.: Rowman & Littlefield, 1996)

4

An Illegitimate Institution

In the decades when the Forest Service was considered a model federal agency the Congress set priorities through the budget process but imposed few statutory limitations on the management actions of the agency. The long-standing mandate for "multiple-use management" was vague enough that it amounted in practice to a wholesale grant of administrative discretion. The judiciary was also content to trust to the professional skills of the Forest Service, seldom intervening in its internal decision making.[1]

A turning point for all this was the Wilderness Act of 1964. Environmentalists did not trust the Forest Service, dominated as it was by a progressive religion of scientific and material progress, to fulfill their plans for wilderness areas. In fact, environmental groups were in this regard realistic in that the very management regime of a wilderness area amounted to a symbolic repudiation of much of the value system that the Forest Service had stood for. In the 1970s, the trend toward outside pressures on and interference with Forest Service management accelerated. Given handles provided by new laws such as the National Environmental Policy Act of 1969, and its requirement for preparation of environmental impact statements, the courts began to intervene routinely in Forest Service administrative matters. With laws such as the Endangered Species Act of 1973, Congress would act on its own to alter sharply the priorities and modes of operation of the Forest Service.

The increasing judicial and legislative involvement in the day-to-day management of the national forests reflected a growing loss of legitimacy for the claims of scientific management. The public and its political and judicial representatives no longer had enough confidence that expert forest professionals could be left on their own to serve the public interest.

The failures of land-use planning in the 1970s and 1980s stemmed in part from this source. Land-use planning was conceived to be a means by which the Forest Service, although now consulting closely with outside groups, ultimately decided the fate of the national forests on scientific forestry grounds. The outside groups, however, were no longer willing to accept the validity of such Forest Service decisions. The scientific claims made by the Forest Service often appeared to be false and in any case there were usually much more than scientific matters at stake. The formal publication of a Forest Service plan thus was typically not the end but merely the beginning of a new round of political struggle, with the formal plan providing a further backdrop for the battles among contending interests and ideas.

The high professional hopes of the Forest Service in the 1990s for ecosystem management implicitly assumed that this newest ecological form of scientific management would finally win scientific legitimacy for agency decisions. The operating assumption of the Forest Service was that the agency lacked legitimacy in the 1970s and 1980s because its actions either were driven by narrow interest groups like the timber industry or because the Forest Service was attempting to impose mistaken theories on the management of the national forests. Now that a more correct form of thinking, as found in the principles of ecosystem management, was to be applied, the social legitimacy of the Forest Service to act authoritatively would be restored. It would mean an end to the severe polarization and gridlock that had characterized the management of the national forests since the 1970s.

In reality, this was not only an untested theory but also one that seems most unlikely to be sustained. Among the obstacles to a new social legitimacy and consensus on the national forests, many of the people who seemingly should be among the greatest enthusiasts for ecosystem management in fact have offered little support. Indeed, vocal segments of the environmental movement are critical, seeing ecosystem management as merely a new guise under which the old imperial Forest Service is attempting to revive its authority, and yet another manifestation of the failed precepts of scientific management. The remaining heirs to the progressive tradition, who still believe in the large benefits of material progress and continue to see the proper goal of Forest Service management as improving human welfare, are also antagonistic to recent agency changes. With ecosystem management also resulting in sharp reductions of timber harvesting, mining, and other traditional commodity uses of the national forests, one is left to wonder where the Forest Service will find any defenders in the future.

ECOLOGICAL IMPERIALISM

A strong believer in the principle of sustaining ecosystem integrity for its own sake, Walter Kuhlmann in 1997 was harshly critical of recent Forest Service efforts to revise its planning regulations in light of the need to make them serve this management philosophy. He found that the 1995 proposed rules for ecosystem planning and management "exhibit the attributes of imperial ecology." The agency had not really escaped from the old scientific management ways of thinking. Indeed, it now exhibited "a level of confidence in new engineering that is similar to the overconfidence in earlier [wild] game and timber management." The government proponents of ecosystem management have "incorporated the findings of the 'new biology' but wield them in a manner similar to Pinchot's promotion of 'scientific forestry' earlier in the century."[2]

While the Forest Service can now talk a good game of ecosystem management, Kuhlmann is unhappy that the agency has not entirely abandoned its old core utilitarianism. It has defined ecosystem management in a way that "converts the management of ecosystems from protection and restoration of biological systems to a multiple use balancing of human socio-economic needs with other values."[3] This subverts, however, the true ethical significance of the fundamental reorientation of management that the Forest Service should be undertaking. In a 1997 law review article, Kuhlmann similarly argued that ecosystem management must focus on "the purely ecological interactions which will determine whether the 'ecosystem,' as that term has well accepted scientific meaning, is thriving or losing ground." This is much different from the Forest Service attempts to say that "we need to consider humans' needs along with, and in some sort of balance with, the needs of the legitimate biological communities that are present in the National Forest System."[4] For Kuhlmann, in short, the ecology must come first; this goal must not be compromised by utilitarian—human-centered—concerns.

Thus, even though the Forest Service may now be recasting its timber harvesting plans to ground them in a language of ecosystem management, these plans will have little greater legitimacy for Kuhlmann than the old timber sale targets, derived from "even flow" and other traditional timber harvest planning. If the old land-use planning was a mere camouflage for the destruction of forest ecologies in the name of a religious dedication to supplying wood to meet the material needs of the nation—raping the land under the cover of scientific management—ecosystem management today seems to be more of the same. Indeed, it may be more insidious, because it appears more benign; destroying the forest today would have better symbolic camouflage. For Kuhlmann any new Forest Service plans to harvest significant amounts of timber for the announced purpose of forest health and ecosystem management would serve mainly to further confirm this overall negative assessment.

Kuhlmann's value system is in fact representative of an influential and vocal part of the environmental movement. The leading environmentalist David Brower commented in 1998 that "I've never forgiven the Forest Service" for a timber harvest clearcut he encountered in his youth, and "I don't intend to." Asked whether he favored abolishing the Forest Service, Brower replied: "I spoke at a Sierra Club banquet once during which I said that the Club had had a hand in founding the Forest Service and now it should help to unfound it—start over on a new track."[5]

In the spring of 1996 the membership of the Sierra Club voted by a two to one margin to set a seemingly radical policy goal, to eliminate all timber harvesting from the national forest system, whatever the specific benefits and costs of any particular timber sale might be. Then, in the fall of 1996 the executive board of the Sierra Club endorsed an equally radical idea, to tear down Glen Canyon dam on the Colorado River, one of the largest dams in the United States and a major source of electric power for the Southwest.[6] Lake Powell, which was formed behind the dam, makes spectacular desert scenery newly accessible and otherwise attracts 2.5 million visitors per year, one of the most popular tourist destinations in the country. However, for the leadership of the Sierra Club, these large human benefits counted for little against the fact that the dam had altered the natural order of the Colorado River. The Glen Canyon Dam, simply put, is a sin, a sacrilege against nature.

Leading environmentalists, to be sure, are usually more cautious about declaring in public that human interests must take a back seat to the physical condition of ecological systems. They know that, if the debate were framed explicitly in those terms, they would probably lose in the wider court of American public opinion.

ENVIRONMENTAL GUERRILLA WARFARE

David Brower pioneered a solution to this problem many years ago. In his wonderful book, *Conversations with the Archdruid*, John McPhee described Brower's environmental battle plan—a very successful strategy, as proven in numerous major victories by the environmental movement over the years. First of all, Brower was driven by an intense passion for his cause. McPhee commented that Brower's standard stump speech was in essence a "sermon" in which "to put it mildly, there is something evangelical." In Brower's belief system, there was no uncertainty about whether, say, the benefits of a proposed development project might exceed its costs. It was a moral, not an economic choice.[7]

Yet Brower did not become the seminal figure in the modern environmental movement merely by his great enthusiasm for the cause or by the power of his preaching. It was his ability to combine such deep moral passion with great strategic shrewdness that made him so influential a figure. In fighting to block a proposed dam in Dinosaur National Monument in the mid-1950s, McPhee considers that Brower single-handedly brought about "the birth of the modern conservation movement." If previous conservationists had spoken of their great affection for nature, Brower now pioneered new and more effective battle tactics. "With a passing wave at the aesthetic argument, he went after the Bureau of Reclamation with facts and figures. He challenged the word of its engineers and geologists that the damsite was a sound one, he suggested that cliffs would dissolve and there would be a tremendous and cataclysmic dam failure there, and he went after the basic mathematics underlying the bureau's proposals and uncovered embarrassing errors."[8]

McPhee soon came to realize that Brower had little real interest in or affinity for mathematics or science. In any case, whether he was right or wrong technically was beside the point. The public had no way of knowing and as McPhee relates, "a man in the public-relations office of the Bureau of Reclamation one day summed up the telling of the story by saying, 'Dave won, hands down.'" Moreover, winning often was aided by the fact that the bureau itself lacked any genuine commitment to scientific management. The bureau was dedicated to and possessed of great skills in high-quality engineering but its engineers lived to build dams for their own sake, as much as Brower hated them for their own sake. If the bureau was legally required to conduct benefit-cost studies, it showed little more interest in the results than Brower had. Thus, as Brower demonstrated to his fellow environmental warriors, uncovering significant economic and other technical errors by the government was surprisingly easy.

Rather than correct the errors, however, modern environmental strategists have often determined to fight fire with fire. As McPhee discovered, "in the war strategy of the conservation movement, exaggeration is a standard weapon and is used consciously on broad fronts." When something worked, "the fact that this was not true did not slow up Brower or the Sierra Club"—at Dinosaur National Monument or in large numbers of environmental battles to come.[9] Moreover, it turned out that the environmentalists were better at public relations than the Bureau of Reclamation and most other government agencies.

Then, and still today, leading environmentalists do not believe that they can win by putting their ethical values for the treatment of nature directly on the table. In environmental warfare, guerrilla tactics work better than frontal assaults. Environmentalists thus concentrate their attacks on hitting the weak points of the opposition, skirmishing here and there, seeking to undermine a fact here or a government statement there, impugning the credibility of this or that critic, and so forth. The goal, as Ho Chi Minh and other practitioners of guerrilla warfare have long understood, is to wear down the willingness to continue the fight of private corporations, government agencies, and any other opponents.

FIGHTING TIMBER HARVESTS

In the fall of 1996, following the severe forest fires of that summer, the Sierra Club saw a significant new threat to its newly announced goal of eliminating timber harvests from the national forests. Significant increases in timber harvests were being suggested under the guise of excess fuels removal and forest fire protection. The Sierra Club promptly put out a warning to its members in the field that "the timber industry is using the current fire season to plead for more access to log our remaining roadless areas, old growth forests, and critical watersheds."[10]

In support of its position of opposition to any new logging, whether motivated by ecological reasons or not, the Sierra Club provided three arguments—arguments intended to be wielded by its members and supporters in upcoming public debates. First, the club release stated that "most of the wildfires burning this year are not in public forest land that would be suitable for timber harvest. In fact, much of the recent wildfires have been in 'cheatgrass' and other low-elevation sage and grasslands."[11] However, the Sierra Club failed to mention that the federal government was being forced to spend $721 million (and state governments another $325 million) in 1996 for controlling forest fires—hardly a minor series of grassland fires as the Sierra Club seemed to be suggesting.

Second, the Sierra Club argued that "timber corporations share the blame for severe fires. Decades of poor forest management—extensive suppression of natural fires and indiscriminate overcutting—have led to inevitable results: commercially logged forests are now more vulnerable to hot and fast, and occasionally catastrophic, fires."[12] However, among most professional foresters the view was precisely the opposite. There is wide agreement that the national forests are a greater fire hazard than industry forests, mostly because intensive private forest management prevented the fuels buildups that has occurred on the federal lands. As Neil Sampson comments, "the best examples of environmentally sound forest management are on industry lands." This is partly because "industry has both the science and the flexibility" to apply effective management techniques that keep the forest clear of excess trees and other unwanted vegetation.[13]

The third and final Sierra Club argument was that "the industry says extensive 'salvage' logging is necessary to reduce fire risk in our National Forests. They don't tell you that most scientists say they are wrong. . . . Logging, including 'salvage' logging, increases fire hazard by leaving behind slash and other wood that is not commercially valuable but that fuels fires."[14] It is true that wood leftovers from timber harvesting at one time created major forest fire problems; prior to World War II, they were a major contributor to widespread forest fires in the West.

However, wood is more valuable today and economics militates against leaving timber behind. Moreover, timber sales today must be carefully designed for removal of excess trees and other fuels and contain tight requirements that companies remove all the fire-prone timber. In some forests, thinning and other harvesting might be followed promptly by prescribed burning to remove any undesired wood residues. The Sierra Club statement also lends itself to the easy misinterpretation that forest health and fuels buildup are false issues manufactured by the timber industry—a view at odds with virtually all current professional forestry opinions and the official views of the government agencies with forest management responsibilities of the Clinton administration.

To be sure, with these sound-bite broadsides the Sierra Club was simply following a proven formula developed long ago by Brower and others. And the strategy is still being widely applied successfully. In a 1994 advertisement in the Spokane *Spokesman-Review*, the Missoula-based Alliance for the Wild Rockies announced that "WHERE THERE'S SMOKE . . . THERE'S LIARS, 'Forest Health' Scare Tactic is Public Forest Ripoff." The ad went on to accuse the Forest Service, Congress, and the timber industry of conspiring to undertake "massive logging operations disguised as thinning to promote forest health and prevent catastrophic wildfires." The Alliance urged the public to "stop the forest butchers" and to "stop voodoo forestry." Another environmental group, the Inland Empire Public Lands Council, argued that "big timber wants you to think the forests need to be 'saved' from fires—with a chain saw massacre. They are using their enormous financial resources—and you, if they can—to sell the big lie."[15]

As such efforts reflect, the environmental movement, or at least a portion of the movement, including some of its most vocal and visible spokesmen, has mostly been unalterably opposed to any significant expansion of fuels removal on western forests, whether it might be justified by ecological or any other purposes. One observer commented that "'forest health' has become a buzzword among timber state lawmakers, but the sound grates on the ears of environmentalists like a chainsaw."[16] Indeed, harvesting of trees on federal land is, for many environmentalists, an unmitigated evil in any form that can be tolerated only to the extent that political or other tactical considerations may simply make it impossible to prevent.

Thus, as Jim Peterson recently commented, many environmentalists regard the forest health issue as simply an "excuse to cut down more trees." However, they have a much different attitude toward fire. "By itself, fire is fine with environmentalists because it is 'natural.'" On the other hand, even the act of salvaging timber that has already burned is opposed because this is an unnatural and thus an immoral act in the same category as "mugging a burn victim."[17]

LAND MANAGEMENT GRIDLOCK

Environmental guerrilla warfare against Forest Service proposals—whether for new types of timber thinning and other harvesting based on ecological considerations or many other actions—can often win by the tactics of delay and obstruction. However, when environmentalists sometimes seek to promote real changes in management, their political opponents have been learning to employ some of the same lawsuits, appeals, and other tactics. The result on the national forests of the West today is pervasive stalemate and gridlock—a "regulatory logjam," as Matthew Carroll and Steven Daniels have described it.[18] The Federal Land Policy and Management Act of 1976, the National Forest Management Act of 1976, the Endangered Species Act of 1973, and many other environmental laws enacted in the 1970s have created so many procedural requirements and handles by which opposition can be expressed that the whole national forest system has come to a virtual state of paralysis.[19]

This result may in fact serve those groups that do not want anything to happen. If the goal is to let "nature run its course," and if no management at all is considered as the operational definition of a "naturalness" policy, the existing federal land system is moving steadily toward this goal. For those who do believe that some form of purposeful management is desirable, however, they have come to perceive an urgent need for major changes in the current land management regime. As Frank Gregg, the former director of the Bureau of Land Management (BLM) in the Carter administration, said in summarizing the discussions at a 1992 conference sponsored by the Congressional Research Service, "We have now amassed a considerable history in participating in and judging the revised system [since the 1970s], and we agree that we are in another generation of dissatisfaction. We have characterized the present as gridlock, polarization, so extreme as to suggest extraordinary urgency in pondering what needs to be done."[20]

The former Forest Service chief Jack Ward Thomas has stated that the Forest Service must deal with "the interacting forces of the myriad of laws that come to bear on Federal land management plus regulations issued under those laws plus the constant upsets in balance that occur with decisions in court case after court case," all of which has "produced a situation that is the antithesis of predictability and stability of Federal land management."[21] Thomas has suggested that Congress might need to charter a new public land commission to revisit the basic statutory foundations of the system. Otherwise, the Forest Service will remain tied in knots.[22]

A tried and true tactic of environmental guerrilla warfare is to demand more facts and other information, if some undesired action seems about to happen. This helps to explain the remarkable fact that, as the General Accounting Office (GAO) recently reported, the Forest Service is today preparing more than 20,000 environmental documents annually, at a cost to the agency of more than $250 million per year.[23] The Forest Service has spent more than $250 million on formal land-use plans for individual forests since enactment of the National Forest Management Act of 1976. Yet, despite all this extensive environmental and other planning, the GAO reports that "the public has not been able to form reasonable expectations about the health of forests over time or about the future availability of forest uses."[24]

THE USE AND ABUSE OF SCIENCE

Although environmental language is often overwrought, the facts often weak, and the scientific arguments often contrived, environmental critics of Forest Service plans for thinning and other new timber harvesting, now said to be justified by ecosystem management, are correct in one fundamental respect. How can the very agency that promoted economically and ecologically misguided policies of fire suppression for almost a century be trusted now to guide the forests out of their problems, ecological or otherwise? How can the same agency that for decades preached a misconceived dogma of timber sales set according to targets based on an "even flow" objective now be given the responsibility to set timber sales according to some new timber harvest policy of its choosing? How can an agency facing a basic conflict of interest—it has many employees who have been trained for and owe their very jobs to the high levels of Forest Service timber harvesting of the past and may be out of work if there is no movement back toward earlier high harvest levels—now be expected to determine the harvest levels of the future in a disinterested and objective fashion?

The management failures that resulted from past Forest Service fire suppression may not, as is often suggested, be due simply to an earlier lack of adequate scientific knowledge. It may be too easy to say simply that the good intentions of the Forest Service have been defeated over the course of the twentieth century by the unexpected complexity of natural processes and the scientific inability to model and otherwise comprehend fully the workings of fire in western forest ecologies. The Forest Service is filled with many devoted public servants and otherwise admirable people. Yet, fire suppression in the West is not an isolated incident; the agency throughout its history has failed to make proper use of sound scientific information. Science has consistently taken a back seat to political and public relations considerations, as the Forest Service has perceived them at any given moment.

As long ago as 1962, Ashley Schiff reviewed the history of the use of scientific knowledge by the Forest Service.[25] Schiff found that, despite the origins of the agency in the thinking of scientific management, the internal culture of the Forest Service was antagonistic to the generation and use of carefully developed scientific information. The Forest Service saw itself engaged in a perpetual political struggle, and in its fierce battles with its many enemies it could not afford the luxury of scientific truth (seemingly mirroring a perception that some environmentalists today also have with respect to their own use of scientific information).

Partly because its authority under the Weeks Act to acquire new forest lands had depended on these claims, the Forest Service almost from its inception had argued that forest conditions could determine levels of water runoff and thus river flows—and in this way could even influence whether river flooding would occur. By the 1930s, the Forest Service was still adhering to this old position in the face of overwhelming scientific evidence to the contrary. The Geological Survey, the leading government agency for hydrologic research, said at the time:

> The changes which have been brought about by streamflow regulation through forestry and agricultural practices over broad areas are in general, so insignificant and tenuous that they are indeterminate. . . . It is a sad commentary on a so-called scientific organization like the Forest Service that during its existence it has never published a report on the role played by vegetal cover on the hydrologic cycle which was in accord with well-established hydrologic principles.[26]

Schiff also investigated the use by the Forest Service of scientific information concerning the ecological workings of fire in longleaf pine forests, an important source of timber in the South. Like some western tree species, the longleaf pine depends on fire for the sprouting of its cones and thus the regeneration of a forest. The obvious management conclusion, recognized by many foresters as early as the 1920s, was that forest fire would be necessary to maintain sustainable forests of longleaf pine. Yet, the Forest Service was then in the process of making the battle against forest fire a moral crusade against uncontrolled forces of evil in the world. The public image it sought to present in this grand struggle—the heroic battler against the menacing threat of forest fire—was a major political asset.

If the actual ecology of longleaf pine forests did not fit the public relations posture, perhaps this particular species was not that important to national timber supplies. Longleaf pine forests could be sacrificed for the greater good of the cause. The Forest Service thus for many years rebuffed attempts to infuse valid fire science into its management of longleaf pines in the South, only capitulating to allow burning of these forests when the pressure of outside scientific opinion finally became too great to resist any longer.

Schiff in 1962 concluded that the Forest Service over its history had all too often been willing to sacrifice scientific objectivity for public relations appeal. Smokey Bear was not just an advertising slogan but a well-crafted way of presenting an image of the Forest Service to the American public. As a result, Schiff explains, forest "administration itself suffered because research was too closely identified, from a spiritual and structural standpoint, with 'the cause.'"[27] In 1955, a chief of the Forest Service, Richard McCardle, had acknowledged the need for new thinking in the agency. As he stated, "we live in different times. We cannot recreate the initial crusade for forestry any more than we can rediscover America. . . . I think our task in the next half century is more concerned with action than with publicity."[28]

Yet, as the sorry history of Forest Service fire suppression in the West—still continued well into the 1990s—shows, not that much has changed since the problems Schiff identified forty-five years ago. The scientific role of fire on the national forests has not been as great a mystery as the Forest Service and its current defenders often suggest. The National Park Service adopted a policy of prescribed burning as long ago as 1968 in Sequoia and Kings Canyon National Parks, reflecting a growing professional understanding, at least as early as the 1960s, of the ecological role of fire. Two professional foresters (one employed at a Forest Service research station) stated in 1996 that "a number of [good] works on fire in natural resources management have been available for decades," going back to the 1940s. Yet despite considerable scientific knowledge to the contrary, "the ecological function of fire has been ignored, denied, or treated as an interesting but inconsequential, academic curiosity by most managers and policy makers" in the Forest Service.[29]

After decades of Smokey Bear, it would, admittedly, have been difficult for the Forest Service to change public attitudes, to admit that it had been embarrassingly wrong, to explain that fire was actually a necessary part of a well-functioning forest system. Rather than face the unpleasant necessity to try to inform the public, the agency instead continued for many more years on its long-standing crusade against fire. It made little effort to alter the traditional attitude both internally and externally that fire "should be regarded as a nuisance, as a destructive agent." It has only been in the mid-1990s, Skinner and Chang explain, and "in response to attempts to define and carry out more comprehensive ecosystem management, [that] the ecological role of fire [has] been generally acknowledged" by the Forest Service.[30]

SURVIVING IN A HOSTILE WORLD

To be sure, the Forest Service did not change because it suddenly came to its senses about the scientific merits of the role of fire in forest ecologies. After all, this knowledge had been available in at least a general way for decades. Rather, the Forest Service faced a new political environment and, as in the past, the use of science would be driven by political and public relations needs. Environmentalists were now rapidly gaining political power, as demonstrated convincingly by their victory in the struggle over the management of old-growth forests in the Pacific Northwest, driven by events relating to the spotted owl. Despite heroic efforts to sustain past levels, timber harvesting, the old mainstay of the Forest Service, was in rapid decline, as total harvest levels on the national forests plummeted by more than two-thirds nationwide in less than ten years. The very survival of the agency might be at stake. Indeed, an influential environmentalist, Ed Marston, reflecting a drastic falloff of public support for the Forest Service, called in 1993 in the *High Country News* for the very abolition of the agency.[31]

Like many others over the years, Marston had been disillusioned by his experiences with the Forest Service. In 1982, he had been involved in a controversy over permitting of a Colorado mine and found that the Forest Service's environmental impact statement was "shameless and contemptuous of the public." He had thought at the time that this was a rare exception and that the Gunnison National Forest, which had prepared the document, was an outlier "rogue forest." Over the years, however, after many further dealings with the agency, he concluded that the Gunnison was a "perfectly average, conforming part of the U.S. Forest Service" culture. The Forest Service was an organization that regularly exhibited "contempt for science" and thus could not "implement a policy that requires good science and ecological integrity." It transferred employees so often that it had "little institutional or human memory" and, under the centralizing influence of laws such as the Resources Planning Act of 1974 and the National Forest Management Act of 1976, had "isolated itself from the ground and from communities." All in all, the Forest Service was "beyond redemption" and therefore "it must die."[32]

The Clinton administration brought many environmental critics of the Forest Service into positions of power, some of them with direct administrative authority over the agency. To be sure, if environmentalists now had the political power, and thus might even represent a threat to the future existence of the Forest Service, the agency was capable of trying to adapt its mission to the new realities. If the old vocabulary of timber production and forage output no longer served the ultimate imperative of institutional survival, a brand-new vocabulary of ecosystem management could be introduced into forest management. After all, Gifford Pinchot almost 100 years ago had been more a skilled political advocate and propagandist than a genuine scientist.[33] His greatest skill had been in employing the progressive rhetoric of scientific management—then the secular religion of America, as environmentalism is contending powerfully for that role in the current era—to build a brand-new government agency in the face of implacable opposition from many people in the West.

If today the rhetoric of scientific management is out, and the language of ecosystem management is in, the Forest Service is still in one sense trying to follow the old model of Pinchot. It is still trying to fit its institutional needs to the most powerful forms of public rhetoric and the political circumstances of the day. Now, however, the public relations and political skills of the agency would have to be devoted to presenting a posture of ecosystem management—of restoring pre–European-settlement forest conditions throughout the West. If this was at odds with the scientific management mission as understood by the agency for most of the twentieth century, it was consistent with the agency's long-standing recognition that its very existence required a successful appeal to public emotions—and to the most influential ideas and causes, the leading popular crusades, of the day.

However, the rest of American society does not have such a large stake in the institutional survival of the Forest Service. Ecosystem management may offer a new attractive package, but its substantive content is still elusive. Ecosystem management wraps the Forest Service in the banner of an attractive image but still leaves an agency of 35,000 employees and a

$2 billion budget with little direction or purpose. The real message of ecosystem management may be that there is no national answer—that each ecology is complex; that ecological workings cannot be reduced to a simple scientific understanding; that trial-and-error decision making must prevail; that social and ecological factors must blend together; that local social values will vary greatly; and that in light of all this local decision making in a site-specific manner is the only way to go. As Phillip Weatherspoon and Carl Skinner, both Forest Service research scientists, put it recently,

> Ecosystem management is increasingly espoused as a guiding concept for managing public lands. Managing for ecosystem integrity and sustainability, however, is more difficult and more fraught with uncertainties than managing for a set of specific outputs. We have much to learn. For many reasons, including the complexity and variability of forested ecosystems and the broad spatiotemporal scale that provides the context for ecosystem management, traditional research cannot provide all the answers. Scientists, managers, and interested members of the public must work together as partners in a process of learning by doing.
>
> A key concept for adaptive management is that we cannot wait for perfect information, because we will never have it. Despite the uncertainties, we must move forward with managing for sustainable ecosystems using the best information we have, knowing that with time we will learn more and be able to manage more intelligently.
>
> We know enough at this point to recognize that most low- to middle-elevation forests of the Sierra Nevada are unacceptable in terms of wildlife hazard, diversity, and sustainability. Regardless of the extent to which pre-settlement conditions are used as a guide to desired conditions, most informed people would agree that these forests generally should be less dense, have less fuels, and have more large trees. Even if we have not precisely identified target conditions, we certainly know the direction in which we should begin moving. That beginning will require a large measure of commitment and hard work. We can adjust along the way as we learn more and become better able to define desired conditions.[34]

If this is what it will take to manage the national forests in the future, it is also unlikely that the Forest Service will be able to succeed in putting into place such an unstructured form of management. Moving forward with imperfect information, operating by trial and error, maintaining wide flexibility, requires trust in the managing institution. The people who are affected by decisions must have a strong sense of basic social legitimacy—of the institution's concern for their welfare, its management capabilities, and its legal basis of authority. The Forest Service may in an earlier time have had such social legitimacy and public trust, but it has forfeited it today.

DEFENDERS OF THE OLD FAITH

The religions of progress have come upon hard times in the twentieth century. There are fewer people today who still believe that material abundance will really bring heaven on earth. However, most people still probably believe that more consumption is better than less, that economic growth is a good thing, that human welfare is the ultimate test of the desirability of a government policy, that human use of the natural world is a proper use, that science has been a blessing overall, that the world is for the most part a better place for most people today than it was for most of previous human history, and various other "utilitarian" and "pragmatic" ideas at odds with ecological fundamentalism. The economics profession, while often carrying these themes into realms of utopian thought, is an active and powerful defender of such values in American intellectual circles.[35]

In the field of environment and natural resources policy, the leading think tank for expressing an economic view of the world has long been Resources for the Future (RFF). The culture of RFF might be described as a moderated progressivism, less utopian than progressive manifestations earlier in the twentieth century and more open to other value considerations but still convinced that economic progress and efficiency represent the appropriate standards for judging government actions. RFF was created in the early 1950s as part of the institutional apparatus of scientific management, designed to supply essential expert information for managing the natural resources of the United States and the world.

By the late 1970s, the leading researchers at RFF in the field of management of the public lands had become convinced that the Forest Service was betraying progressive ideals. The most prominent RFF spokesman for this viewpoint was Marion Clawson, perhaps the leading land and natural resource economist of the past fifty years. In 1948 Clawson had become the director of the Bureau of Land Management (BLM— formed in 1946 by a merger of the Grazing Service and the General Land Office). He was forced out of office by the incoming Eisenhower administration despite his protestations that the directorship of the BLM should be a nonpolitical, professional appointment—an early example of the failure of the politics and administration dichotomy favored by progressive political theorists.[36]

In the 1970s Clawson served on the Presidential Panel on Timber and the Environment and directed much of his subsequent professional attention to forestry issues.[37] From these experiences he concluded that the Forest Service was giving short shrift to the progressive values of efficiency and maximization of economic benefit from the national forests. Instead, the agency usually did whatever it saw as politically expedient at that moment. Typical of the resulting agency misallocation of resources, "the pattern of expenditures by regions and by forests strongly suggests that too much money is being spent on poor sites and not enough on good ones." Clawson was one of the first people to point out that the Forest Service timber program was filled with what are now called "below-cost" sales. As he wrote in *The Economics of National Forest Management*, "it is difficult to justify timber management that costs more than it returns, especially since nontimber values are as likely to be reduced as to be increased thereby."[38] All in all, Clawson would conclude in 1976 in the pages of *Science* magazine that the management record of the Forest Service was "disastrous."[39]

Clawson's RFF colleague, John Krutilla, was less critical publicly of the Forest Service, less confrontational in manner, and tended to couch his criticisms more in professional language. However, his views were no less damning. He declared in 1979 that "there is need to provide the 'correct' level and mix of the various resources which the national forests are capable of producing [but] up until the present the instincts and proper impulses of the [forestry] profession expressed themselves somewhat more as high motives and sincere exhortations than as the application of operational criteria."[40] In other words, the Forest Service had always been more concerned about things like Smokey Bear than achieving a sound scientific understanding of fire ecology or achieving an economically efficient allocation of the resources of the national forest system.

Krutilla proposed that the Forest Service in the future should abandon its failed management approach of the past and henceforth adopt an operationally meaningful and precise—a valid "scientific"—basis for decision making: The new mission of the Forest Service (actually, the old progressive mission realized for the first time) should be "to manage the national forests . . . in order to maximize benefits"—in short, to "pursue economic efficiency."[41] Krutilla seemed to suggest in such writings (rather naively, it must be said) that the previous failures were due simply to some past misunderstandings. Now that he and other economists were showing the Forest Service the light, the agency would finally be able for the first time to fulfill the progressive mission that so far had eluded it.

However, the efforts of Krutilla and other economists had little impact. By the mid-1980s another leading natural resource economist, Ronald Johnson (at Montana State University), would write, "criticism of the land management policies of the U.S. Forest Service has become epidemic." He found that "there is growing evidence that the Forest Service has promoted timber harvesting in areas where no private firm could profitably operate"—much as the Bureau of Reclamation had constructed many dams that no private firm would have built. Johnson further reflected the general view of economists who had examined the management record of the agency: "By emphasizing multiple use and designing timber management programs based on biological rules, the Forest Service has managed to disregard economic efficiency criteria."[42] If progressive conservationism was the "gospel of efficiency," some kind of modern devil had seemingly infected the minds of those members of the forestry profession who had been assigned to oversee the management of the Forest Service.

Roger Sedjo, a leading national expert on forestry policy, is today the heir at RFF to the tradition of Clawson and Krutilla. Given RFF's longstanding prominence as a leading advocate of scientific management of forests and other natural resources (if based on economic science), it is not surprising that Sedjo was one of the thirteen members of the Committee of Scientists appointed in December 1997 by Secretary of Agriculture Dan Glickman. However, the committee's report largely rejected the value tradition of economic analysis that RFF has long represented. Economics puts a value on the forests for what they can provide in goods and services for human consumption; the committee strongly advocated an opposite "ecosystem management" view that the national forests should be managed to achieve a particular physical condition for its own sake. Human well-being may be relevant to management decisions but ultimately functions mainly as a potential constraint on ecosystem management options (it is necessary to recognize that policies imposing economic costs that are too high might be politically infeasible and thus could not be adopted in practice).

Hence, it is not surprising that Sedjo in effect dissented from the report—and from the current directions in Forest Service policy and management in the Clinton administration.[43] Similarly, another old-style progressive who also believes in putting human welfare first, the former governor of Idaho, Cecil Andrus, recently commented that in the current political climate "with the Democrats, we might see totally impractical restoration schemes adopted as a sop to militant preservationists." (His view of the Republican Party was equally skeptical, seeing it as dominated by "ultraconservative Western politicians" who would feel no sense of loss in seeing "species condemned to extinction.")[44]

Alone among the members of the Committee of Scientists, Sedjo filed a separate statement of his views that was included with the report, if not a formal dissent.[45] His real dissent came in the form of an earlier discussion paper published by RFF that addressed the contents of the forthcoming Committee of Scientists report, as they were already becoming apparent. As Sedjo summarized his objections in late 1998:

> The Committee of Scientists has suggested that the management of the forests for biological sustainability ought to be the desired objective of management. Further, an objective of managing the forests to keep it within the historical range of variability is to move management in the direction of returning to pre-European forest processes and functions. The objective involves a "mission shift" away from a focus on outputs, dramatically reducing certain outputs, not only timber but other outputs as well, such as recreation. But, what do the American people want from their National Forests? Probably a host of things. It is probably accurate to say that Americans want naturalness and an element of wildness. They surely want many of the ecological services provided by forests including watershed protection, erosion control and wildlife habitat. The American people might even be supportive of a program that identifies the priority responsibility of the National Forest System as that of maintaining a sustainable ecosystem, while the responsibility for timber production is shifted to private producers and foreign lands.
>
> [Yet], in my view such an approach is, in effect, an obituary for the Forest Service. It is doubtful that, in the absence of significant tangible outputs, there is sufficient public support to generate serious budgets for a program such as that suggested by the Committee of Scientists Report. Although many people may support such an approach at one level, it is doubtful that this support could bring together the type of constituency that has the power for generating substantial and continuing budgets for these types of management activities. The services generated by the activities would be difficult for the public to perceive on a regular basis and the major direct financial beneficiaries would be the biologists employed in the process. Although major environmental groups are supporting facets of the Committee of Scientists proposal, some of the major national groups oppose timber harvesting of any type, including that necessary to meet other objectives, e.g., wildlife habitat. Because of their persistent distrust of the motives of the Forest Service, it is problematic that these groups would support with enthusiasm the large budget necessary for the management of biological sustainability. The likely outcome would be the erosion of the Forest Service budget with active management being supplanted with custodial management and protection.[46]

Sedjo clearly thinks that a Forest Service that disavows an interest in providing services for human benefit to serve the users of the national forests—that is left, in effect one might say, with a "spiritual" purpose—faces a very uncertain future. Indeed, he suggested that "perhaps it is time to 'think the unthinkable,'" and ask whether the Forest Service should be abolished. As he stated, today "the dialogue should be expanded to seriously consider whether the federal land management problems of the 21st Century may not require the creation of new streamlined integrated organizations to replace the outmoded agencies of the past century."[47]

In short, it is not only environmentalists, timber industry representatives, western members of Congress, and many others who are unhappy with the current Forest Service. The list also includes economists and other remaining defenders of the old progressive faith in the values of economic efficiency and progress, believers in the legitimacy of using nature for human purposes and in the methods of scientific management. The leading members of the progressive economic "priesthood" also find little in the current Forest Service to justify its continued existence.

CONCLUSION

Yet another longtime close observer of the Forest Service, Randal O'Toole, commented in 1997 that "the U.S.D.A. Forest Service will be 100 years old in 2005—if it survives that long. There is a good chance that it won't."[48] In O'Toole's view, the decision of the Clinton administration to impose an outsider political appointee, Mike Dombeck, on the Forest Service as its new chief, formally symbolized the end of the ethos of professional Forest Service management. (Dombeck had worked earlier in his career in the Forest Service but in a lower-level position at that time and had been away for a number of years.) Yet it was the very goal of scientific management that had initially justified the centralization of administrative authority for the national forests at the federal level.

As long as it was accepted that management decisions should be made by experts with scientific skills and knowledge, it was reasonable to argue that the resources to assemble these experts and to put their technical skills to work could best be marshaled at the federal level. The federal government was best positioned to apply "objective" forestry knowledge throughout the nation. However, if the aspirations to scientific management are to now be seen as a misplaced utopianism among many such misplaced ideals of the twentieth century, the source of social legitimacy of the Forest Service will be gone. The agency may encounter the same fate as other "socialist" enterprises that did not survive the 1990s. The Forest Service will be regarded by many of those affected by its decisions as an illegitimate institution. If that perception spreads too widely, as O'Toole suggested, the days of the agency may well be numbered.

NOTES

1. See Paul W. Hirt, *A Conspiracy of Optimism: Management of the National Forests Since World War Two* (Lincoln: University of Nebraska Press, 1994).

2. Walter Kuhlmann, "Can the Precautionary Principle Protect Us from Imperial Ecology," *Wild Earth* (Fall 1997), pp. 68, 69–70.

3. Ibid., p. 69.

4. W. Kuhlmann, "Making the Law More Ecocentric: Responding to Leopold and Conservation Biology," *Duke Environmental Law and Policy Forum* (1997), quoted in Kuhlmann, "Can the Precautionary Principle Protect Us from Imperial Ecology," p. 69.

5. "Interview with David Brower," *Wild Earth* (Spring 1998), pp. 35–36.

6. James Brooke, "In the Balance, the Future of a Lake," *The New York Times* (September 22, 1997), p. A14.

7. John McPhee, *Conversations with the Archdruid* (New York: Farrar, Straus and Giroux, 1971), pp. 79, 83.

8. Ibid., p. 165.

9. Ibid., pp. 37, 165.

10. IN THE FIELD: Sierra Club Action #265B—"Cutting Through Another Timber Smokescreen," Sierra Club website, posted on September 10, 1996.

11. Ibid.

12. Ibid.

13. Personal interview with author, Washington, D.C., March 28, 1997.

14. Sierra Club Action #265B—"Cutting Through Another Timber Smokescreen."

15. Press materials quoted in "A Season of Fire," *Evergreen* (Winter 1994–1995), pp. 52–53.

16. Larry Swisher, "Commentary: Lawmakers Debate 'Forest Health,'" *Lewiston [Idaho] Morning Tribune* (August 24, 1992), p. 5A. Quoted in Jay O'Laughlin, "Forest Ecosystem Health Assessment Issues: Definition, Measurement, and Management Implications," *Ecosystem Health* vol. 2, no. 1 (March 1996), p. 33.

17. Jim Peterson, "In This Issue," *Evergreen* (Winter 1994–1995), p. 5.

18. Matthew S. Carroll and Steven E. Daniels, "Public Land Management and Three Decades of American Social Change: Thoughts on the Future of Public Lands and Public Demands," in *Multiple Use and Sustained Yield: Changing Philosophies for Federal Land Management,* the proceedings and summary of a workshop convened on March 5 and 6, 1992, Washington, D.C., prepared by the Congressional Research Search, Committee Print No. 11, Committee on Interior and Insular Affairs, U.S. House of Representatives (December 1992), p. 60.

19. For a casebook of public land law, see George Cameron Coggins, Charles F. Wilkinson, and John D. Leshy, *Federal Public Land and Resources Law,* 3d edition (Westbury, N.Y.: The Foundation Press, 1993).

20. Frank Gregg, "Summary," in *Multiple Use and Sustained Yield: Changing Philosophies for Federal Land Management,* p. 311 (see note 18).

21. Jack Ward Thomas, "The Stability of Instability," speech to the University of Montana, Missoula, Montana, 1995.

22. See also R. W. Behan, "The Irony of the Multiple Use/Sustained Yield Concept: Nothing is so Powerful as an Idea Whose Time Has Passed," in *Multiple Use*

and Sustained Yield Management: Changing Philosophies for Federal Land Management.

23. General Accounting Office, *Forest Service Decision-Making: Greater Clarity Needed on Mission Priorities,* testimony to Congress by Barry T. Hill, Associate Director (Washington, D.C., February 25, 1997), p. 28.

24. Ibid., p. 31.

25. Ashley L. Schiff, *Fire and Water: Scientific Heresy in the Forest Service* (Cambridge: Harvard University Press, 1962); for a similar story with the respect to the failures of Forest Service timber predictions, see Sherry Olson, *The Depletion Myth: A History of Railroad Use of Timber* (Cambridge: Harvard University Press, 1971).

26. Quoted in Schiff, *Fire and Water,* p. 139.

27. Schiff, *Fire and Water,* p. 169.

28. Quoted in Schiff, *Fire and Water,* p. 162.

29. Carl N. Skinner and Chi-Ru Chang, "Fire Regimes, Past and Present," in *Status of the Sierra Nevada, Volume II,* Sierra Nevada Ecosystem Project, Final Report to Congress (Davis: University of California, Wildland Resources Center Report No. 40, March 1997), p. 1062.

30. Ibid.

31. Ed Marston, "It's Time to Clearcut the Forest Service," *High Country News* (September 20, 1993), p. 13.

32. Ibid.

33. See Olson, *The Depletion Myth.*

34. C. Phillip Weatherspoon and Carl N. Skinner, "Landscape-Level Strategies for Forest Fuel Management," in *Status of the Sierra Nevada, Volume II,* pp. 1487–89.

35. See Robert H. Nelson, *Reaching for Heaven on Earth: The Theological Meaning of Economics* (Lanham, Md.: Rowman & Littlefield, 1991).

36. Marion Clawson, *From Sagebrush to Sage: The Making of a Natural Resource Economist* (Washington, D.C.: Ana Publications, 1987).

37. *Report of the President's Advisory Panel on Timber and the Environment* (Washington, D.C.: Government Printing Office, April 30, 1973).

38. Marion Clawson, *The Economics of National Forest Management* (Washington, D.C.: Resources for the Future, 1976), pp. 78, 86.

39. Marion Clawson, "The National Forests," *Science* (February 20, 1976), p. 766.

40. John V. Krutilla, "Adaptive Responses to Forces for Change" (paper presented at the annual meeting of the Society of American Foresters, Boston, Mass., October 16, 1976), p. 6.

41. John V. Krutilla and John A. Haigh, "An Integrated Approach to National Forest Management," *Environmental Law* (Winter 1978), p. 383. Krutilla devoted much of his professional efforts in the 1970s and 1980s to developing the technical apparatus to enable the Forest Service to adopt an economic mission for the national forests. This would require comprehensive calculation of benefits and costs for all potential actions on the national forests. See Michael D. Bowes and John V. Krutilla, *Multiple-Use Management: The Economics of Public Forestlands* (Washington, D.C.: Resources for the Future, 1989).

42. Ronald N. Johnson, "U.S. Forest Service Policy and its Budget," in *Forestlands: Public and Private,* ed. Robert T. Deacon and M. Bruce Johnson (San Francisco: Pacific Institute for Public Policy Research, 1985), p. 103.

43. See Roger A. Sedjo, "Ecosystem Management: An Uncharted Path for Public Forests," *Resources* (Fall 1995).

44. Cecil D. Andrus and Joel Connelly, *Cecil Andrus: Politics Western Style* (Seattle, Wash.: Sasquatch Books, 1998), p. 130.

45. Roger A. Sedjo, "A View of the Report of the Committee of Scientists," in Committee of Scientists, *Sustaining the People's Land: Recommendations for Stewardship of the National Forests and Grasslands into the Next Century,* A report to the Secretary of Agriculture and the Chief of the Forest Service (Washington, D.C.: Department of Agriculture, March 15, 1999), p. 183.

46. Roger A. Sedjo, *Forest Service Vision: or, Does the Forest Service Have a Future?* Resources for the Future Discussion Paper 99-03 (Washington, D.C., October 1998), pp. 8–9.

47. Ibid., p. 11.

48. Randal O'Toole, "Expect the Forest Service to Be Slowly Emasculated," *The Seattle Times* (May 7, 1997).

5

Why Decentralization

If the management of the national forests is not part of the practice of science, what then is it? The answer, it would seem unavoidably, is politics in one form or another. If social values and moral visions are in basic dispute in national forest decision making, what other means than the political process might be employed to resolve the value disagreements? In its best and highest forms, as leading philosophers since Aristotle have long said, politics is the art of shaping and maintaining the values of a community.

When Secretary of Agriculture Dan Glickman appointed a Committee of Scientists in 1997 to rethink the basic workings of the Forest Service decision making, this was a throwback to the failed ideas of scientific management—and thus unlikely to succeed. For one thing, it would inevitably appear disingenuous because the political leadership of the Forest Service during the Clinton administration has seldom shown much commitment to scientific management—at least when it did not suit some other political objective. Indeed, there was a political purpose in the designation of a Committee of Scientists. First, by controlling the "scientists" selected, the Clinton administration could exercise substantial influence over the likely recommendations, even while claiming the recommendations would be blessed with neutral scientific authority. The narrower (and probably more important) political purpose was simply to pursue a delaying tactic, providing an excuse for refusing to heed pressures for a new independent public land commission or to cooperate with efforts by the Republican Congress to design a new legislative charter for the Forest Service.

If it is necessarily a political act, the relevant community for most elements of land and resource management need not be the nation as a whole. There is a great deal of difference between politics at the federal level and at the local level. Federal politics is today dominated by national television networks and other media that distort as often as clarify the real forest issues. If decisions for the forests of the West are made in Washington, most democratically elected representatives will be far removed from the places where their decisions take effect. Many members of Congress will have never visited the national forests where their votes will be determining future policy. They are likely to have little idea what policy issues, typically posed in abstract and symbolic terms at the national level, are likely to mean when translated into on-the-ground results in the West.

Because local people have such limited contact with most political representatives at the national level, they must rely on various intermediary groups to express their political preferences. Thus, in Washington it is inevitable that industry trade associations, environmental groups, large law firms, and others of the city's lobbying infrastructure will have a central role in decision making. However, these groups themselves are often well removed from actual decisions. Moreover, they have their own organizational imperatives that may conflict with the interests of their members— including a strong interest that decisions should remain at the national level, where their own jobs are located and where their lobbying skills have been honed.

When it comes from the federal government, money tends to be seen as "free." If the state of Colorado can attract $100 million in federal funds to build a new federal project, almost all of the money will come from taxpayers outside Colorado. Thus, any $100 million of federal money for virtually any project located in Colorado will be a net benefit to the state, as long as the project does not do outright harm. Colorado politicians in Washington, like politicians from every other state, will be judged by their ability to "bring home the bacon." Cumulatively, the problem might be described as creating a budgetary "tragedy of the commons" at the federal level.

Competition among individual political representatives for local projects produces high federal expenditures and high tax rates, even though taxpayers as a whole might actually prefer—and collectively might derive greater benefit—from keeping their money at home and their federal taxes lower. However, like a grazing commons, the workings of individual political incentives at the national level can lead to an overall undesired national budget and tax result—an "overgrazing" of the federal treasury.

Such misplaced incentives have been much in evidence in national forest management. It is a main reason why the West has long tolerated the pervasive federal presence in managing its forests and rangelands. There are simply too many financial benefits to give up the existing system easily, especially without concrete assurances that other parts of the nation would reciprocally give up their federal benefits as well.[1] Fire money, as seen in chapter 1, is a good example of this federal showering of dollars on the West that is a large part of the economic base of many rural communities.

Yet most of the tasks of national forest management do not really involve issues of national significance. National forest decisions typically involve the kinds of matters that elsewhere in the United States would be decided either privately or by a local planning and zoning board— whether to allow this or that proposed use on this or that piece of land next year. It falls to federal officials to decide how many cows should be allowed in a given pasture on the national forests in the month of July. Until the progressive era with its grand plans for central scientific management of the resources of the nation, a vision that ended up overthrowing the traditional American scheme of federalism, it would have been unimaginable that any such small-scale decisions should be made at the federal level.

Environmental policies generally involve issues that are more regional or local than national. In the past few years, a number of national study groups have recommended the significant decentralization of environmental responsibilities in the United States. A 1995 report of the National Academy of Public Administration concluded that "EPA and Congress need to hand more responsibility and decision-making authority over to the states and localities. . . . The principle is simple: one size does not fit all. Those states that are capable and willing to take over functions from the federal government should have full operational responsibility."[2] Similarly, in a study of the Endangered Species Act, the New York Academy of Sciences recommended that "environmental management takes place on the land, not in Washington. Hence, the locus of [endangered species] policy making, implementation, and management must be much more decentralized."[3] By comparison with clean air or endangered species policies, the management of ordinary national forest lands is yet more local in character. Unlike air or water pollution, national forest actions typically do not involve impacts that spill over the boundaries from one state to another.

Whether one accepts principled federalism arguments for decentralization or not, there is one practical reality that should trump almost any other consideration. The existing national forest system, as testifiers to Congress, the General Accounting Office (GAO), many academic researchers, environmental critics, numerous spokesmen for user groups, and many others have been saying, is now broken. Moreover, there is little prospect of fixing it at the federal level. The many federal politicians and executive branch officials who continue to assert otherwise are either trapped in the thinking of the past, unable to imagine any basic alternative to the present system, or may simply be protecting their own (or others') jobs or other perquisites.

WINNING LEGITIMACY LOCALLY

Social legitimacy for forest management seemingly will have to be achieved today through different routes than making claims to scientific authority. On the headwaters of the Feather River in California, at the initiative of local government officials, the "gang of seven"—including Forest Service employees, representatives of a few key state and local agencies, and a local environmentalist—was formed in 1985 to practice what subsequently would be deemed "coordinated research management." Given all the failures of the past, the group perceived a local attitude of "pervasive cynicism about the possibilities for change in resource management." An outside coordinator was later hired who made no pretense of being scientifically "neutral, but rather is explicit about her personal and professional commitment to a vision of economic and ecological sustainability."[4]

This local group sought to avoid polarizing disputes about broad policy "issues" with symbolic overtones and instead concentrated its "priority on actions," trying to keep the discussions focused on specific projects that are "concrete and grounded." It managed to gain the cooperation of skeptical local landowners—who had "fears of coercion, loss of control, or being forced to compromise fundamental values"—by adopting a requirement that "all projects are initiated on a voluntary basis." Such a general "pragmatic stance" and "experimental approach"—a "dynamic and ground-based approach to learning ideas" from all involved parties—also proved "especially important in facilitating the participation of landowners in . . . projects by reducing the divisions between 'expert' and 'nonexpert' knowledge and the associated resentment caused by perceptions of 'expert arrogance.'"[5]

This Feather River effort managed to implement a number of specific watershed improvement projects and to achieve "reduced tensions and increased cooperation between public agencies and private landowners, and between agencies themselves"—objectives that the Forest Service in its own efforts has seldom been able to accomplish in recent years.[6] The Forest Service does not try and is not able to limit itself to actions voluntarily accepted by affected parties, to abandon claims to final authority grounded in specialized expertise, or to commit itself to a specific ecosystem mission closely tailored to the local needs of a specific area. The Forest Service has not been able to build the bridges of trust, and to gain local acceptance for the legitimacy of its actions, that the Feather River group, including a wider representation of views and acting collegially on an ad hoc basis, was able to achieve.

Leading ecologists now tell us that expectations for scientific understanding of forest systems should be lowered. Kathryn Kohm and Jerry Franklin comment that "scientists, managers, and stakeholders must appreciate the idiosyncratic nature of each forest stand and landscape, as well as the limitations of general theory." The misplaced confidence of past forestry professionals has been replaced by "humility as a basic attitude," a result of so many past "surprises and basic new insights into forest composition, structure, and function [that] have been the hallmark of recent decades." As troublesome as it might be for national forest managers trying to function under fierce political pressures, it is simply necessary to face the fact of "the very tentative state of our current knowledge and the iterative nature of learning."

Indeed, Kohm and Franklin endorsed the new concept of "adaptive management," agreeing with other proponents that adaptive management is "the only logical approach under the circumstances of uncertainty and the continued accumulation of knowledge."[7] The Committee of Scientists similarly declared that "for the foreseeable future, decisions on appropriate management of natural resources will be made in the context of considerable uncertainty about the outcome of those actions. Where risks are high and uncertainty about outcomes is great, active adaptive management will be needed." In essence endorsing a much greater willingness to experiment on a small scale, the committee recommended that "implementation of adaptive management approaches will speed up the process of learning how ecological systems function and will decrease the likelihood of large-scale management errors."[8]

In a world of adaptive management, based much more on trial and error, requiring frequent changes of course as further knowledge develops, and in which there is much greater humility about the capabilities of scientific understanding of complex ecological and economic systems, a large central bureaucracy such as the Forest Service may simply not be capable of functioning. The Forest Service may never be able to implement a set of forest purposes that will be difficult to define in a lasting fashion and may vary greatly from place to place across the West.

One federal agency, the Natural Resources Conservation Service (formerly the Soil Conservation Service), has been an exception to the general disillusionment with federal actions of recent decades. As Douglas Kenney reports, the old soil "conservation districts provide a highly practical organizational model for Federal-State-local cooperation" in natural resource management. The key to their success has been that these districts have operated through mechanisms of local governance; they have "historically not been used as a vehicle for unwanted regulatory action." Rather than the club of federal power, soil conservation districts "have operated on a system of positive incentives (i.e., Federal funding and technical assistance being provided to landowners who voluntarily agree to implement conservation measures)."[9] The burgeoning watershed management movement in the West has borrowed heavily from the operating methods of the old soil conservation districts.

THE QUINCY LIBRARY GROUP

While the Forest Service, the Congress, and other national actors have been creating policy and management gridlock at the national level, other local groups in the West have also been forming in the 1990s—virtually in desperation—with the hope of working out answers to problems that national institutions seem incapable of resolving. They are saying in effect that, if the ones who have the formal authority will not serve them, they will act on their own. To be sure, even assuming that local groups can reach agreement on forest management issues where outsiders cannot, they must then face the question of how to get the Forest Service and other centralized land management institutions to act in accord with their local agreement.

One such local group, the Quincy Library Group in the Sierra Nevadas of northeastern California, took the bold step of asking the Congress to enact into law its own locally developed forest plan.[10] The participants in the Quincy group included longtime environmental lawyer and activist Michael Jackson, local government officials, timber industry representatives, and other local leaders. In 1997, Ed Marston described it in the pages of the *High Country News* as "the most serious challenge in decades" to the familiar centralized ways of doing things of the organized national environmental groups.[11] National environmental groups in fact mobilized to oppose the Quincy Library plan, seeing it as an opening wedge toward much greater local control of the national forests. A total of 140 national and regional environmental organizations declared their opposition to the legislation. Nevertheless, following a fierce political struggle in the Congress, President Bill Clinton signed a bill to go forward with the Quincy forest plan in the fall of 1998.

The Quincy Library Group started from a recognition that the local national forests in northeastern California faced major ecological and resource problems that required decisive management actions. In an earlier era the Forest Service would have been expected to work with the various interests to broker appropriate management solutions. However, the participants in the Quincy Library discussions now found that the agency was no longer capable of fulfilling this role. Moving into the vacuum, there were new holders of power for the national forests but they were too fragmented, too far removed from the local scene, and/or too busy with other more pressing concerns "to settle a dispute in an obscure corner of the Sierra Nevada range." As a result, as Marston commented, the local interests came to the conclusion that their only choice was "to deal directly with each other or to remain in perpetual struggle and gridlock."[12]

The basic forest problem they faced was little different from many other national forests of the West. As Marston explains, a century of "fire suppression and overgrazing" had led to a large and historically unprecedented "accumulation of fuel, especially in the drier forests." Prescribed burning would generally be unacceptable because in the current condition of the forest there is too much risk that "even small fires will quickly grow to catastrophic, landscape-scale conflagrations that will destroy all trees and habitat."[13] Hence, instead of prescribed burning, the Quincy group developed detailed plans for a program of selective thinning and logging of certain forest areas. The idea would be to reduce significantly the future risk of fire, while harvesting enough timber to keep the local mill functioning and its workers with jobs.

According to a Wilderness Society analyst, the new plan would about double the current level of timber harvests. Because the timber is not worth much in the current unhealthy condition of the forests, and given the high administrative costs for the Forest Service of holding timber sales, this analyst also estimated that the federal government might eventually have to contribute as much as $83 million to fulfill the Quincy plan.

By following their plan, as Marston observes, the members of the Quincy group hope "to return almost 3 percent of California to what it calls a pre-settlement state." Instead of the current "thicket of 1,000 or more trees per acre," and once the forests have been cleared of the dense mass of excess fuels, it will be possible to return more closely to the ecological workings of fire of the past, leading to more parklike conditions for trees where "a small number of survivors" are able "to grow large and old."[14] In short, the Quincy Library Group is not proposing any radical innovation in forest thinking; its plans are in many respects a reflection in one particular locality in the West of the wider thinking of most recent forestry studies and government agency reports, as discussed above in chapters 1 and 2.

Why, then, was it necessary to bypass all the regular institutional apparatus of public land management and to take the radical step of going directly to Congress to obtain the authority to implement a solution?

Why should legislators in Washington have to enact into federal law, in effect, a local land-use plan involving a few California national forests? As Marston comments, the Forest Service is today "a weakened, disoriented agency that used to run the national forests." As its claims to social legitimacy grounded in scientific management have been undermined, others have stepped in to challenge successfully its authority. As a result, "today, the [national] forests are run by judges, by environmentalists working through the Clinton administration, and by the timber industry working through Congress."[15] However, with this fragmentation of authority, the overall result is an absence of any effective management.

Marston found that the local forest supervisor on the Lassen National Forest, Kent Connaughton, did not contest this assessment. As Connaughton explained to Marston, until recently timber harvesting had provided a "clarity" of Forest Service mission. Connaughton recognized that a new era had arrived in which the management focus was now on "the biological condition over large landscapes." As this forest supervisor commented, "I have an idea about where this landscape needs to go—toward the more natural conditions that once existed." However, there was "great chaos in how to do it," because the scientific understanding of forest workings was so weak, authority was so fragmented, and the institutional paralysis of the Forest Service so great. Indeed, the many existing constraints would effectively prevent "a forest from moving decisively in any one direction."[16]

A key question today is whether local efforts such as that of the Quincy Library Group will find an institutional framework in which they will be able to fit their activities in a more routine way. It is difficult to imagine that the Congress has either the will or the capacity to enact into law a separate plan for each national forest, as it is developed by a local group of national forest users. The Congress could, however, set up procedures by which future local bodies such as the Quincy Library Group might be formed and officially chartered. These groups could assume real responsibilities for developing and implementing forest plans, perhaps going further to play a role in selecting top managers, proposing budgets, and making other key forest management decisions.[17]

A WORLD OF VALUE PLURALISM

Congress is being forced to act because, as noted above, in its essence national forest management comes down to a political act and Congress is the only available political body that can make final decisions for federally owned resources. Forest Service management is not mainly a technical set of decisions, and ecosystem management, for all the high hopes, suffers from familiar liabilities of earlier understandings of scientific management. It is doubtful that ecosystem management will be capable of producing a management consensus that the broader society will easily follow. Even if it should prove possible to win a considerable degree of public acceptance of the objective of achieving a forest condition corresponding to pre-European times—despite the many scientific and philosophical (theological) objections to this vision—there is not likely to be a similar agreement on the path for getting there. The most feasible path to this end, widespread removal of excess fuels through an expanded Forest Service program of thinning and other increased harvesting of national forest timber, is unacceptable to much of the national environmental movement.

Thus, in the absence of some major new and unexpected development, the prospect is for continued polarization and gridlock. In a background review of recent national forest management for the Sierra Nevada Ecosystem Project, Larry Ruth, professor of environmental policy at the University of California at Berkeley, offered a pessimistic assessment. The National Forest Management Act of 1976 confronted the agency with "conflicting forest management goals," a problem compounded by "conflicting demands of the public." It remained a "riddle" how the agency should respond to the welter of conflicting pressures it faced. Whatever the agency did, it would "face certain scrutiny," much of it critical, and its opponents would have no reluctance to use a wide variety of "legal and administrative mandates" for their own purposes.[18]

The result had been that the Forest Service in the Sierra Nevada region had been "unable to implement either broad policies or land-management plans that survive longer than a few years." Whenever the agency had developed "plans and management activities poised to have a substantial impact on the ecosystem," the outcome had been that these plans "were prevented from being fully implemented." Given the complexity of the legal and political environment that the Forest Service faced, "no proposal for managing the national forests of the Sierra Nevada thus far has elucidated a strategy that will demonstrably satisfy the ecological, socioeconomic, legal, and political criteria by which these policies are judged." In short, the Forest Service—conceivably because it was in an impossible position—was thus far failing in what should be its fundamental goal, to ensure "long-term sustainability for the natural resources and ecosystems" of the Sierra Nevada national forests.[19] Ruth did not offer any particular grounds for greater optimism about the future.

With the Forest Service lacking the social legitimacy to make its decisions stick, and the courts institutionally ill suited to a coordinating policy and management role, the political process—meaning in the case of the national forests the Congress—is the one remaining possibility. There has in fact been considerable recognition in the Congress that the management of the national forests is today failing. The Forests and Public Land Management Subcommittee of the Senate Energy and Natural Resources Committee in 1995 held ten hearings around the United States on national forest management.[20] It was the most comprehensive effort in many years by the Congress to address the problems of the national forest system. Near the end of the process, the chairman of the full committee, Senator Frank Murkowski, commented that "nobody is defending the status quo," nobody is saying that the existing system "is not broken." Based on testimony of dozens of witnesses, it was apparent that there are "different views of what is broken, what needs fixing, and how to fix it. But I have been overwhelmed by the universal dissatisfaction with the current status."[21]

Yet perhaps reflecting the legacy of a century of scientific management thinking, the Senate has approached its task as though its goal should be the establishment of a new national policy direction for the national forests. As it has tried to fulfill this goal, the same policy disagreements and value conflicts that have prevented the Forest Service from managing successfully have also prevented the Congress from legislating successfully. The error of the Senate, and the Congress as a whole, is to assume that there should be some national policy for the national forests. The inability of the Congress to pass any meaningful legislation, or of the Forest Service to achieve effective management, say much the same thing. The message is that there is no longer enough policy and value consensus in the United States to decide issues of national forest management on a national basis, in terms of one national set of values or vision for the forests implemented for the whole country.

This is the view now of James Giltmier, an architect as a Senate staffer of key national forest legislation of the 1970s, and a longtime observer of the policy-making process for the national forests. Giltmier stated in 1998 that "the vast forested areas of America are as diverse as the nation itself. Perhaps this is the heart of the enduring management challenges." Observing that the Forest Service today is "paralyzed" by the many conflicting demands being placed upon it, Giltmier suggested that "it may simply be impossible for all sides to reach agreement on a national forest policy."[22]

It may still be possible to find agreement, however, at the local level. There is likely to be a greater agreement on values locally. Issues can be addressed at the local level in less symbolic and more practical terms. The on-the-ground conditions and results will be visible there for all to see. If management fails, it is the local people who actually suffer the direct consequences. The old saying, "necessity is the mother of invention," reflects a basic truth. Indeed, the members of the Quincy Library Group arrived at a plan that, if proposed broadly for the entire nation, would surely have failed. As noted above, the forest plans developed by the Quincy group involved a substantial increase in timber harvesting from levels of the past few years, based on economic, environmental, and fire policy considerations.

NATIONAL-LEVEL OBSTRUCTIONISM

The greatest obstacle the Quincy Library Group and other local efforts have faced has been the desire of leading environmental organizations to nationalize the significance of local proposals and actions. A report to the Western Water Policy Review Advisory Commission noted that the increasing local "reliance on consensus decisionmaking is also of concern to some parties, since this requirement may prompt watershed initiatives to selectively exclude dissenting voices from the collaborative effort (for fear of creating groups that are unable to make decisions) and can encourage 'lowest common denominator' decision making." National environmental organizations in particular may be excluded from the new "consensus-based processes" because they are not physically present in the local area and because such processes tend to "'de-legitimate' public conflict and litigation, strategies upon which many environmental groups have become highly dependent."[23]

It thus is not surprising that, as Mark Sagoff noted, the Quincy legislation "greatly angered national environmental organizations," including the Audubon Society, the Sierra Club, and the Wilderness Society.[24] The Sierra Club described the bill as "a disastrous law" that could "radically alter how all our National Forests are managed," abdicating responsibilities mandated by laws such as the National Forest Management Act in favor of a new "local control." However, the "National Forests belong to all Americans, not just those who live in nearby communities." Noting that the Quincy Library plan would significantly increase timber harvests, the Sierra Club stated that "MORE LOGGING is not the solution needed for our national forests. . . . It is the problem."[25]

In strongly opposing the Quincy legislation, Michael McCloskey, the chair of the Sierra Club, acknowledged that the organization distrusted local groups to exercise management control, declaring that the bill was "designed to disempower our constituency, which is heavily urban."[26] Louis Blumberg of the Wilderness Society argued that the bill "excludes 99 percent of the Americans who have an equal stake in national forests."[27] According to Sagoff, tactically these organizations employed their usual rhetorical flamboyance, portraying "rural westerners

[as] easily snookered by slick talking industry representatives. According to one newspaper report, literature from national groups often refers 'to well-intentioned Bambi consorting with ravenous Godzilla, and naive chickens inviting sharp, high powered foxes into the coop.'"[28] The common use of such language by environmentalists is incompatible with the approaches of local "civic environmentalism" because it is specifically designed to sharpen disagreements and heighten tensions, rather than to diffuse conflict in order to reach local agreement.[29]

In the case of Quincy Library, for the most part the national environmental groups have not sought to engage the debate in terms of the specific merits of the local Quincy plan for the local forests—other than to say that the work of the Quincy group raises many unanswered questions (as if this would not be true of almost any major action, no matter how much it is studied). Rather, typical of what happens when forest policy issues are raised to the national level, they have argued that the efforts of the Quincy group should be seen in terms of the national precedent that would be created for applying the same approach throughout the United States. Posed in these terms, Congress would surely have rejected the Quincy efforts—or virtually any other plans.

THE NEW POLITICS OF VALUES

An inability to resolve deep value conflicts at the national level is apparent in many other areas besides public land policy. Gay rights groups seek a formal public acceptance of their lifestyle, but prominent Christian organizations fight these efforts. There is no more national agreement—and no more ability to resolve the issue—on the future course of abortion policy than of national forest policy. The great American "melting pot" no longer holds such allure.

Robert Bork, in his early career at Yale Law School, was a student of antitrust law, a member of the law and economics movement. His interests partly reflected the fact that in the 1960s domestic policy debates were focused on economic questions—how to maintain a high rate of economic growth and how to pursue the war on poverty. Reflecting a broader social belief in the benefits of economic progress, it was widely assumed that poverty was a problem that could be solved by economic means— that alleviating the material deprivation of the inner cities would end crime, drug dependency, marital instability, gang warfare, and other social problems there. After thirty years of experience, however, there is now a different perspective. Today, the *Washington Post* states in a matter-of-fact way that "as common sense suggests and social science affirms, improving children's futures [in the inner city] has more to do with time and values than with income."[30]

Reflecting this redirection of national concern from economic affairs to cultural and value matters, Bork now spends much less time studying economics and sees the basic issues confronting the United States in the following terms. "We, or a large proportion of our population, have adopted a secular religion that 'celebrates emotion, deplores reason and above all reveres the victim.'" While the domestic debates of the 1960s seemingly were about economic and other "rational" public policy matters, at a deeper level Bork now thinks that there was a "cultural and spiritual revolution" taking place at that time. To his regret, this revolution has taken hold now among opinion leaders in many walks of American life: "schools and colleges, sexual relations and family life, churches, the media and entertainment industry."[31]

As Bork now sees matters, "in our current state of affluence, social and cultural issues are more important to the good life" than continued material progress. The more urgent task now is to "restore sanity and morality to our lives," curbing the influence of the secular religions introduced in the 1960s. For Bork, therefore, the central policy issues of the current period are culturally driven, matters like "educational curricula, the feminization of the military, the understanding of the family, the proper spheres of reason and emotion, and much more."[32] He could easily have added to his list the following: Will the national forests be used to serve human purposes or manage to achieve an ecological state desirable in its own right? Will the goal of ecological management be to achieve a forest condition that eliminates signs of European civilization (thus offering a strong negative moral judgment on this civilization)? Or will the goal be some positive vision of a future forest condition created by human action (nature as a "work of art") that offers widespread recreational opportunities and other forms of direct use?

Where Bork and many others go wrong is to think that these kinds of issues should be resolved at a national level—whether the policy question is national forest management, teaching of U.S. history in public school, or divorce law. The debate can be held in part nationally, and leading intellectuals can and should compete on a national (and international) stage. But the bottom line should be decided locally. As Bork is correct to perceive, these questions are fundamentally matters of religion, whether the values are grounded in traditional Christian and Jewish religions, or in older secular religions like the progressive "gospel of efficiency," or in newer secular faiths like the environmental gospel. To attempt to impose national values everywhere across the United States—to impose a national religious standard of values where there is no national religious consensus—is a formula for social division and bitterness.

When domestic policy debates were centered on economics, it was more plausible to argue that a national economic system required national approaches. When economic disagreements were about the dividing up of the material outputs of the national economic system, it was not so difficult to split an economic pie—so much for labor unions, so much for business, and so forth. When the disagreements are about basic social (religious) values, achieving compromise is more difficult. How is it possible to split the differences on a question of morality, say, the circumstances in which there is a legitimate right to kill, as some see abortion? Even assuming a form of compromise can be conceived, those who are willing to compromise are all too easily seen as infidels to the cause. The world has recently seen in the case of the former Yugoslavia, how religious differences can inflame other disagreements and lead to irreconcilable conflicts.

In managing the national forests, there is no reason that Mormon Utah should reflect all the same forest values as the neighboring state of Nevada, where prostitution and gambling have long been legal. These two states have much different histories and cultures, as every western state differs from every other western state in some significant respects. If forest policy is politics in one form or another, and politics is in significant part a matter of defining the values of the community, it would seem that there should be differing forest policies from state to state. To be sure, the states in the West themselves often contain multiple communities within their boundaries that may differ significantly in history and culture among themselves. In Mormon Utah, Park City is an old mining community where Mormons were once few and far between and hard drinking and prostitution flourished.

The religious tradition in Western civilization has always had a difficult time reconciling the fundamental commitment to monotheism (which teaches there is one and only one absolute truth) with the reality of religious pluralism. The monotheist believes that he (or she) knows God's one plan for the world, and to accept other plans could be virtually to admit the devil into the discussion. In a pluralist world this is a formula, however, for religious warfare, of which Western civilization has seen all too much, including the Thirty Years War in the seventeenth century and terrible wars of secular religion in Europe in the twentieth century. The avoidance of such outcomes would seem to require an agreement to suspend religious certainty in the public arena (as seen in American ideas of separation of church and state), or an agreement to separate and to go different ways (to "divorce" rather than remain religiously "married").[33]

EDEN VERSUS NOAH'S ARK

If we demand national answers, the necessity of imposing these answers on unwilling objects of national policy requires at least making a claim that they should be "objective." Forcing one person's religion on another as a government mandate would violate long-standing American political ideals. Yet even remaining within the value framework of contemporary environmentalism (on which there is hardly consensus), there will be policy issues inside this framework that defy any objective resolution.

Consider, for example, how it might be possible to give an "objective" answer to the following problem. One goal of environmental values, as discussed in chapter 2, is to recover the conditions preceding European settlement. A second equally important goal is to protect and restore the populations of native plant and animal species of North America. The Endangered Species Act of 1973 gives the government extraordinary powers to act in the pursuit of this second goal. The difficulty is that the two goals—each seemingly reflecting basic values for which any compromise is difficult—can yield opposite policy recommendations.

The GAO thus recently found itself puzzling over the following dilemma. In the more eastern parts of the range of the spotted owl in Oregon and Washington, one finds the familiar ecological story of past fire suppression leading to an invasion of Douglas firs and the loss of the historic ponderosa pine forests. According to the precepts of ecosystem management, the goal of management here should be to restore the original ponderosa pine forest that preceded European settlement and the disruption of natural ecological processes by fire suppression. However, the newer Douglas fir forests, the result of human manipulation of the forest, now provide a good habitat for the spotted owl. Indeed, the Endangered Species Act might well be taken to preclude the removal of the Douglas fir forest to restore the historic ponderosa pines. As the GAO commented, in places where "ponderosa stands have largely been replaced by abnormally dense stands of Douglas fir, . . . many of the Douglas fir stands cannot be removed because they now provide habitat for the threatened northern spotted owl."[34]

Which should it be—maximum effort to preserve an endangered species population or decisive management actions to restore original ecosystem conditions? If there is no "objective" answer, why try to impose one answer through national policy required everywhere? Why not let the local people most directly affected work out their own local solution?

Such circumstances may occur widely. Animal species—even rare and endangered ones—do not necessarily have the aversion to a human presence that modern wilderness advocates feel. It was recently revealed that the Pinehurst number 2 golf course in North Carolina, designed by Donald Ross and one of the most famous in the United States (it is the site of the 1999 U.S. Open, bringing tens of thousands of spectators), is also a favored habitat for the endangered red-cockaded woodpecker.[35] The woodpeckers like the forest edges with large trees alongside of generally open areas provided by a golf course. Perhaps building more golf courses on the national forests might provide the financial capital needed to take actions that would also serve to advance significantly the restoration and maintenance of red-cockaded woodpecker populations.

Contrary to a common perception, clearcutting and other forms of timber harvesting can contribute significantly to biological diversity by creating the disturbance conditions required by some key species. In North Carolina, botanist Alan Weakley, searching in the early 1980s for rare plant species, felt discouraged to discover a forest area recently clearcut and abandoned. Revisiting the site in 1996, he found to his surprise that, although the area remained treeless, fully seventeen rare plant species had colonized the old clearcut. One species, Cooley's meadowrue, was federally listed as endangered; the new meadowrue colony discovered by Weakley on the old clearcut was only the twelfth known to exist in the United States. As Bruce Stein and Stephanie Flack of the Nature Conservancy comment with respect to this and other similar reports, "sometimes rare species can turn human disturbances to their advantage."[36] Who is to decide whether forests should be clearcut to promote endangered species?

Five researchers at the Yale School of Forestry and Environmental Studies summarized the state of scientific knowledge concerning the relationship between biological diversity and ecosystem stability as follows:

> Attempts to unveil the relationships between the taxonomic diversity, productivity and stability of ecosystems continue to generate inconclusive, contradictory and controversial conclusions. New insights from recent studies support the hypothesis that species diversity enhances productivity and stability in some ecosystems, but not in others. Appreciation is growing for the ways that particular ecosystem features, such as environmental variability and nutrient stress, can influence biotic interactions. Alternatives to the diversity-stability hypothesis have been proposed, and experimental approaches are starting to evolve to test these hypotheses and to elucidate the mechanisms underlying the functional role of species diversity.[37]

Given the awkwardness of the tensions posed between current interpretations of "ecosystem management" and the imperatives of endangered species preservation, some groups have attempted to paper over the conflict by simply assuming that the conflict does not exist. The Committee of Scientists, for example, asserted on the one hand that a main policy goal should be to restore "historic" ecosystem conditions and simultaneously another main goal should be to preserve "focal species" of plants and animals—like rare and endangered species listed under the Endangered Species Act. The committee argued that "the key characteristic of a focal species is that its status and time trend provide insights to the integrity of the larger ecological system." The committee was honest enough, however, to admit that it was making some heroic assumptions: "available knowledge of species ecologies and their functional roles in ecological systems is so limited that it is not always possible, a priori, to unambiguously identify focal species."[38]

Other conflicts among core values may be unavoidable. Using prescribed fire in the management of some national forests may contribute significantly to air pollution, resulting in a certain number of additional deaths—a number for which precise statistical estimates can be developed by government analysts. How many human deaths can be tolerated in order to make forest ecologies function more "naturally"? Introduction of grizzly bears into Idaho or other wild areas will cause some people to hike in a fearful state of mind in backcountry areas and a few deaths over the long run. How much increase in human anxiety or danger to human life is acceptable? Such decisions should be made by those who will bear the consequences, not by distant bureaucracies.

In the Bible, we can be sure that God would not have asked Noah to build his Ark if it had meant taking us farther away from the Kingdom of Heaven. Although many environmentalists seem to want to look to the science of ecology to find a new modern substitute for God, the actual science is not so cooperative. There can in fact be direct conflicts between "ecosystem integrity," as it is currently being interpreted, and the protection of rare and endangered species. If a choice is necessary, which will it be—or at least how will it be made? Neither environmental science nor environmental theology at present seems to be able to shed any clear light here. If there is no one answer, attempts to impose national answers by government fiat will in the end lack social legitimacy, appearing rather as naked exercises in coercion.

The growing success of local watershed groups, by contrast, has reflected their ability to establish, as Kenney writes, "moral authority." Watershed groups operate in a culture of informal understandings impossible to achieve in the legalistic and regulation-driven world of federal natural resource agencies. The watershed groups in fact renounce reliance on "formal authorities" and the regulatory coercion associated with such traditional forms of authority as neither "needed nor desired." The ethos of watershed decision making includes instead a new blend of communitarian and libertarian impulses—that actions by each party should be taken "voluntarily," which may succeed in an arena where "each party feels a compelling need to support collective efforts to improve resource management."[39]

To be sure, although this approach is new in the American West today, reflecting a newfound rejection of the centralizing and authoritarian strategies of scientific management, it has a much older lineage. The central theme of Elinor Ostrom's classic analysis in *Governing the Commons* is the widespread ability of many local communities throughout history to work out common solutions without either formal property rights or formal regulations.[40] If left to themselves, local groups have long demonstrated an impressive ability to solve their problems through voluntary means, as long as the bonds of a common culture are sufficiently strong to maintain trust ("moral authority") and the scale of decision making is not too large.

This approach would never work today in the United States at a national level but watershed decision processes, as Kenney explains, "take on a decidedly different nature when the parties are only 20 miles apart and members of the same civic and social organizations" and there is frequent opportunity for "face-to-face interactions." The willingness and ability to find workable compromises is much greater locally than in larger forums with "separate parties [that] never meet and that have little appreciation of the others' situation." As a result, "management efforts organized at the scale of small watersheds are potentially more likely to achieve [the] 'moral authority'"—the political legitimacy based on the presence of trust—that is today necessary to any form of decisive natural resource actions.[41]

THE GOSPEL ACCORDING TO LEOPOLD

Aldo Leopold is often described as the patron saint of the modern environmental movement. The concepts of ecosystem management, as now being put into practice on the national forests by the U.S. Forest Service, are in fact to a significant degree restatements of much of what Leopold had to say. Leopold is the new prophet.[42] The essence of Leopold's vision is that human beings should apply a new morality to the forests and other lands. Leopold's famous "land ethic" argues that human beings should not be principally concerned for their own material or other narrow welfare but should recognize a basic moral imperative to maintain the forests (and other lands) in a proper ecological condition.

As a current interpreter of his thought explains, Leopold believed that "all parts of the land or biotic community, thus all parts of forests, have value and are 'good;' which means that all parts have ecological value and aesthetic value. Moreover, the land as a whole has such value, as do forests as wholes." A further implication was that "ethical status and concern should be extended to all parts of the land, and thus to all parts, components, processes and organisms in forests, not just to the human social community." It follows, therefore, according to Leopold's reasoning, that "some parts of the land, thus some parts of forests and some forests, have a right to continued existence, and to continued existence in a natural or 'wild' state." Finally, for policy makers on the national forests, all this would mean that "humans and thus foresters have special moral or ethical responsibilities, of an individual sort, to the land and its components, and thus to forests and their components."[43]

The Forest Service in its recent policy pronouncements and the Committee of Scientists in its 1999 report have been following in the path of this gospel according to Leopold. But what about other people who follow other gospels, perhaps finding an appropriate vision of land stewardship in, say, the biblical gospel according to Mark or the gospel according to Luke? Leopold was the proponent of a particular "land ethic," but there is more than one ethical vision possible for the national forests and other public lands.[44]

For example, Thomas Bonnicksen, a respected professor at Texas A&M University, perceives that "zealots within the agencies, encouraged by some preservation groups and ideologues in universities, have taken over our National Park and Wilderness areas and converted them into their own quasi-religious temples." They have renounced the "original purpose of providing for 'the enjoyment of the people'" and instead are now aiming to "satisfy the spiritual needs of a small but influential subculture." This subculture believes in an ethic that "people may enter these sanctuaries to see the forces of nature at work, but they must not interfere with these forces"—even though there is not a "shred of scientific evidence" that a policy of noninterference will restore earlier "natural" conditions. In short, for Bonnicksen, federal "Park and Wilderness managers no longer need a degree in science to manage resources—they need a degree in mythology."[45]

The philosopher Mark Sagoff has written that with the benefit of hindsight it is increasingly apparent that many past policy and management issues relating to nature were really a twentieth century version of the "wars of religion." The progressive "gospel of efficiency," which provided the ethos in which the Forest Service was founded, was part of a general "faith in material progress" of the early part of the twentieth century. As far back as the Enlightenment, many people had come to believe that human beings had acquired "the means to build the Heavenly City on earth, primarily by conquering nature and thus ensuring limitless material progress."[46]

Gifford Pinchot saw his own efforts in terms of such a great spiritual quest. The United States, as the industrial leader of the world, was leading the way to a "future uplifting of the nations." This country was "the greatest human power for good" on earth, showing the way through rational behavior and economic progress to the future salvation of the world.[47] However, as Sagoff comments, following World War I, and then World War II, the Holocaust, and many other horrors of the twentieth century, there was a "collapse of this faith" in the redemptive powers of material progress in Western civilization. Yet the old assumptions remain "the moral basis for welfare economics" and, at least until recently, for the professional culture of the Forest Service.[48]

The bitterness of the past clashes between environmentalists and the Forest Service is typical of religious warfare (fortunately fought mostly in this country with words rather than guns). For Cecil Andrus, the disputes over land use on the national forests and other public lands called to mind another place of religious warfare; as he commented, "drawing up maps on the use of lands is about as easy in the American West as it is in Bosnia."[49] The difficulties of new-style environmentalists and old-style progressives in working together have resulted from two factors: (1) the conflicting tenets of mutually distinctive faiths, and also (2) the mutual tendency to camouflage religious disagreements in scientific rhetoric, thus making any common exploration of the underlying theological differences all the more difficult.

If the members of the environmental movement had limited themselves to criticisms of the merits of the founding Forest Service vision of scientific management, or of the moral claims of the gospel of efficiency, they would in fact have been on solid ground. They would also have found many surprising allies, including libertarians for whom central government authority justified by the claims of scientific management is seen as posing a basic threat to individual freedoms.[50] However, environmentalists did not stop at criticisms of progressive excesses of faith. All too often, they have ended up seeking to substitute one scientific religion—based on misleading claims to a scientific status—for another.

The environmental movement started off as a decentralized struggle of local citizens against central planners seeking to impose their grand designs. In the early days, environmentalists in neighborhoods and other local areas organized to fend off highways, dams, power plants, and all manner of other development projects, often justified in the name of scientific management. Today, however, the situation is frequently reversed. The Environmental Protection Agency (EPA) seeks to impose its air and water quality control plans on local citizens, justified in the name of science. The strongest local protests are no longer against highway departments but are now often directed at environmental agencies such as the EPA and the Forest Service.

The "wise use" movement today is the closest heir to earlier populist movements in the West, with environmental agencies now taking the place of the capitalist financiers who incurred the wrath of earlier generations of populists. The environmental movement increasingly has sought to employ federal power to command results it could not achieve locally on its own. As they have turned to federal authority, it is a great irony that environmentalists now find themselves often repeating the old argument that centralization of management authority is necessary in order to implement the one valid truth, the truth provided by science. Environmentalism now claims in effect a unique access to the mind of God, reflecting the common substitution in the modern age of scientific truth for the earlier role of Judeo-Christian religion.

However, similar to Donald Worster's doubts about any effort to ground a moral vision in the teachings of ecological science, Sagoff considers that "as an object of scientific inquiry" the idea of the ecosystem offers a morally "pointless hodgepodge" in a world characterized by "constantly changing associations of organisms and environments."[51] Ecological or any other science offers a system of thought for explaining the physical details of the world, not for finding ethical value in the world. Hence, even if it worked better as a predictive science, ecological science would in itself be incapable of providing sound policy grounds for preserving forests, maintaining biodiversity, or saving other parts of nature for its own sake.

As Sagoff says, "it is largely for moral—ethical, not prudential, reasons—that we care about all our fellow creatures." Sagoff believes strongly that forests and other parts of nature should be preserved but that the grounds for protecting nature do not "have anything to do with human well-being or welfare as economists understand that term"—or as foresters have traditionally conceived their professional mission in utilitarian terms as well. Nature should not be preserved because it betters the human condition in a narrowly self-interested sense; it is not a matter of increasing "utility," however measured. Rather, nature should be protected and preserved because, morally and ethically, it is the right thing to do. In traditional religious terms, one might say that God has so commanded.

Hence, despite all the scientific claims and the legal maneuvering in current public land controversies, as Sagoff argues, "the debate between ecological and economic theory [and traditional forestry] is largely a moral and theological debate."[52] Many environmentalists view the world in much the same spirit as those more traditional Christian theologians who look to the "God of Jesus Christ [who] is opposed to the idols we make of self, nation, race or economic production."[53] For theologians of such views, traditional and secular alike, the progressive gospel of efficiency is one such false idol based on a materialist heresy of the potential for re-making human nature through economic progress.

Yet, if management decisions for the national forests are now to be un-derstood as requiring a theological inquiry at least as much as a scientific set of determinations, there will be major implications for the allocation of political authority over these lands. With science there can be at least the hope of a national (or international) consensus. In matters of religion, no one claims—or wants—that there should be one national religion, espe-cially in a country as large and diverse as the United States.

The only answer would seem to be to decentralize the management of the national forests. It is not a perfect solution but it offers at least the pos-sibility that there will be greater homogeneity of values among those af-fected locally by forest management decisions—and thus there will be less necessity for land managers to try to reconcile basic value conflicts. To the extent that there is greater agreement at the local level on the basic goals and mission of forest management—on the appropriate "land ethic," or "stewardship ideal," whether that of Aldo Leopold, St. Paul, or any other figure—the essence of the management task will become more feasible.

THE WATERSHED MOVEMENT

Perhaps the vanguard of such a future decentralization movement can be found in the current innovations in political authority today occur-ring in many parts of the West at the watershed level. Indeed, as Marston estimates, there are "hundreds" of local groups in the West that are now functioning to seek to resolve watershed management issues that have defied the efforts of higher level institutions.[54] In 1995, the Natural Resources Law Center at the School of Law of the University of Colorado documented the extent to which many local groups were being organized to find better management answers to immediate wa-tershed problems—there was currently a "widespread proliferation" of such local watershed groups across the West.[55] In many cases, the need to resolve forest fire, timber harvesting, and other forestry issues was among the driving concerns within the watershed. The University of Colorado Law Center in 1996 issued a report on this development, in-cluding capsule summaries of the manner of formation and activities of fully seventy-six groups.

There were three common reasons for the formation of a local watershed group. First, there was often a "desire of watershed residents for more input and control in managing resources." Second, this was often closely related to the fact that local citizens perceived an existing "inability of government agencies to resolve problems in the watershed." And third, the most frequent area of special concern to local residents was "economic development issues"—what would be the future of the local economy and what could be done in the watershed to influence its direction.[56]

Watershed groups had been formed in various ways.[57] In some cases, local citizens had taken the initiative; in other cases, government agencies had perceived the need for greater local involvement. These government agencies recognized that, in an environment of widespread skepticism and distrust of government, the ability to develop and implement effective policies depended on closely consulting with local groups and obtaining their approval. If claims to scientific expertise were no longer sufficient to establish social legitimacy, it would be necessary to look to some other legitimizing source. When existing political institutions could not serve this purpose, whole new political mechanisms might have to be established. Local watershed groups were in effect politics in a new form and context—and it was in such "places" that greater public trust could now be found and politics might be made to work.

One reason why existing government institutions were not working was that they often simply had the wrong boundaries. A watershed group, because it was created in an ad hoc fashion, could be designed to meet the actual geographic scope of the watershed resource needs at issue. For example, the Tri-State Bear River Watershed Project had to deal with a river basin whose geography was described as follows:

> The Bear River originates in the Uinta mountains of north central Utah and flows north into southwestern Wyoming, back into Utah, again into Wyoming, and then into Idaho. In Idaho, some water from the river is diverted into Bear Lake, and then the water flows or is pumped back into the natural channel north of Bear Lake. After passing Bear Lake, the river turns south and again flows into Utah where it finally empties into Great Salt Lake.[58]

In short, no existing local government or state government was constituted to deal effectively with the watershed management problems of the Bear River. If government agencies were often failing, perhaps it was because some of them never had a suitable jurisdictional set of boundaries for the political and management tasks they were now being asked to perform.

Even where a watershed might lie within the same state or local government, there was still often much jurisdictional fragmentation. Because of their pervasive federal presence in the West, the Forest Service and the Bureau of Land Management often hold significant lands in the same watershed. If conflicts arise, these agencies do not report to the same cabinet secretary in Washington; in theory, the president is the only federal official with the authority to resolve a dispute between the two agencies definitively. Moreover, their relationships historically have often been characterized by as much rivalry as cooperation. They have operated in many areas under different policies and regulations. Then, intermingled with federal lands might be extensive private lands, state-owned lands, and lands owned by a local government. Each has its own separate management organization and leading policy concerns.

For example, in California the Mokelumne River Watershed Project was formed to address problems of water quality attributed by some groups to the effects of timber harvesting. The initiating parties (and funders of the effort) were the California Department of Forestry and Fire Protection and the California Board of Forestry. The public sector members of the project included the following: the U.S. Bureau of Land Management; U.S. Forest Service; East Bay Municipal Utility District, Calaveras County; Amador County Department of Water Resources; Central Valley Regional Water Quality Control Board; California Department of Fish and Game; California Water Resources Control Board; and the California Department of Forestry and Fire Protection. Private sector members of the group included the Georgia Pacific Corporation, the Pacific Gas and Electric Company, and a number of individual livestock operators.

In effect, the Mokelumne River Watershed Project was a new political mechanism bringing these diverse parties, whose activities might otherwise be little connected, together to address the resource management concerns of the full watershed. While this group has no formal authority, if it is successful, it may achieve greater political legitimacy in its area of concern than any existing governing institution or political body. As the Natural Resources Law Center commented, groups focused on watersheds are more likely to encompass the "problemshed" for issues of water quality, water supply, and fish and game habitat. As a result, they encompass "the areas in which the problems exist, more completely than political jurisdictions." In this way they can "promote effective communication and coordination for overlapping [governmental and private] activities and avoid duplication of effort and conflicting regulations."[59]

The Applegate Partnership is located in a timber-rich area of southwest Oregon. Owing to the spotted owl and other environmental controversies, the relationships among environmentalists, the timber industry, and government agencies had reached a state of "warlike atmosphere" in the surrounding Applegate basin. With support from the Oregon Watershed

Health Program, the partnership was formed to at least bring these contending parties together to talk about their differences. Ecologically, the Applegate basin is suffering from "many years of logging, road building, fire suppression and drought." As a result, like many other forests throughout the West, these forests have "become young, overcrowded, insect damaged and at high risk of catastrophic fire." Despite the urgency of corrective steps, the involved parties "vehemently disagree over how the forests should be managed."[60]

In other such situations in the West, matters have reached a seemingly permanent state of gridlock. The Natural Resources Law Center reports that the Applegate Partnership has at least succeeded to the extent that "now people are learning to listen and compromise in a less adversarial manner."[61] The Forest Service and Bureau of Land Management, unable to act on their own, are seeking the public support of the partnership for an accelerated program of timber salvage and thinning sales, designed to serve both forest health purposes and to keep the local timber economy alive. In one case, the partnership worked with the Forest Service to get an injunction lifted on timber harvesting in an area where trees still standing had previously been killed by fire. As in the case of the Quincy Library Group, to be sure, such efforts of local environmentalists to reach compromises with the timber industry and other local interests have led national environmental organizations to oppose further such efforts by the Applegate group or others who might follow in its steps.

Achieving political legitimacy for such controversial actions requires educating all the local players on the full technical, administrative, and other grounds for the decision.[62] Local people are no longer willing simply to put their trust in the experts. As a result, the old decision-making model—the experts consult with the locals to understand their values and preferences and then the experts ultimately decide—no longer works. In the new model being practiced by watershed groups, experts help out by providing essential information but their role may go little further. Politicians and other nontechnical people then use this information to reach the final decision.

For example, in the Yampa River Basin Partnership in northwest Colorado, "the experts were utilized to inform the participants about basic scientific and technical issues important to the watershed." Thus, "the technical experts did not dominate, and sometimes did not directly participate, in group decision making. Instead, they provided information and options so the decision makers could make informed decisions."[63] Science is no longer the controlling force in forest decision making; rather, the scientific representatives are now simply one party to the discussion.

The Natural Resources Law Center summed up its review of this important new local institutional mechanism in the West as follows:

> The emergence of collaborative watershed efforts throughout the western states is a relatively recent phenomenon. The phenomenon is a response to the failure of traditional governmental approaches to address resource management issues in a manner that recognizes the problemshed, and the interrelationships of the issues, to coordinate and cooperate effectively among agencies and across the problemshed and to involve citizens and non-governmental groups in decision making in a meaningful fashion early in the decision process.[64]

Mark Baker and William Stewart find that at one time in its history the Forest Service had maintained "robust informal relationships with community and political leaders." However, this informal way of operating was "gradually supplanted by the formalized involvement methods mandated in the Resources Planning Act" of 1974, as modified and supplemented by the National Forest Management Act of 1976. These acts were based on the old scientific management model and attempted to stiffen the legal requirements to ensure that appropriate scientific management procedures were in fact followed in the management of the national forests.[65] Thus, the National Forest Management Act required the preparation of comprehensive land-use plans throughout the national forests, with decisions based in the end on scientific criteria.

However, even though the 1970s laws also contained new mandates for public participation, according to Baker and Stewart, the result of this effort has been a "loss of legitimacy and trust" for the Forest Service. The only way to rectify this situation will be to decentralize management authority significantly:

> [New] outreach efforts may help improve public awareness, [but] public trust will probably not be regained without some devolution of planning authority to the district and forest level which allows substantive public involvement, and without an "error embracing" attitude and the concomitant organizational openness this attitude requires. Public confidence and trust, once lost, is hard to restore. However, and perhaps paradoxically, as the social and political environment in which the Forest Service operates becomes more complex and contentious, the importance of maintaining institutional legitimacy becomes increasingly important.[66]

The Western Water Policy Review Advisory Commission recommended in 1998 an urgent effort to promote new governance "mechanisms that help integrate the management of river basins and watersheds across agencies, political jurisdictions, functional programs and time." This approach should build upon "the tremendous increase in the number of local watershed initiatives and groups, and the great energy and creativity they bring to resolving resource problems." These local groups operated under "a type of pragmatic democracy" that reflected a "basic philosophy . . . to involve as many parties as possible in consensus-based decision-making processes." It was at the local level that "individuals are most likely to recognize unsustainable use first." Local groups were providing "a community-based forum for resolving . . . some of the most difficult kinds of [land and] water conflicts"—conflicts that had defied all the recent efforts of federal natural resource agencies guided by traditional assumptions and employing traditional modes of operation.[67]

The key to the success of the new groups was that "they are achieving success often without regulatory intervention and with very meager funding because they capitalize on the sense of ownership and obligation to others that exists foremost at the community level." With political legitimacy, many things are possible; without it, the current resource management gridlock is virtually inevitable. Increasingly, it is federal agencies that are losing legitimacy; it is local groups that are gaining the social authority to resolve local problems—if sometimes tapping into federal and state resources and skills.

CONCLUSION

Over the 200-year history of the public lands, the Congress has seldom initiated bold new policy directions.[68] Rather, it has been more likely to ratify and further encourage developments that were already well advanced. The Homestead Act of 1862, for example, was not a new idea. Settlers had been moving onto public lands for decades and then acquiring ownership subsequent to their physical occupancy and cultivation of the land. For many years the federal government had condemned this practice as illegal squatter occupancy. But it had no practical way of combating the squatter on a distant frontier and would eventually be forced to acquiesce in the occupancy. The Homestead Act simply confirmed, legitimized, and further extended this preexisting de facto system. Similarly, the Mining Law of 1872 and the development of appropriations law for western water emerged from informal arrangements devised by settlers to allocate rights to the use of resources among themselves.

Today, there is a spreading informal decentralization of authority taking place on the national forests and other federal lands of the West. It is part of a broader development for natural resources in the West where since the 1970s "the dominant trends in Federalism have encouraged a partial transfer of authority from Federal to State, from legislative and executive to judicial, and, more recently, from public to private."[69] If the past is a guide, such evolving informal processes of decentralization and privatization may be followed in the next few decades by a more formal reconstitution of governance of those parts of the rural West with extensive federal lands. It would in part recognize that the scientific management and other ideas on which the existing system of federal lands and resources is based have long been antiquated, and that this system is no longer capable of meeting the basic needs of the West.

NOTES

1. See Robert H. Nelson, *Public Lands and Private Rights: The Failure of Scientific Management* (Lanham, Md.: Rowman & Littlefield, 1995), chs. 6 and 7.

2. National Academy of Public Administration, *Setting Priorities, Getting Results: A New Direction for EPA* (Washington, D.C.: April 1995), p. 2.

3. New York Academy of Sciences, *Science and Endangered Species Preservation: Rethinking the Environmental Policy Process* (New York: August 1995), p. 18.

4. Jonathan Kusel, "Coordinated Resource Management," in *Status of the Sierra Nevada, Volume III*, Sierra Nevada Ecosystem Project, Report to the Congress (Davis: University of California, Wildland Resources Center Report No. 38, June 1996), pp. 1067–69.

5. Ibid., pp. 1068–71.

6. Ibid., p. 1071.

7. Kathryn A. Kohm and Jerry F. Franklin, *Creating a Forestry for the 21st Century: The Science of Ecosystem Management* (Washington, D.C.: Island Press, 1997), p. 5.

8. Committee of Scientists, *Sustaining the People's Lands: Recommendations for Stewardship of the National Forests and Grasslands*, A report to the Secretary of Agriculture and the Chief of the Forest Service (Washington, D.C.: Department of Agriculture, March 15, 1999), p. 40. Another leading advisory group that strongly endorsed the approach of "adaptive management" was the Western Water Policy Review Advisory Commission. See *Water in the West: Challenge for the Next Century*, Report of the Western Water Policy Review Advisory Commission (June 1998), p. 6–40.

9. Douglas S. Kenney, *Resource Management at the Watershed Level: An Assessment of the Changing Federal Role in the Emerging Era of Community-Based Watershed Management*, Report to the Western Water Policy Review Commission (October 1997), pp. 6, 63.

10. See Mark Sagoff, "The View from Quincy Library: Civic Engagement in Environmental Problem Solving," in *Civil Society, Democracy, and Civic Renewal*, ed. Robert K. Fullinwider, (Lanham, Md.: Rowman & Littlefield, 1999).

11. Ed Marston, "The Timber Wars Evolve into a Divisive Attempt at Peace," *High Country News* (September 29, 1997), p. 8.

12. Ibid., p. 12.

13. Ibid., pp. 11, 12.

14. Ibid., p. 11.

15. Ibid.

16. Quoted in Ed Marston, "The Timber Wars Evolve into a Divisive Attempt at Peace," *High Country News* (September 29, 1997), pp. 11–12.

17. See Robert H. Nelson and Mary M. Chapman, *Voices from the Heartland: New Tools for Decentralizing Management of the West's Public Lands*, Points West—Special Report (Denver, Colo.: Center for the New West, December 1995).

18. Larry Ruth, "Conservation and Controversy: National Forest Management, 1960–95," in *Status of the Sierra Nevada, Volume II*, p. 160.

19. Ibid.

20. U.S. Senate, Subcommittee on Forests and Public Land Management, Committee on Energy and Natural Resources, "Federal Forest Management," *Hearings on the Forest Service Reinvention and National Forest Planning Regulations*, S. Hrg. 104-182 (Pt. 1 and Pt. 2) (Washington, D.C.: Government Printing Office, 1996).

21. Statement by Honorable Frank Murkowski, U.S. Senator from Alaska, before the Subcommittee on Forests and Public Land Management, "Federal Forest Management," Hearings on the *Forest Service Reinvention and National Forest Planning Regulations* (Pt. 2), p. 355.

22. James Giltmier, "Evolution of an Agency," *Forum* (Summer 1998), pp. 7, 10. See other articles in this issue of *Forum* in a special section, "Policy in a Thicket," relating to the future of the national forests.

23. Kenney, *Resource Management at the Watershed Level*, p. 58.

24. Sagoff, "The View from Quincy Library," p. 169.

25. Sierra Club Action, Vol. II, #135, "IN THE WOODS—The Quincy Library Bill Means More Logging in Your National Forests," Sierra Club web site, posted July 22, 1997.

26. Cited in Sagoff, "The View from Quincy Library," p. 169.

27. Ibid.

28. Ibid., p. 171.

29. See Dewitt John, *Civic Environmentalism: Alternatives to Regulation in States and Communities* (Washington, D.C.: Congressional Quarterly Press, 1994).

30. Katherine Boo, "Painful Choices: Denise Jordan Is Off Welfare and Loves Her Job. But What About Her Daughter?" *Washington Post* (October 19, 1997), p. 1.

31. Robert H. Bork, "Good Reasons for Despair on the Right," *The Wall Street Journal* (October 9, 1997), p. A18. See also Robert H. Bork, *Slouching Towards Gomorrah: Modern Liberalism and American Decline* (New York: HarperCollins, 1996).

32. Bork, "Good Reasons for Despair on the Right."

33. See Robert H. Nelson, *Reaching for Heaven on Earth: The Theological Meaning of Economics* (Lanham, Md.: Rowman & Littlefield, 1991), ch. 8.

34. General Accounting Office, *Western National Forests: A Cohesive Strategy is Needed to Address Catastrophic Wildfire Threats*, GAO/RCED-99-65 (April 1999), p. 42.

35. "Rare Birdies: Endangered Woodpeckers Live on the Site of Next Week's U.S. Open Golf Tournament," *Sports Illustrated*, June 14, 1999.

36. Bruce A. Stein and Stephanie R. Flack, "Priorities: The State of U.S. Plants and Animals," *Environment* (May 1997), p. 37.

37. Kris H. Johnson, Kristiina A. Vogt, Heidi J. Clark, Oswald J. Schmitz, and Daniel J. Vogt, "Biodiversity and the Productivity and Stability of Ecosystems," *TREE* (September 1996), p. 372.

38. Committee of Scientists, *Sustaining the People's Lands*, p. 39.

39. Kenney, *Resource Management at the Watershed Level*, p. 54. See also Douglas S. Kenney, "Are Community-Based Watershed Groups Really Effective?" *Chronicle of Community*, Northern Lights Institute (Winter 1999). The *Chronicle of Community* is generally an excellent source of current information on local group efforts in western natural resource management.

40. See Elinor Ostrom, *Governing the Commons: The Evolution of Institutions for Collective Action* (New York: Cambridge University Press, 1990).

41. Kenney, *Resource Management at the Watershed Level*, pp. 54–55.

42. See Robert H. Nelson, "The Religions of Forestry," *Journal of Forestry* (April 1998).

43. Peter List, "The Land Ethic in American Forestry: Pinchot and Leopold," in *The Idea of the Forest: German and American Perspectives on the Culture and Politics of Trees*, ed. Karla L. Schultz and Kenneth S. Calhoon (New York: Peter Lang, 1996), p. 38.

44. See Boris Zeide, "Another Look at Leopold's Land Ethic," *Journal of Forestry* (January 1998).

45. Thomas M. Bonnicksen, "Fire Gods and Federal Policy," *American Forests* (July/August 1989), p. 16.

46. Mark Sagoff, "Muddle or Muddle Through?: Takings Jurisprudence Meets the Endangered Species Act," *William and Mary Law Review* (March 1997), pp. 968, 976, 979.

47. Gifford Pinchot, *The Fight for Conservation* (Seattle: University of Washington Press, 1967), p. 95.

48. Sagoff, "Muddle or Muddle Through?" p. 980.

49. Cecil D. Andrus and Jeol Connelly, *Cecil Andrus: Politics Western Style* (Seattle: Sasquatch Books, 1998), p. 135.

50. Robert H. Nelson, "Is 'Libertarian Environmentalist' an Oxymoron?: The Crisis of Progressive Faith and the Environmental and Libertarian Search for a New Guiding Vision," in *The Next West: Public Lands, Community, and Economy in the American West*, ed. John A. Baden and Donald Snow (Washington, D.C.: Island Press, 1997).

51. Sagoff, "Muddle or Muddle Through?" p. 901.

52. Ibid., pp. 911, 991.

53. Douglas F. Ottati, "God and Ourselves: The Witness of H. Richard Niebuhr," *Christian Century* (April 2, 1997), p. 346.

54. Marston, "Timber Wars Evolve into a Divisive Attempt at Peace."

55. Natural Resources Law Center, School of Law, University of Colorado, *The Watershed Source Book: Watershed-Based Solutions to Natural Resource Problems* (Boulder: 1996), p. 1-2.

56. Ibid., p. 1-23.

57. Jo Clark, *Watershed Partnerships: A Strategic Guide for Local Conservation Efforts in the West*, Prepared for the Western Governors' Association (February 1997).

58. Natural Resources Law Center, *The Watershed Source Book*, p. 2-173.

59. Ibid., pp. 2-7, 2-8.

60. Ibid., p. 2-51.

61. Ibid., p. 2-53.

62. See Julia M. Wondolleck, *Public Lands Conflict and Resolution: Managing National Forest Disputes* (New York: Plenum Press, 1988).

63. Natural Resources Law Center, *The Watershed Source Book*, pp. 1-42, 1-43.

64. Ibid., p. 1-63.

65. See Dennis C. Le Master, *Decade of Change: The Remaking of Forest Service Statutory Authority during the 1970s* (Westport, Conn.: Greenwood Press, 1984).

66. Mark Baker and William Stewart, "Ecosystems under Four Different Public Institutions: A Comparative Analysis," in *Status of the Sierra Nevada, Volume II*, p. 1364.

67. *Water in the West: Challenge for the Next Century*, Report of the Western Water Policy Review Advisory Commission (June 1998), pp. xxx, 3-41, 6-5.

68. See Paul W. Gates, *History of Public Land Law Development* (Washington, D.C.: Government Printing Office, 1968).

69. Kenney, *Resource Management at the Watershed Level*, p. 3.

6

Lessons in Western Political Economy

The national forests constitute about 20 percent of the land area of the eleven westernmost of the lower forty-eight states. The Bureau of Land Management (BLM) in the Department of the Interior manages another 25 percent of the land in the West. Combined with national parks, wildlife refuges, and other federal systems, total federal land is almost 50 percent of the land area of these western states.[1] When the federal presence is so large, the fundamental governance arrangements for federal lands must be considered as a key element of a de facto "political constitution" of the western states themselves.

This chapter describes some realities of the political and economic circumstances of the western United States. It does this by way of a background for the next chapter in which the development of alternative basic political arrangements for the lands now in the national forest system will be briefly explored.

THE POLITICAL CONSTITUTION OF THE RURAL WEST

For the rural areas of the West, where federal lands dominate the landscape, it is not farfetched to say that these lands have a unique political system seen nowhere else in the United States. The limited amounts of private land are often surrounded by a sea of federal land. In the extreme case of Nevada, where 77 percent of the total area of the state is federal land, a number of counties are well over 90 percent federal.* In such areas, the citizens in practice look to Washington, not the state capital, for much of their governance.

There is a de facto legislature for much of the rural West and a de facto executive branch, both located in Washington. To be sure, the makeup of these branches is unlike anything found in standard political theory. For many practical purposes, the effective legislature for the public land areas of Wyoming consists of the one elected member of the U.S. House of Representatives, along with the two elected members of the U.S. Senate. In this informal governing system, the effective "governor" of the national forest lands of Wyoming is the chief of the Forest Service (in conjunction with political appointees in the Office of the Secretary of Agriculture)—and for the BLM lands of Wyoming, it is the secretary of the Interior. These executive branch officials, like the territorial governors of old prior to statehood, are not elected but are appointed by the president.

As a result of this informal governance structure for areas of the West with extensive public lands, the public officials actually elected at the state and local level in the rural West have less real responsibility than their counterparts elsewhere in the United States. The real authority over large acreages within their local jurisdictions lies in Washington. When politicians can make promises but have neither the power to deliver nor the obligation to raise the money to pay for them, it encourages a political climate of rhetorical excess. A number of western politicians have in fact become masters of a political style grounded in what Wallace Stegner once described as the characteristic attitude of the West: Tell the federal government to "get out, and give us more money."[2]

In some measure, the unique political and management structure for the rural areas with extensive public lands might be rationalized based on progressive-era theories of governance. The progressives in fact sought to minimize the role of democratic politics in the administrative tasks of government. As a technical undertaking, the management of the lands should be turned over to the experts. Mere "politicians" were likely to be driven by short-term considerations reflecting the pressures of "the special interests." Thus, in the progressive scheme of things, it did not pose such a problem that a small handful of elected politicians for practical purposes have often constituted the relevant political decision-making body for the extensive public land portions of the

---

*The percentages of federal land in the individual western states are as follows: Alaska—45.6%; Arizona—41.5%; California—44.6%; Colorado—36.0%; Idaho—60.6%; Montana—27.5%; Nevada—77.1%; New Mexico—33.9%; Oregon—51.8%; Utah—63.1%; Washington—24.1%; Wyoming—48.5%. See Bureau of Land Management, U.S. Department of the Interior, *Public Land Statistics, 1997* (Washington, D.C.,: March 1998), pp. 7–8.

West—that no full-fledged popular democracy has ever existed over these areas.

CONGRESSIONAL REALITIES

Yet progressive thinking is only a small part of the story today. Why have the residents of the rural West continued to accept the long-term limitations on normal democratic prerogatives? Partly it is that the western members of Congress in Washington have a strong incentive to perpetuate the arrangement. Some of them may speak from time to time of wanting a "Sagebrush Rebellion" but in reality it is very much in the self-interest of every western member of Congress—Democrat and Republican alike—to maintain the public land status quo.[3] Constituency service is a main reason that most incumbent members of Congress normally are reelected with little danger of losing. The control over small details of public land governance, exercised ultimately through Washington, provides the western members of Congress with widespread opportunities for constituency service.

The members of Congress from the West, unlike ordinary state and local legislators, can often operate without any real budget constraint. They do not have to raise the funds to pay for the local types of programs they deliver—programs that elsewhere in the United States are delivered by state and local governments and have to be paid for by state and local taxes. Instead, in the West the many federal programs of a local character are paid for by the rest of the nation. The advantages of this arrangement have been so great that it has served the interests of western states to maintain the national forest and public land status quo, even though it may deny them full democratic participation in the governance of the lands.

These advantages to the West are closely tied to the disproportionate political power that the West holds in the U.S. Senate. In total, excluding California, eleven other western public land states have 45 percent of the land area of the United States.* However, they have only 9 percent of the U.S. population. Yet because of the constitutional workings of the Senate, these eleven states with few people nonetheless have 22 percent of the votes in the Senate.

Wyoming has 3 percent of the population of New York State, but an equal number of senators. After Republicans took over the Senate in the 1994 elections, in the next Congress Westerners chaired various Senate

---

*These eleven states are Alaska, Arizona, Colorado, Idaho, Montana, Nevada, New Mexico, Oregon, Utah, Washington, and Wyoming.

committees: Appropriations (Mark O. Hatfield, Oregon), Budget (Pete V. Domenici, New Mexico), Judiciary (Orrin G. Hatch, Utah), Energy and Natural Resources (Frank H. Murkowski, Alaska), Rules and Administration (Theodore F. Stevens, Alaska), Veterans Affairs (Alan Simpson, Wyoming), and Indian Affairs (John McCain, Arizona). When Republicans control the Senate, the West assumes a role in that body approaching the political power associated in an earlier period of American history with dominance by southern Democrats.

To be sure, on the other side of the U.S. Capitol, except for California, the presence of the West in the House of Representatives is limited. Alaska, Wyoming, and Montana have only one representative; Nevada and Idaho have two. In the eleven public land states noted above, the West has a total of thirty-nine representatives, equal to 9 percent of the House. Yet on the whole the western numerical strength in the Senate is more than sufficient to compensate for the political weakness in the House. The Congress operates by the rule of "you scratch my back today, I scratch yours tomorrow." When the president wants to pass some legislation, western Senate votes are numerous and available for negotiation. This all translates into a large number of political chips held by western Senators at any given time.

From a national point of view, making political payoffs to the West can be socially efficient. Making political deals with the West may represent sound public policy making because otherwise nationally important legislation might not be able to muster enough support to be enacted. The constituents of western Senators who stand to benefit from all this merely happen to be at the right place at the right time; they can call in a financial windfall of federal money that dates as far back as the Constitutional Convention of 1787 and the Connecticut "great compromise" that set the terms for a bicameral legislature. Moreover, in sparsely populated western states, it does not take a great deal of federal money to have a significant impact on the state.

Of course, the West is not the only region of the country to benefit from federal largesse. Similar political incentives can be found operating in many other federal program areas besides the public lands. It is simply that these incentives and the associated political behavior of "rent seeking" are found in exaggerated form in the West, owing significantly to the presence of the national forests and other public lands.[4]

WHO OWNS THE NATIONAL FORESTS?

Land tenure historically has often operated under large myths. A distinguished student of the history of the land laws of England once wrote that over many centuries "the history of our land laws, it cannot be too often repeated, is a history of legal fictions, with which the Legislature vainly endeavoured to keep pace until their results . . . were perforce acquiesced in as a settled part of the law itself."[5] For example, in the United States one might say that a farmer "owns" his land. However, on metropolitan fringes of major cities where no-growth pressures are strong, some municipalities have zoned farmland to prevent most development. Since development rights constitute the greatest value of the land, it would actually be more correct to say that the municipality "owns" much of the farmland—although the farmer retains some residual specific rights, including the right to continue farming.

In the western United States, actual "ownership" of the national forests may be well removed from nominal ownership. The federal government nominally owns the lands but the main beneficiaries may lie elsewhere. One of the main prerogatives of ownership of a physical asset is the right to retain the financial dividends produced by that asset. Regarded in that perspective, it is a misnomer to say that the federal government actually "owns" the national forests. The financial data reveal a much different picture.

If the "citizens of the United States," or the "taxpayers," were the actual owners of the national forests, one might expect this ownership to result in significant amounts of money flowing into the U.S. Treasury. The national forests contain an immense wealth of natural resources. It is difficult to put a precise dollar value on these resources, but the Forest Service once estimated the total capital asset value of the national forest resources in 1990 to be equal to $182 billion (equal on average to about $950 per acre for the 192 million acres of the national forest system).[6] If the national forests were a normally productive resource asset, and could be expected to yield a positive rate of return of around 5 percent per year, the expected net income to the U.S. Treasury from the national forests would then be about $9 billion per year.

In reality, the Treasury instead annually experiences large net outflows from the national forests, creating large financial losses for federal taxpayers.[7] The picture can be quickly summarized. The main source of revenue—typically 80 percent or more in the 1980s—on the national forests has long been and still is timber harvesting (even despite recent sharp declines in timber harvests). The General Accounting Office (GAO) in November 1998 released an accounting analysis of timber financial flows from the national forest system, the great majority involving lands in the West.[8] According to the GAO (which based its calculations on Forest Service data), as shown in table 6-1, the incoming payments to the U.S. Treasury over the three-year period from 1995 to 1997 derived from national forest timber harvests equaled in total

Table 6-1.   Timber Sales Receipts and Distributions, Fiscal Years 1995 through 1997
(Dollars in Millions)

Fiscal year	Total	Amount distributed for specific Forest Service purposes	Amount distributed to states	Amount deposited in the General Fund of the U.S. Treasury
1995	$682.0	$392.9	$257.4	$31.7
1996	610.9	448.4	106.1	56.4
1997	558.0	399.1	89.7	69.2
Total	$1,850.9	$1,240.4	$453.2	$157.3

Source: General Accounting Office, Forest Service: Distribution of Timber Sale Receipts, Fiscal Years 1995 through 1997. GAO-RCED-99-24 (November 1998), p. 7.

only $157.3 million. As shown below in table 6-2, total outflows to pay for timber management from the U.S. Treasury over the same three-year period equaled $1.2 billion.

Gross federal outlays from appropriated funds formally charged to timber management on the national forests, in short, were about eight times the gross revenue returns from timber to the U.S. Treasury. As Randal O'Toole once wrote of the Forest Service, "In terms of assets, the agency would rank in the . . . nation's 500 largest corporations. . . . In terms of net income, the Forest Service would be classified as bankrupt."[9]

The GAO and Forest Service data, moreover, do not include as costs many items that might in fact properly be charged to the timber program. The data do not include, for example, the costs of forest fire protection, a main purpose of which historically has been to protect the timber supplies of the national forests. Over the three years from 1995 to 1997, a total of $1.8 billion was spent by the Forest Service for forest fire protection and

Table 6-2.   Timber Sale Costs, Fiscal Years 1995 through 1997 (Dollars in Millions)

Outlay	1995	1996	1997	Total
Sale preparation	$121.3	$153.5	$135.8	$410.6
General administration attributable to sales	100.1	125.5	125.3	350.9
Analysis/documentation	45.7	50.5	65.8	162.0
Harvest administration	51.3	53.3	50.4	155.0
Silvicultural exams	22.5	19.8	21.1	63.4
Transportation planning	16.0	13.3	15.1	44.4
Appeals/litigation	2.9	1.6	4.1	8.6
Appeals/litigation (indirect)	4.6	3.1	3.5	11.2
Total	$364.4	$420.6	$421.1	$1,206.1

Source: General Accounting Office, Forest Service: Distribution of Timber Sale Receipts, Fiscal Years 1995 through 1997. GAO-RCED-99-24 (November 1998), p. 8.

suppression.[10] If one-half of forest fire protection costs are assigned (perhaps somewhat arbitrarily) to timber management, the appropriations for the expense of running the timber program from 1995 to 1997 are greater than $2 billion, compared with $157.3 million in gross revenue from timber sales returned to the U.S. Treasury.

It is not that the timber program did not earn much more in timber sale revenue. From 1995 to 1997, total timber sale revenue equaled $1.85 billion. However, fully $1.7 billion of this revenue never reached the Treasury because it was placed in various off-budget special accounts. As shown in table 6-3, the largest single payment, $493 million, went to the Salvage Sale Fund. Another large amount, $464 million, went to the Knutson-Vandenberg Fund for reforestation. And significant additional amounts, including $129 million for purchaser credits for roads, went to still further special accounts (the road purchaser credit is money subtracted from timber sale payment obligations as credit for private road building by the winning timber sale bidder, and thus the money never actually comes into the government's hands).

All these off-budget accounts generate spending activities but in each case the money outflows equal the revenue inflows into the accounts (at least over the longer run). There is one party, however, that experiences large net revenue gains. Under existing law, 25 percent of gross timber sale receipts are turned over to the local county in which the timber sale occurs. During the period 1995 to 1997, these (mostly) western counties received direct money payments of $453 million from timber sales on the

Table 6-3. Distribution of Timber Sales Receipts, Fiscal Years 1992 through 1997 (1997 Dollars in Millions)

Fund or account	1992	1993	1994	1995	1996	1997
Knutson-Vandenberg Fund	$278.1	$301.8	$230.1	$183.4	$156.7	$123.8
Salvage Sale Fund	218.6	208.4	183.9	139.0	198.9	155.6
Purchaser road credits	100.2	71.0	73.2	50.1	42.2	36.9
Associated charges	63.9	47.8	37.2	31.9	33.7	46.7
Interest and penalties assessed	2.6	2.1	0.9	0.9	1.7	0.9
National Forest Fund	568.9	456.6	451.1	307.3	190.8	190.7
Total	$1,232.3	$1,087.7	$976.4	$712.6	$624.0	554.6

Source: General Accounting Office, *Forest Service—Distribution of Timber Sales Receipts, Fiscal Years 1995 through 1997.* GAO-RCED-99-24 (November 1998), p. 19.

national forests—almost three times the total payments to the U.S. Treasury. Since the counties did not incur much in the way of expenses for these sales, the $453 million was mostly net revenue for them, in contrast to the billion-dollar losses incurred by the U.S. Treasury.

So one might again ask, based on net revenue or earnings flows, who actually owns the national forests? It would seem that the counties in which the forests are located might be said to own the largest number of "shares" in the national forests. It is the counties that collect the largest financial "dividends" of any group.

EMPLOYEE OWNERSHIP

To be sure, this would be only a partial answer because counties received only $453 million out of the $1.7 billion in timber sale revenues that escaped the Treasury. As noted, more than $1 billion went to various special accounts.[11] Who benefits from these accounts? Nominally, one might say that they support necessary mitigation actions—such as reforestation costs paid for from the Knutson-Vandenberg Fund—for the negative effects of timber harvesting. However, there is considerable flexibility in spending the Knutson-Vandenberg funds, and much of the money goes to cover operating costs of Forest Service administration. Moreover, even when the money is spent on the ground, it is spent off budget by the Forest Service in ways that the agency can control. Knutson-Vandenberg and other funds greatly increase the discretionary funding available to the Forest Service to be utilized for various special purposes, bypassing the normal appropriations process altogether.[12]

If Forest Service timber sales actually returned any real profits to the Treasury, such an arrangement of financial autonomy might be desirable—a way of taking the Forest Service outside the normal political log rolling and rent seeking and giving the agency the management flexibility to operate efficiently and effectively. However, given the large losses on timber sales, a more realistic view is to consider that Knutson-Vandenberg and other special account moneys are more like "play money" for the employees of the Forest Service. These funds allow the employees to have high-paying jobs in attractive rural locations—jobs in fact much coveted by many people. The special funding accounts not only pay for the salaries of many of these employees but also give them considerable ability to spend money on their own pet projects.

Hence, another de facto "shareholder" in the national forests, one might say, in addition to the local western counties, consists of the employees of the Forest Service itself. The Forest Service might be regarded as a small exercise of socialism within the larger free-market economy of the United States. In the socialist countries of Eastern Europe and the former Soviet Union, when it came time to break up money-losing state enterprises, an allocation of shares had to be made in the newly privatized firms. Politically, the feasibility of privatization depended in part on achieving a reasonable match between new shareholders and past beneficiaries. Typically, a major portion of the shares in the newly privatized firms went to the managers and employees. It was a reflection of the reality that in the real world of socialist economic practice, in contrast to the utopian aspirations of socialist theory over the course of the twentieth century, the real beneficiaries of socialism tended to be the managers of socialist enterprises, along with some of the favored workers. Like the U.S. Forest Service, they were among the actual "owners" of the money-losing state enterprises in Eastern Europe and the former Soviet Union.

To be sure, just as communism could die suddenly in the revolutionary year of 1989, the traditional political economy of the national forest system is not immune to change. The traditional "ownership" arrangements of state enterprises have been based on informal understandings and the realities of political power at any given moment. They often require the support of an ideology (or secular religion) to justify them. As we saw in 1989 in Eastern Europe and the former Soviet Union, all this can collapse with remarkable speed. In the cases of both the former Soviet Union and the Forest Service, however large the differences in other respects, one can say that a regime based (formally, at least) on values of material progress and scientific management faced a crisis of social legitimacy. In both cases, the process of working through the full consequences of this loss of legitimacy has only begun—and many large mistakes are still being made.

AN AMERICAN "REVOLUTION OF 1989"

The Forest Service—like many Russian state enterprises—has thus far managed to escape the formal privatization or devolution that was the fate of many other state enterprises in other countries in the 1990s. However, "ecosystem management"—whatever its many failings of both concept and practice—is working a slow revolution in the circumstances of the Forest Service. By shifting the focus of management attention away from the actual uses of the forests (and the revenues that these uses predictably produce), and instead focusing on the physical condition of the forest, the traditional economic returns to the West from the national forests are falling rapidly. In all the confusion, much as the economy of the former Soviet Union is today not a great deal more than half the size it was in

1989, the numbers show that the national forests in the United States in 1999 are producing around half or less their economic output of 1989. The annual financial report of the Forest Service for fiscal year 1997 (issued in July 1998) documented the dramatic developments of the past decade.[13] Timber harvests on the national forests had long fluctuated from year to year but overall had stayed fairly steady for several decades prior to 1989. In 1989, however, they began to fall rapidly, declining from 12 billion board feet in 1989 to 3.3 billion board feet in 1997. Moreover, the quality of the timber in 1997 was much inferior—40 percent of the timber harvested in 1997 consisted or "dead and dying trees, and trees of less than sawtimber size," compared with only 20 percent in 1989. These revolutionary developments—the mounting evidence of some kind of "quiet revolution" that seemingly occurred in 1989 on the national forests—has had dramatic consequences as also recorded in a number of other key economic measures of timber and forest management activity on the national forests.

- Total timber revenues from the national forests fell from $1.5 billion in 1989 to $885 million in 1994, and then to $577 million in 1997.
- For the first time ever (by its own accounting methods), the Forest Service lost money ($15 million) on its "forest management program" in 1996. In 1997, losses on the forest management program rose to $89 million.
- By the Forest Service's own calculations, jobs associated with national forest timber harvest activities fell from around 100,000 jobs in 1991 to around 50,000 jobs in 1997, an employment decline of 50 percent in only six years.
- The generation of income to individuals and companies associated with national forest timber harvest activities fell from an estimated $5.5 billion in income in 1991 to about $2 billion in 1997, another drop of startling speed.
- By Forest Service calculations, a formal economic measure of social benefit, the "net present value" of timber program activities, fell from around $950 million in 1991 to around $250 million in 1997.*

Perhaps the most remarkable event is the trend in a comprehensive estimate that the Forest Service calls its calculation of "All Resources Net Present Value (NPV)" associated with its forest management program.

---

*The "net present value" differs from "net income" —which was negative for 1997—in that the latter addresses only financial flows in the current year while the former includes estimates of discounted economic values over all future years as a result of this year's timber program activities.

When pressed to justify the large losses associated with its timber program (much larger when calculated by other accounting methods than those employed by the Forest Service itself), the Forest Service has typically argued that it is misleading to focus on the timber program as an isolated program. Roads, for example, the Forest Service argues, serve many purposes, in addition to providing access to timber sale areas. Roads open the forest up, for example, to hunters and fishermen who can gain easy entry to favored locations.

In order to encompass the full range of side benefits associated with road building and other aspects of its forest management activities, the Forest Service thus calculates an estimate of "All Resources NPV." As calculated by the Forest Service, this All Resources NPV does transform the 1997 loss of $89 million for the timber program alone into a large gain for all resources combined. However, equally telling is the trend in this estimate of overall net benefits from all the forest uses associated directly or indirectly with timber program activities. By the Forest Service's own calculations, the All Resources NPV has fallen from more than $1 billion in 1991 to $345 million in 1997.

Because the All Resources NPV includes estimates for the values associated with recreation, grazing, and other traditional outputs of the national forest system, in addition to timber, the drop in this number is the one single best indicator of the revolutionary impact of ecosystem management on the national forest system. The fall in this economic measure of direct outputs from timber management (including timber "stewardship" and much of the forest management activities of any kind) has been 65 percent from 1991 to 1997. If the goal of ecosystem management was to shift the orientation of the national forest system from serving the demands of users to achieving a given physical condition of the ecosystem for its own sake, the Forest Service has apparently been succeeding very well in the 1990s.

Ross Gorte of the Congressional Research Service has estimated the potential impact of declining timber harvests on another affected party, the end users of wood products in the United States. Federal timber historically has supplied about 20 percent of U.S. softwood timber supplies, but recent harvest declines have reduced this share to 6 percent. Based on historical experience, lumber demand is fairly inelastic with respect to changes in price (especially in the short run), implying that small changes in supply can have significant price impacts. Drawing on previous economic research, Gorte estimates that lumber prices could rise by about four times the percentage reduction in timber supplies. This suggests that the federal harvest reductions of the past decade—if there had been no other compensating increases in harvests from other sources—could have caused an increase in lumber prices of more than 50 percent. Then, going

further to eliminate the remaining federal timber harvests could potentially cause a further 25 percent increase in lumber prices.[14] To be sure,
significant increases in timber harvests from U.S. private forests and increased imports from Canada, Latin America, and other countries (all this
involving displaced environmental impacts from federal lands in the
United States) have increased nonfederal supplies considerably and diminished the likelihood of any such price increases of these magnitudes
occurring. Moreover, the price increases are likely to be the largest in the
short run. In the long run, both producers and consumers will find ways
to adjust to any sharp rise in timber prices and thus to dampen the effects
(as the rapidly rising and then rapidly falling oil and gas price experience
of the fifteen years following the OPEC price shocks of the 1970s dramat-
ically illustrated).

AN AGENCY WITHOUT A CONSTITUENCY

In a novel political and social experiment, the Forest Service is seemingly
putting to the test a concept of spurning many of the very groups that traditionally provided it with political support in the Congress and other political arenas. One of its most important past supporters, the part of the
timber industry that historically depended on national forest sales, is rapidly disappearing. (Large industrial forestry firms such as Weyerhaeuser
generally have little stake in national forest timber harvests because they
own their own forests, are well provided for the future with standing timber, and in fact can often benefit from cutbacks in federal timber supplies
because of the resulting overall increases in timber prices.) The levels of
livestock grazing and mining are diminishing on the national forests, and
many environmentalists would like to eliminate these activities altogether
as well.

Another traditional beneficiary group from national forest management
is the local counties of the West. With timber sale revenues on the national
forests declining rapidly, their 25 percent share of gross revenues has
been falling correspondingly. The Clinton administration has understood
that this loss of county revenue represents, perhaps more than disaffected
timber companies dependent on federal supplies (and their workers), a
serious political threat. For one thing, unlike the timber industry, the
counties cannot be counted on to disappear as revenues from the national
forests decline. Indeed, complaints of local county officials are likely to
continue and perhaps grow.

In 1999 the Clinton administration therefore proposed to "decouple"
Forest Service payments to counties from timber sale revenues. If this
proposal is enacted (an uncertain prospect as of this writing), the counties would be guaranteed significant levels of funding from the national

forest system that would be independent of timber sale revenue and would instead be paid by direct Treasury appropriations. It would be yet another entitlement program, in this case serving western local governments.

Recreationists are less impacted by the trends of the 1990s, but the management philosophy of ecosystem management suggests that future improvements in recreational use will be incidental to activities pursued for other reasons. More intensive forms of recreation such as ski resorts are likely to face the same future as timber harvesting. Even more benign recreational uses such as rock climbing in wilderness areas are at risk; the Forest Service has recently proposed that the use of permanent anchors by climbers could be banned in the future as inconsistent with the "natural" objectives sought.

Recreation has provided little revenue to the national forest system, despite the large increases in visitor days over the past few decades. The Forest Service estimates the total market value of recreational use of the national forests at more than $4 billion per year. However, total fees collected from 830 million recreational visitors to the national forests in 1995 were only $46 million, about 1 percent of the market value.[15] As bleak as the timber program economics has been, even money-losing timber sales have at least covered a significant portion if less than 100 percent of program costs. The recreation fees have been about 30 percent of recreation costs on the national forests (by Forest Service calculations, which are bound to be conservative in assigning costs).

Yet, however much the Forest Service may lose traditional constituency support, it will always have one very important political asset. As long as the Forest Service continues to serve as a conduit for approximately $2 to $3 billion per year in federal funds into western states, it may not make a great deal of difference what the Forest Service actually does with the money, or the efficiency with which that money is spent. Ideally, the money should be usefully spent and it should generate positive benefits, but for western politicians the most important consideration of all is that it should be spent somehow and somewhere in the West. If the $2 to $3 billion were dropped in dollar bills from airplanes, it might not be optimal, but many of the economic benefits to the West would be almost as great as they are at present.

The economic trends in terms of real outputs from the national forests may all have been sharply downward in the 1990s but there is one trend that did not decline as rapidly. The funding for the national forest system in 1990 was $3.1 billion and has remained in this vicinity since then. The Republican senators from the West experienced deep frustration in that the Clinton administration defied their best efforts to control the policy priorities of the Forest Service. It was a new era in this regard. However, while the western Senators may have bluffed and blustered, the Clinton administration knew that in the end they were not likely to shoot themselves in the foot. There is nothing to be gained for the West by cutting the budget for the national forest system. Even under the workings of ecosystem management, high paying salaries to Forest Service land-use planners, biologists, and other ecosystem managers—while perhaps not typical Republican voters—are the ones who do still help to hold up rural economies (and the Republican voters who sell goods and services to the biologists) throughout the West.

THE EXAMPLE OF LIVESTOCK GRAZING

Livestock grazing is another good illustration of the political and economic realities today in the American West. It is also an area where the costs of grazing administration have seemingly become for some people the end in themselves. Grazing of livestock on the national forests and other public lands has never generated much money for the Treasury. In 1998, less than $15 million was collected in grazing fees on the national forests (and a similar amount from grazing on lands managed by the BLM).

Nevertheless, the grazing use of the national forests plays an important role in the operation of many individual western ranches. Livestock grazing has been important politically since the beginning of the Forest Service in 1905. Many of the fiercest political controversies surrounding the national forests—especially before World War II and the rise of timber harvesting as a major forest activity—involved the grazing of cattle and sheep.[16]

Under a system that dates back to the beginning of the twentieth century, private ranchers are assigned particular portions of the national forests to graze their livestock ("allotments" that fall within well-defined boundary lines on the ground). Some allotments are grazed in common but most are assigned to a single rancher. If a rancher sells his private lands and other "base property," by long-standing custom the grazing access to "his" (or "her") national forest allotment is routinely transferred to the new ranch owner. The grazing use of the national forest land is frequently integral to the operation of the private ranch property.

The same grazing system exists on the public lands managed by the BLM. The same rancher in some cases will hold both Forest Service and BLM grazing permits. When the private lands of the rancher are sold, the sale value of the private ranch property will reflect the accompanying assurance of access to complementary public land grazing. If this public land grazing were not available, many private ranch properties would lose hundreds of thousands, or in some cases millions, of dollars in sale value, perhaps half of the value for many ranches.

The Forest Service and the BLM accommodate similar amounts of livestock grazing on their lands, about 8.1 million "animal unit months" (AUMs) per year on the national forests and 9.0 million AUMs on BLM lands. There are more data available on some of the economics of BLM grazing and other land management.[17] However, the basic picture examined below for BLM lands is representative of the economics of national forest grazing as well.

The federal fee for grazing use of public land is the same on both national forest and BLM lands, equal in 1998 to $1.35 per AUM. By the estimates of the most recent comprehensive appraisal, the average market value of public land grazing is about $6.50 per AUM. Holders of public land grazing permits often temporarily sublease their grazing "rights" to other ranchers for $5 to $10 per AUM. Given that the BLM has about 9 million AUMs per year of livestock grazing, total government revenue from BLM lands is about $13 million per year, and the private market value of grazing on BLM lands is about $60 million per year.

The total resource management budget for the BLM lands and resources approaches $700 million per year. The public land agencies keep track of some costs by output activities such as livestock grazing, but much of their budgets are included within planning, preparing environmental impact statements, personnel functions, and many other kinds of general overhead functions. Nevertheless, by making some assumptions, it is possible to estimate the full costs of BLM grazing—about $200 million per year. This estimate may in fact be conservative because $200 million is less than a third of the total BLM resource management costs, and livestock grazing in one way or another drives much of the administrative duties of the BLM.

The key facts thus are as follows. The BLM collects $13 million in revenues but spends perhaps $200 million to administer the livestock grazing program. However, even if the BLM collected the market value of grazing, it would collect only $60 million. Ranchers receive a subsidy, but it is much less than the full cost of BLM grazing administration. Most of the cost of administration would be unrecoverable under any economic system. Like the Forest Service spending for national forest management, it might be said that the purpose of the grazing program is to support a large number of desirable jobs that the BLM is able to provide for its employees in desirable rural locations of the West. In this respect, BLM spending also contributes significantly to the general economic welfare of the rural West.

If livestock grazing on public lands were regarded as a policy decision based on economics—if BLM operated like a private firm—the optimal strategy would be clear-cut: Declare the BLM grazing program (and Forest Service grazing, too) bankrupt and shut it down as soon as possible. Alternatively, one might concede that ranchers using national forest and

BLM lands for as much as a century or more have acquired a de facto "right" and should be compensated for any cancellation of grazing. It is not the ranchers who have insisted on all the planning and other procedural steps and turned livestock grazing on public lands into a grounds for political warfare, thus driving BLM administrative costs for the grazing program into the stratosphere.

Ranchers do sell AUMs on a permanent basis from one to another, so there is a capital value of an AUM that can be observed in a market. The average capital value for permanent acquisition of a public land AUM is about $50 today in the West.[18] The total capital value of BLM grazing thus is probably less than $500 million (for the 9 million AUMs on BLM land). Given BLM administrative costs for grazing of about $200 million per year, it would in concept be possible to do a complete "compensated buyout" of all BLM grazing with about two-and-one-half years' worth of grazing administrative expense. After that, federal taxpayers would realize a savings of the full $200 million in BLM administrative costs every year into the future.

As it has evolved, in short, there is nothing economic about the public land grazing program. It can be justified only as part of the cultural heritage of the West. The cowboy is part of the national mythology of America and ranching is a remaining symbol of the era of western settlement. Ironically, in this respect livestock grazing on the public lands works much like the goal of ecosystem management, seeking a land outcome for its own sake that is unrelated to the direct economic values obtained from the uses of the land. Maintaining rancher lifestyles perhaps falls into the same category as endangered species, driven by the same kinds of noneconomic policy goals. It may be that Americans simply regard ranchers as an important part of the western landscape like wolves and grizzly bears. Perhaps, therefore, they do not mind subsidizing rancher use of the public lands—a set of "virtual cowboys" to match the "virtual nature" that so many environmentalists are attracted to.

This view is far from universally shared, however. Historically, many environmentalists have long sought to curb or eliminate livestock grazing from the public lands, seeing grazing as an environmental and aesthetic offense. Edward Abbey once wrote "I'm in favor of putting the public lands livestock grazers out of business." Abbey had a litany of reasons but the most important was that "the cattle have done, and are doing, intolerable damage to our public lands—our national forests, state lands, BLM-administered lands, wildlife preserves, even some of our national parks and monuments. . . . [The cattle are] transforming soil and grass into dust and weeds."[19] Cattle impacts on riparian areas in the arid Southwest have been particularly damaging.

More recently, however, there has been at least a partial change of thinking, as some leading environmentalists have decided that cattle ranching is better than new second homes and subdivisions. It is a western version of the efforts more common in the East to preserve agricultural lands in the face of development pressures.

Environmentalists have also been rethinking their long-standing opposition to any recognition of the presence of rancher grazing on public lands as a salable "right." Given a choice between buying out ranchers with compensation and continuing to fight to remove livestock grazing by "kicking the ranchers off the land," environmentalists in the past have always opted, one might say, for the coercion strategy. To pay ranchers to stop committing a "moral offense" against the land, as most environmentalists have seen the matter, would be to commit a still graver injustice.

However, since 1995 a number of leading environmental strategists have been shifting their position, often arguing that a buy-out strategy is more practical. Environmentalists perhaps need to learn to pay more attention to the bottom line, to put up cash if necessary to rid the environment of harms that result from cattle ranching. Dave Foreman thus proposed in *Wild Earth* in 1995 to "buy out grazing permittees in Wilderness Areas, National Parks, Wildlife Refuges, and other reserves." This would be, Foreman now thought, "the most practical and fairest way to end grazing in wilderness."[20]

Buying out ranchers need not—should not, in my view—be done by the federal government.[21] Buying out livestock grazing would cost, based on current market value for AUMs, about $3 to $4 per acre on average, and less in some lower quality locations for public land grazing. This amount is easily within the reach of environmental organizations such as the Nature Conservancy. Local environmental groups could also organize to raise funds as needed. The ability to raise the funds privately to buy out public land grazing provides a healthy test of the environmental benefits actually present versus the grazing value to the rancher.

For several years, a group of prominent spokesmen for the ranching industry in the West met with leading environmentalists to discuss the possibility of a new land-tenure arrangement for use of the forage resource on public lands.[22] The discussions concerned the possibility of the government issuing a "lease" to the use of the public land forage, perhaps for a period such as thirty years. At present, grazing permits legally can only be held by livestock ranchers. However, according to the proposal on the table, the new leases could have been held by anyone—an elk hunting club, a land trust, the next-door neighbor who wants to control the view, as well as a cattle rancher. Any forage lessee could halt livestock grazing altogether, or might decide to alter livestock grazing to make it less environmentally damaging. The lessee could sublease to a rancher under new terms that might be set by an environmental organization holding the forage lease to public land.

In order to cut down on the large administrative costs of public land grazing, which also greatly inhibit the flexibility for any form of "adaptive management" in forage use on the public lands, another arrangement under discussion would have turned to much greater use of performance standards. As long as the forage lessee could meet the performance standards for rangeland trend and condition, he or she would have had much wider discretion to manage for whatever the intended forage use. The idea was that the BLM and Forest Service should seek to avoid the micromanagement of individual grazing allotments that has characterized their approach of the past few decades.

In the end, the ranchers and environmentalists participating in the negotiations were unable to agree on the full details of such a system and the negotiations broke down in 1999. There had been, however, considerable prior agreement in principle on several broad directions of future grazing policy for public lands that would rely more heavily on market forces.* The very fact of the willingness of ranchers and environmentalists to sit down together at meetings occurring over several years to discuss radical changes in the current system reflected a common deep dissatisfaction with the results of this system.

TOWARD A NEW LAND TENURE

The existing institutional arrangements for the national forests, BLM lands, and other public lands are largely a product of history. Given an opportunity to start all over again, the boundaries and organizational arrangements for these lands would surely be much different. The extent of federal authority for the public lands is inconsistent with long-standing

---

*Several of the key principles actively considered by the group included: (1) current grazing permits might be replaced by new "public land leases" for diverse allowed uses, including grazing as only one among these uses; (2) the term of the new public land leases might be increased significantly, perhaps to thirty years; (3) public land leases should be available to any party, whether in the livestock business or not; (4) measurable and practical standards that address such rangeland factors as soil stability, water quality, riparian conditions, and fish, wildlife, and plant habitat should be established and applied as minimum requirements on the use of the rangeland resource by the public land lessee, whatever use was being made of the land; (5) holders of public land leases should enjoy wide flexibility in their management and use of rangelands within the bounds set by resource objectives that would address the full spectrum of public values; and (6) an effective and predictable enforcement system should be firmly in place to ensure that public land leases comply with the applicable standards and environmental sidebars.

American federalism principles—even in the much weakened form in which American federalism survived into the twentieth century. In this new era in the twenty-first century, one might imagine applying a few simple federalism tests.[23]

- Activities on the federal lands that involve mostly state and local concerns should be managed at state and local levels.
- Activities that are mainly commercial, like harvesting of timber on a sustained rotation basis, should be transferred to the private sector.
- Those lands that involve major national interests, like most national parks or some wilderness areas, should remain in federal management.

If these criteria were applied to the existing federal lands, perhaps 80 percent would be shifted to state and local management or to private ownership.

Politically, however, there are many obstacles to the implementation of any such principles. A well-defined set of beneficiaries exists—many of whom have a large stake in the current institutional arrangements of the public lands. The benefits to these groups have been won and sustained by hard political struggle over many years, if not decades. Ranchers, for example, have maintained low grazing fees and access to grazing use of public lands in the face of strenuous opposition of many environmental groups. Current public land ranchers, despite some occasional rhetorical suggestions to the contrary, oppose either any transfer of lands to states and local governments or to the private sector. They fear that they might lose their low grazing fees (states typically charge two and three times the federal fee at present). Even more important, the arrangements for automatic reissuance and easy transfer of federal grazing permits are based on long-standing informal understandings with federal administrators. If states took over current federal grazing lands, there would be no firm guarantees (unless explicitly provided in a transfer agreement) that new state administrators would respect the old federal practices.

Western politicians often denounce the overbearing regulations and other devices by which the federal government exercises control over much that happens in the West. Their political rhetoric sometimes suggests that they would like the federal government to get out of the picture. However, in the past whenever concrete proposals have been made to this effect, the opinion leaders of the West have quickly backed away. They have been fearful that there is too much money at stake, and too many uncertainties associated with major institutional changes in federal land management practices, to justify giving up the federal landlord.

In 1995, following the Republican takeover of the Congress in the fall elections of 1994, Representative James Hanson of Utah introduced legislation to give western states the option to take possession of BLM lands. There was nothing mandatory; it would have been up to each state. Even this moderate proposal received little support among fellow Westerners. Republican members of Congress were reminded by their constituents of the many financial and other risks to the region involved.

Table 6-4 shows estimates of the fiscal impacts that western states would have realized in 1992 from a transfer of BLM lands to their ownership.[24] These estimates were based on several simplifying assumptions—including that the states would earn the same revenues and incur the same administrative costs as the federal government.[25] In that case, most western states would have lost money in 1992 by agreeing to take ownership of BLM lands, typically on the order of $20 to $30 million per year. The largest loser would have been Alaska, reflecting the vast acreage of BLM land in that state and the few revenues earned there from the public lands. California would have suffered a negative fiscal impact of $25 million and Idaho of $40 million.

The two big exceptions would have been New Mexico and Wyoming, reflecting the presence of large oil, gas, and coal reserves in these states

Table 6-4.   Estimated 1992 Net Fiscal Impact on Western States if All BLM Surface Estate and the Federal Mineral Estate Had Been Transferred to the States (Millions of Dollars)

State	Additional revenues	Additional costs	Net fiscal impact
Alaska	$4.8	$108.3	–$103.5
Arizona	1.8	33.5	–31.7
California	30.4	55.5	–25.1
Colorado	43.3	57.2	–13.9
Idaho	5.5	45.8	–40.3
Montana	24.7	54.0	–29.3
Nevada	18.6	54.6	–36.0
New Mexico	124.6	49.5	+75.1
Oregon	110.2	120.1	–9.9
Utah	29.7	51.6	–21.9
Washington	1.2	2.0	–0.8
Wyoming	180.2	55.9	+124.3
Total	$575.0	$688.0	$–113.0

Source: Robert H. Nelson and Mary M. Chapman, *Voices from the Heartland: New Tools for Decentralizing Management of the West's Public Lands,* Points West—Special Report (Denver, Colo.: Center for the New West, December 1995), p. 11.

owned by the federal government. In 1992 federal revenues from energy mineral leasing totaled about $240 million in New Mexico and $350 million in Wyoming. Half of these revenues at present are already transferred to the state where the lease is located. Thus, the gain to a state from taking full ownership of the mineral rights would equal only the other half of current federal energy revenues. Yet, given the large energy leasing revenues currently received by the federal government in New Mexico and Wyoming, this gain is much more than sufficient to compensate for the increased administrative costs to the states that would be associated with new state management responsibilities for former BLM lands.

Much as ranchers and environmentalists have been exploring radically new options, a few western leaders have begun to reconsider the traditional western attitude toward the federal government of "get out and give us more money." It reflects, in part, a recognition that the current state of land management gridlock is harmful to state interests; the federal government can no longer respond effectively to the expressed needs of the West. Second, during the period of large federal budget deficits in the 1980s and 1990s, there was increasing resistance at the federal level to continuing the large net flow of dollars to the West. Demands grew, for example, for wider imposition of charges for the use of public lands. This has been reflected in the recent doubling since 1996 of total federal revenues collected from national park entrance and other recreation fees. At the same time, as the fastest growing part of the United States, the West boomed economically in the 1990s, providing the financial resources to assume new land management responsibilities. Finally, under the Clinton administration federal administrators have often acted in ways that alienated western political leadership, undermining the traditional close working relationships between members of Congress and the public land agencies.

Some more thoughtful Westerners have also shown a new principled concern that the continued federal dominance of the rural West keeps this region of the country in a state of perpetual political adolescence. If the West truly wants to resolve some of its problems on its own, it may have to show a greater willingness to assume the responsibility for finding and implementing the solutions itself. Daniel Kemmis served as the Democratic majority leader of the Montana Senate and then mayor of Missoula. Kemmis has been a prominent advocate of greater western autonomy in its land and resource management, necessarily requiring a curtailment of the historic federal role. As he wrote in 1990, the West:

> cannot transcend its colonial heritage until it gains a much more substantial measure of indigenous control over its own land and resources. But it can neither gain nor exercise that control until the left and the right gain enough trust in each other, and establish a productive enough working relationship, to en-

able them to agree, at least roughly, on what they would seek to accomplish
if they had such control. . . . Until that happens, . . . the end of those federally
controlled debates is always a less satisfying way of inhabiting the place than
any of the participants would have chosen. As more and more people become dissatisfied with this less-than-zero-sum solution of the procedural re-
public, it is time to look the alternative in the face.[26]

CONCLUSION

There are strong grounds for making basic changes in the institutional
arrangements for the management of the public lands—for writing a
new political constitution for much of the rural West. However, the resistance to change is also powerful. Most government programs develop a set of beneficiaries who gradually come to hold firm expectations that the benefits will continue. In the extreme cases, they regard
the continuing receipt of past benefits as a virtual "right."[27]

Any new political constitution for the rural West will itself have to be a
political act, reflecting compromises of various sorts. In theory, given the
large waste associated with the current federal land system, it would be
possible to make every involved party a winner. In practice, it may never
be feasible to ensure that everyone will be better off but there can still be
many winners. The transition to a new set of institutional arrangements
will have to be crafted to avoid imposing large costs on any group. Each
state will have to perceive that the citizens of that state on balance are better off than they are at present.

Yet all this is in concept doable. Devolution of much of the national forest and other federal lands can be a win-win change all around. Thus far,
it has been the political imagination and leadership in the West that have
been lacking. The next chapter offers the outline of a practical devolution
plan for the West.

NOTES

1. Bureau of Land Management, U.S. Department of the Interior, *Public Land
Statistics, 1997* (March 1998), pp. 7–8.

2. Wallace Stegner, *The American West as Living Space* (Ann Arbor: University
of Michigan Press, 1987), p. 15.

3. See Robert H. Nelson, "Why the Sagebrush Revolt Burned Out," *Regulation*
(May/June 1984).

4. See John Francis and Richard Ganzel, eds., *Western Public Lands* (Totowa,
N.J.: Rowman and Allenheld, 1984).

5. Frederick Pollock, *The Land Laws* (London: Macmillan, 1883), p. 62.

6. Forest Service, U.S. Department of Agriculture, *The Forest Service Program for Forest and Rangeland Resources: A Long-Term Strategic Plan,* Recommended 1990 RPA Program (Washington, D.C.: U.S. Forest Service, May 1990), p. 6-53.

7. See Holly Lippke Fretwell, *Public Lands: The Price We Pay* (Bozeman, Mont.: Political Economy Research Center, August 1998).

8. General Accounting Office, *Forest Service—Distribution of Timber Sales Receipts, Fiscal Years 1995 through 1997,* GAO/RCED-99-24 (November 1998).

9. Randal O'Toole, *Reforming the Forest Service* (Washington, D.C.: Island Press, 1988), p. 14.

10. General Accounting Office, *Federal Lands: Wildfire Suppression and Suppression Expenditures for Fiscal Years 1993 through 1997,* GAO/T-RCED-98-247 (August 4, 1998), p. 8.

11. See Ross W. Gorte and M. Lynne Corn, *The Forest Service Budget: Trust Funds and Special Accounts,* Congressional Research Service Report No. 97-14 ENR (January 3, 1997).

12. See Forest Service Employees for Environmental Ethics, *Who Says Money Doesn't Grow on Trees—The Knutson-Vandenberg Act: How the U.S. Forest Service Misuses a Little Known Law to Siphon Millions of Public Dollars from the Forest to the Bureaucracy,* (Eugene, Ore.).

13. U.S. Forest Service, Department of Agriculture, *National Summary: Forest Management Program Annual Report, Fiscal Year 1997* (Washington, D.C.: U.S. Forest Service, July 1998).

14. Ross W. Gorte, *Federal Timber Harvests: Implications for U.S. Timber Supply,* Congressional Research Service Report No. 98-233 ENR (March 10, 1998), pp. 4–6.

15. Forest Service, U.S. Department of Agriculture, *Report of the Forest Service, Fiscal Year 1995* (Washington, D.C.: U.S. Forest Service, June 1996), pp. 9–11.

16. E. Louise Peffer, *The Closing of the Public Domain: Disposal and Reservation Policies, 1900–1950* (Stanford: Stanford University Press, 1951).

17. See *Inside the Bureau of Land Management: Timber, Minerals, Recreation, and Grazing,* special issue of *Different Drummer,* edited by Randal O'Toole and published by the Thoreau Institute (1998).

18. See L. Allen Torell et al., "The Market Value of Public Land Forage Implied from Grazing Permits," in *Current Issues in Rangeland Economics—1994,* ed. Neil R. Rimbey and Diane E. Isaak, Papers of the Western Research Coordinating Committee—Range Economics (Moscow, Idaho: Idaho Agricultural Experiment Station, University of Idaho, October 1994), p. 80.

19. Edward Abbey, "Even the Bad Guys Wear White Hats: Cowboys, Ranchers and the Ruin of the American West," *Harper's* (January 1986), pp. 52–53.

20. Dave Foreman, "Around the Campfire," *Wild Earth* (Fall 1995), pp. 2–3. See also Andy Kerr, "The Voluntary Retirement Option for Federal Public Land Grazing Permittees," *Rangelands* (October 1998).

21. See Robert H. Nelson, "How to Reform Grazing Policy: Creating Forage Rights on Federal Rangelands," *Fordham Environmental Law Journal* vol. VIII, no. 3 (1997).

22. I was a regular participant in these discussions, which began in February 1996 in Reno, Nevada, and continued into the summer of 1999 before finally breaking down. Other participants included Jason Campbell, Cathy Carlson, Frank Gregg, Karl Hess, Fran Hunt, Truman Julian, Brad Little, Jeff Menges, Bill Myers, Fred Obermiller, Rose Strickland, Johanna Wald, and Brent Atkins (deceased).

23. Similar proposals for public land devolution are offered in Alexander F. Annett, *The Federal Government's Poor Management of America's Land Resources*, Heritage Foundation Backgrounder No. 1282 (Washington, D.C.: Heritage Foundation, May 17, 1999).

24. See Robert H. Nelson, "Transferring Federal Lands in the West to the States: How Would It Work?" *Chronicle* (Center for the New West: Denver, Colo., Winter 1994–1995). These estimates were updated from Robert H. Nelson and Gabriel Joseph, "An Analysis of Revenues and Costs of Public Land Management by the Interior Department in 13 Western States—Update to 1981," Office of Policy Analysis, U.S. Department of the Interior, September 1982.

25. Similar estimates are developed in Ross W. Gorte, "BLM Revenues and Expenditures," Memorandum to Allen Freemyer, House Committee on Resources, July 28, 1995. Gorte, who is a specialist in natural resources policy at the Congressional Research Service, estimated that western states cumulatively would experience a negative fiscal impact of $111 million per year from taking over BLM lands. New Mexico and Wyoming, however, would have large positive fiscal impacts due to revenues from federal energy leasing.

26. Daniel Kemmis, *Community and the Politics of Place* (Norman: University of Oklahoma Press, 1990), pp. 127–28.

27. See Robert H. Nelson, "Private Rights to Government Actions: How Modern Property Rights Evolve," *University of Illinois Law Review* vol. 1986, no. 2 (1986).

7

A New Political Constitution for the Rural West

In the United States, the political legitimacy of government rests ultimately on its democratic foundations. According to the traditional American principles of federalism, the relevant democratic electorate should be those people who would gain the benefits and bear the costs of a government action.

However, for the rural areas of the West where federal lands dominate the landscape, the workings of the democratic process are unlike anywhere else in the United States. The West has continued to live with its unusual governing system because of the large practical advantages to the West from continuing federal land ownership. Most of all, the federal government makes large expenditures in western states that have been sufficient to compensate the West for other liabilities of the federal presence.[1] Yet another key factor has been that many private individuals and groups in the West know the federal system and how to make it work for them and are skeptical about any major changes. As many Westerners think, "the devil you know is better than the devil you don't."

Today, however, as the management of federal lands appears increasingly ineffective, and as the West has greater economic resources, the time may have come to revisit the issue of an appropriate set of political institutions for the rural West where federal lands often dominate the landscape. The Western Water Policy Review Advisory Commission, finding that water and land management issues—both often present on the national forests—were increasingly intertwined, called for a broad scale "reevaluation of the role of the federal government" in the West. It should reflect the fact of "the widespread recognition that [the federal] historical mission of western settlement has been fulfilled."[2]

167

As the preceding chapters have shown with respect to the Forest Service, the Commission reported that the "federal water agencies are [also] caught in a fundamental paradigm shift which affects their ability to fulfill their traditional missions and to adapt to new missions." Indeed, much as the managerial capabilities of the Forest Service have been undermined in recent years, "the performance of federal agencies charged with water management is the subject of intense and justifiable concern at the present time." It was important to understand the historical reality that "most of the federal agencies with significant water and land management responsibilities in the West emerged in an age in which agencies (in all subject matters) were looked to as impartial, scientific decisionmakers, a concept underlying much of the progressive conservation era" early in the twentieth century. However, as the commission now found, "over time, this idea has lost popular support," undermining the political legitimacy of the federal resource management agencies and their ability to act.[3] The current situation was one of

> a growing number of parties involved in decisionmaking [that] have the legal and political resources to influence policymaking efforts, resulting in an increasingly large number of interests with the power to veto, or at least impede, proposed actions. The simultaneous growth in the number of parties with veto power, considered along with the growing difficulty of crafting positive-sum solutions and the largely unmet need to address the interrelationships among resource issues, means that the act of making essential decisions—the primary purpose of all mechanisms for governance—is more difficult than ever. The result is gridlock.[4]

In light of the close interconnections among land, water, and other resource management issues, the task today facing the West, as the commission reported, is one of "changing the way resource management decisions are made." This will require rethinking traditional basic assumptions with respect to "adequacy of representation, the locus of decisionmaking authority, the processes of decisionmaking." In the past, reflecting the underlying assumptions of scientific management, policy reformers in the natural resource field had typically perceived their job as an exercise in administrative reorganization and in making other administrative improvements, drawing heavily on the methods and knowledge of the field of public administration. In light of the new focus on political legitimacy and the basic character of decision-making processes themselves, it was now apparent that the job of improving natural resource management involved making recommendations ultimately concerning "questions of governance." The core problem facing the West today in the management of its natural resources is one of "crafting efficient, equitable and universally acceptable mechanisms of governance."[5]

On the national forests, key political issues to be addressed in any such reworking of basic governance arrangements should include the following: If management of the national forests is a political act, what political body should have ultimate responsibility for overseeing management of these forests? Congress does not have the institutional capacity to review each land-use plan for each national forest. If Congress does not oversee zoning and planning on private lands elsewhere in the United States, why should Congress be the ultimate political body to oversee the full details of national forest decision making—at least in so far as decisions there do not involve endangered species, national parks, or other concerns involving a major national interest?

If final political authority in the rural West is to be shifted closer to the local level, how might this be done? The Quincy Library Group was a self-appointed body. There were people in the local area who complained that the members of the Quincy group did not adequately represent the community. National environmental groups complained that they had had no representation at all. While the Quincy group may have had no alternative under its informal working arrangements, other such groups in the future may have to operate within more structured procedures under which the grounds for establishing local political legitimacy are more clearly spelled out. Should counties and other local governments, as the existing holders of political authority at the local level, be given a greater role in managing the national forests (and other federal lands)? Should significant portions of the national forests perhaps be transferred directly to the ownership or management of existing local governments? Should parts of the national forests be privatized, leaving them in a status under which they would then be subject to state and local taxation and regulation?

Alternatively, rather than relying on existing instruments of governance, should a brand-new political structure be improvised at the local level throughout the West? It could reflect the history of the national forests, their special character, and the differences in their geography and traditional uses, as compared with most other rural lands in the United States. For example, this new set of governing arrangements might take as a beginning point the current proliferation of watershed groups, using them as a base and giving them a more formal status as part of an evolving new political constitution for the rural West. If newly formed institutions at the local level are to be given real political power, how might the selection of the participants in these institutions meet the clear expectation in the United States that any political authority must rest on a valid foundation of democratic principles?

Should members, say, of watershed groups be elected locally? Is it sufficient to argue that democratic requirements can be met because the president of the United States is democratically elected and he appoints the heads of cabinet agencies and other federal officials, and they might then select the membership of future watershed or other local decision-making groups? At present, this is the working procedure being followed by the Interior Department in forming the Resource Advisory Councils (RACs), which might eventually evolve to assume a broader political role.[6]

DECENTRALIZATION IN THE SHORT RUN

A path for decentralization of political authority for the national forest lands can be approached from a short-run and a long-run perspective. I propose below a short-run strategy that recognizes existing political constraints, including the incremental character of social and administrative change that characterizes the American system. The proposal thus would build on a number of existing institutions and political and economic circumstances.[7] As a proposal, it is merely one possibility being put on the table for discussion, leaving wide room for further modification and refinement.[8]

In the short run, I propose that the national forests remain in federal hands, but most decision-making power should be transferred to individual national forests. These forests would be responsible for defining their own management objectives—ecological, economic, or otherwise. Indeed, it is only by a clear transfer of real political authority to the local level that any effective management is likely in the future. In the numerous western national forests with major problems of excess fuels buildup, and resulting fire hazards, the local forest managers would be responsible for deciding whether prescribed burning, commercial thinning, other mechanical treatment of the forest, no action at all, or still other possible actions would be taken.

The local national forest would also be required to raise the money to pay the costs associated with the management of the forest.[9] In order to obtain the revenues for this purpose, the managers of each national forest would have the freedom to set their own recreation, grazing, and other user fees, and to collect other charges as they determined to be appropriate. They could offer timber for sale under a seal bid or an oral auction system of bidding competition or other sale procedures of their choosing. They could solicit voluntary contributions of funds from private profit and nonprofit wildlife, hunting, and other organizations. They could enter into cooperative agreements with state and local governments. In short, the local forest would be financed in much same way that a typical private organization in a rural area today would be.

If management costs were assumed by the federal government, even as decision making was decentralized in other respects, the local incentives would be perverse. Rather than to find "good" projects, localities would find it in their interest simply to maximize the amount of federal money coming into the local forest. However, the federal government is not likely to be willing to write blank checks. If national taxpayers pay for local projects, national political representatives will reasonably enough insist on maintaining oversight of local decisions. Federal financing of national forest operations thus inevitably also means ultimate federal accountability and control over forest decisions on the ground, acting to defeat the very purposes of decentralization.

Assuming revenues must be raised at the forest level, I further propose that for each national forest a local board of directors be appointed to oversee its management. The actual administration of the local national forest would probably continue to be performed mainly by existing Forest Service personnel (although likely reduced considerably in numbers from current levels). However, the new board of directors would set the basic policy directions, much like the board of directors of a private corporation. It would also be responsible for hiring the forest supervisor, reviewing the budget for the national forest, and overseeing other specific areas of responsibility.

The membership of the board would have to include reasonable representation from the various users of the local national forest, including in a typical case timber companies and workers, ranchers, hunters, fishermen, miners, hikers, off-road vehicle users, and other types of recreational users. Environmental, taxpayer, and any other national and regional groups having a general concern for the quality of management of the national forests—independent of any specific use objectives—might be offered representation on the forest board of directors as well. Some of the positions on the national forest board might be chosen by direct election from among the memberships of the involved groups.

In order to smooth out cash flow problems, local national forests would be able to borrow from a loan fund administered by the Forest Service. However, any money borrowed by a forest would have to be repaid at the borrowing rate of interest of the federal government (in recent years about 5 to 6 percent). The local national forest would also have authority to go into the commercial bond market, if it preferred to obtain funds in this fashion, and to pay back the bonds over time.

It is often remarked that no management reform will work if the current confused and overlapping structure of federal environmental laws is left in place. However, the needed rewriting of laws such as the Clean Air Act and the Clean Water Act would have to occur in another time and place. The local national forest organizations, just as any other state or private party, would be required to comply with these laws—including the Endangered Species Act. However, local forests would no longer have to comply with the complex and burdensome procedural laws for decision making that apply specifically to federal management of natural resources. Thus, the failed land-use planning and other decision-making apparatus imposed by the National Forest Management Act of 1976 would be abolished. Local national forests would still be required to prepare environmental impact statements, but judicial review of the adequacy of such statements would no longer occur—the same position generally taken at present by environmental organizations with respect to the preparation of regulatory and economic analysis documents.

Management of formally designated wilderness areas would continue to be a federal responsibility, reflecting common rules to be applied throughout a national wilderness system. Any important changes made by local forests in management in wilderness areas would have to be approved at a regional or national level of the Forest Service. Existing livestock grazing permits would continue in place. Mining claims previously filed would be processed under existing national law for mineral discovery on public lands, and appeals could be directed to the federal appeals process and the federal courts.

In order to put such a scheme of national forest decentralization into actual operation, many other details would have to be worked out. Whatever the specifics, the basic management responsibility for the individual national forest (and/or the Bureau of Land Management [BLM] district) should be devolved in a meaningful way to the local forest level. It is only at this level, and among people who live on and near the land, and often know each other, that there is likely to be much agreement on the goals of forest management and on the best way to achieve these goals. Without some acceptance of goals there can be no true accountability. And without accountability, the management of the national forests is likely to continue to fail to meet even minimal requirements for efficiency and effectiveness.

SIMILAR PROPOSALS

The steps proposed here are not new. A number of students of the public lands in the West have advocated the creation of a management regime for the national forests along these lines.[10] Environmental writer Tom Wolf of Colorado College finds that:

> We are squandering the best and the brightest of our forest-resource managers. We are forcing those who remain in the agencies to witness the

trashing of our neglected public lands. Frustrated and hamstrung, many of today's finest mid-level managers are leaving the Forest Service.

We should turn management of public lands over to public-private, non-profit regional conservation trusts. If funded by net receipts from local operations, such trusts could do what private businesses do—react quickly to reward or punish managers as their achievements merit. Here in the Sangre de Cristo Mountains, for example, we could let the market set appropriate fees for access to our world-class [mountain climbing] rock. That money could liberate our pros to be pros—it could provide managers with the funds they need to do the job right. Some in Congress already see this. There are a few experiments under way.

[We need to] take the next step—not toward a mega-agency, but toward a series of much smaller ones. These experiments could and should mean the end of the national Forest Service. Let a thousand local Forest Services bloom.[11]

Released in 1999, the *Second Century Report*—organized under the leadership of Randal O'Toole—proposed experimentation with five options for significantly altering the management regime on the national forests. These options were labeled "entrepreneurial budgeting," "collaborative governance," "collaborative planning," "forest trusts," and "rate board." The *Second Century Report* focused its efforts on designing a new set of "governing structures" and a new "budgetary process" for the national forests. A new organizational design was necessary in order to correct the current problem that "top-down governance structures promote polarization and discourage people from working with the agency at the local level because of the risk that a higher level would overturn the decisions. The budgetary process encourages people to view both the national forests and federal funds as a commons, available to those who stake their claims."[12]

Each of the proposed five pilot approaches would involve substantial decentralization of the budgetary process and decision making generally. Under "entrepreneurial budgeting," forest managers would have the freedom to set user fees and to keep the money locally. In turn, they would be expected to fund the management of an individual national forest from the revenues collected on that forest. Under "collaborative governance," a board would be appointed to assume some of the functions of a board of directors. Under the "forest trust" model, these changes would be carried further, converting each national forest to an actual trust status with a board of trustees appointed by the Secretary of Agriculture.[13]

In a related model, each local forest might be organized as a public corporation. The Port Authority of New York, the Postal Service Corporation

at the federal level, and many other public corporations have been created over the years to provide a degree of insulation of business-like activities from ordinary politics. As long ago as 1957, Marion Clawson proposed that the public lands should be managed as a public corporation.[14]
They could raise their own money, if necessary, in financial markets and
earn the revenues to cover their costs. Other students of the public lands
have since made similar proposals, including John Beuter and Dennis
Teeguarden.[15] Rather than one public corporation for all the national
forests, the most promising version of this approach would decentralize
management to create numerous public corporations at the level of individual national forests.

   The Federal Lands Task Force of the Idaho State Board of Land Commissioners also recommended experimentation with new forms of decentralized management within the framework of continued federal land
ownership. The Task Force offered three models: the "trust alternative,"
the "collaborative alternative," and the "cooperative alternative." Each of
the alternatives would be designed to replace the "current Washington,
D.C. centered, lawsuit-driven, land management structure that hinders decision making and allows little flexibility in conflict resolution."[16] The
most far-reaching changes would occur under the trust model, involving
the designation of a trust beneficiary to receive the income from the national forests and a board of trustees to oversee their management to ensure that this income-earning function was realized.

STATE AND LOCAL FIRE PROTECTION

As in other respects, management of forest fire illustrates broader problems and issues that arise with respect to the decentralization of the management of the national forests. Moreover, given the large sums of money
being spent by the federal government for fire management, any workable plan for decentralization of national forest management would have
to address the matter of policies for forest fire.

   A recent study found that "increasingly in recent years, federal wildland fire-control agencies have been put into the position of having to assume responsibility for structure protection during major wildfires."
However, protection of homes, businesses, and other structures is not a
Forest Service or federal government responsibility; that is supposed to
be the job of state and local fire departments. The study authors considered that spending of federal resources to protect residential and other
properties was creating an inequity in that federal "taxpayers at large pay
for these fire-protection services."[17] It also meant the diversion of federal

resources from the actual jobs they were supposed to be doing: managing and protecting the national forests and other natural resource assets of the federal lands.

Reflecting such concerns, an internal Forest Service staff paper in 1995 proposed that there should be a clarification and redefinition of federal versus state and local responsibilities for forest fire control and suppression. The guiding principles for this new forest fire policy and management regime would be as follows:

> (1) Fire protection on State and private lands is the responsibility of State and local governments, (2) homeowners have a personal responsibility to practice fire safety, (3) the role of the Forest Service is stewardship of adjacent National Forests, cooperative assistance to State and local fire organizations, and cooperative suppression during fire emergencies.[18]

That is to say, the protection of life and property is best assigned to that level of government where this task can most effectively be accomplished. Local fire departments bear the principal responsibility for putting out fires that threaten physical structures. They have the ability and the responsibility to enact building codes, adopt zoning, regulate land use, and take other actions involving private land that can reduce the risk that buildings will be located in forest areas where they may be exposed to a large risk of forest fire—and where governments at all levels may inevitably be forced to bear large costs if a forest fire does break out.

The police power to address such matters is a state and local function in the American constitutional scheme. The most important role of the federal government historically has been to pick up the check for much of the cost of fighting forest fires in the West, even when these fires mainly threatened property holdings on the edges of urban areas on private lands. When the federal government pays in this fashion, the incentives for responsible behavior by other parties diminish.[19] State and local areas have even been known to experience economic booms sustained by federal disaster funding.

It might still be argued that, whatever the economics, federal forest fire fighting—and other federal agency management activities—serve important ecological functions for the national forests. If forest fires were allowed to burn more freely, it would destroy much existing vegetation, wildlife habitat, and other natural features. However, as ecological understanding has advanced in the twentieth century, there has been a new recognition of the constructive—indeed, essential—role of forest fire in ordinary ecological processes. The expensive Forest Service organization built over the course of this century to suppress fire has not only been economically wasteful but also ecologically harmful. Federal fire policy, like the construction of Bureau of Reclamation dams or the provision of agricultural subsidies for the conversion of wetlands to farmland, is yet another example of a federal activity doing significant harm to the environment that is sustained at large cost to the national taxpayer.

Forest fire is one more graphic example of how federal management of the national forests has failed, whether measured by the original progressive goal of efficient use of resources or by a more contemporary goal of environmental quality and ecological well-being. Suppressing fire has failed even in terms of its own narrow objectives. Past suppression has created national forest conditions today in which larger, more dangerous, and more destructive fires are likely to break out in the future. At the same time, the long-standing policy of fire suppression has made the national forests less healthy, less productive, and less biologically diverse—the three criteria by which the federal government now says the success of ecosystem management should be judged.

In light of all this, the Forest Service should act to phase out of many of the forest fire responsibilities it is currently assuming in urban "interface" areas in the West, a step that will require a renegotiation of some existing intergovernmental agreements. Additional resources and technical assistance could be provided to the western states in order to improve their capabilities for an expanded fire-fighting role. The agency itself has stated a goal that "the Forest Service no longer assumes primary [forest fire] protection responsibility in urbanized and developing rural areas."[20] The secretaries of Interior and Agriculture in their joint 1995 report on federal fire policy endorsed a qualified move in this direction. "The role of Federal agencies in the wildland/urban interface includes wildland firefighting, hazard fuels reduction, cooperative prevention and education, and technical assistance. No one entity can resolve and manage all interface issues; it must be a cooperative effort. Ultimately, however, the primary responsibility rests at the State and local levels" for protecting private lands and physical structures.[21]

Such proposals should be carried further. State and local governments might assume responsibility for protecting not only state and local lands but also federal lands. If a fire breaks out today at a federal building in New York City, it is the city fire department, not a federal entity, that puts out the fire. In the past, the Forest Service had a large incentive to provide its own fire protection, because it had very valuable supplies of timber at risk. As timber harvesting has declined rapidly in importance, however, the protection of the wood supplies of the forests from burning up has become a much lower priority.

Indeed, if the management goal for the national forests is now to achieve some desired state of the forest ecological condition, fire suppression often no longer serves that goal. The most compelling reasons for controlling fire on federal lands now is the threat that the fire will spread to state and local lands, where lives could be lost, homes and other physical structures destroyed, and other large property damages incurred. Yet, if state and local governments are given the responsibility for protecting private lands and structures from fire, they will have ample incentive to suppress fires on federal land that could pose a major danger of spreading beyond federal boundaries.

It would be unrealistic, to be sure, after many years of the federal government spending hundreds of million of dollars per year for fire suppression in the West, to simply cut this money off. Rather, the federal government should transfer most of it to the western states in a firefighting block grant. However, this block grant should remain a transitional measure. Federal funds for fighting forest fires might be continued for, say, twenty years, but these funds gradually decline over that period until eventually reaching zero.

The federal government then would retain only the annual funding it needs for prescribed burning and other direct uses of fire for well-defined management purposes. The fire protection block grant to the states thus might, for example, initially provide 80 percent of the average federal fire budget (presuppression and suppression combined) of the past five years. The states would then be responsible for arranging for emergency forest fire control and suppression within their own boundaries, including most fires that broke out on the federal lands.

The federal forest fire apparatus, to be sure, may have the greatest existing experience and technical skills in fighting forest fire of any current body. The federal fire-fighting organization could therefore be reconstituted as a private enterprise (or possibly a public corporation) that could contract out its services to the states, as the states saw fit to hire these services with their new block grant money. State contracts might be signed on an individual fire-by-fire basis with the new fire fighting organization, leaving the state to decide in each case of a forest fire whether special outside assistance would be needed.

Alternatively, a state might sign a longer term contract with a new firefighting corporation to provide any fire-fighting services as needed in the state—like a contract to receive future medical services from an HMO. This would have the character of an insurance policy, in that the amount of money spent by the fire-fighting corporation would be highly variable from year to year. Yet another alternative would be for the state to purchase a forest fire insurance policy from a private insurance carrier, with sufficient coverage to reimburse the state for large and unexpected forest fire-fighting expenditures in any given year.

There might remain some situations where a national interest in the management of the national forests would dictate suppression of forest fire. In such cases, the federal government could contract with state fire authorities, or with new private fire-fighting entities. The end result would be that the federal government would largely retire from the business of fighting fire in the West. The job would be taken over by the western states and by private parties. On a transitional basis, transfer of existing federal forest fire funds to states would help to pave the way to the full-fledged implementation of a fully decentralized system.

HOW TO DISMANTLE THE FOREST SERVICE

In raising the possibility that the Forest Service would be abolished by 2005, Randal O'Toole suggested that the Forest Service might be merged into a consolidated federal land management agency within the Interior Department.[22] A more appropriate long-run policy would be to dismantle the Forest Service by transfer of most of the national forest lands to new owners outside the federal system altogether. As part of this process, most of the BLM lands should also be transferred to new nonfederal owner-ship.[23] The Western Water Policy Review Advisory Commission in 1998 found a need for "fundamental change in the structure of the federal government" in the West, where its presence has been pervasive for a century or more. Taking a longer run view, the commission members declared that "we anticipate that during the next century, the federal resources management agencies will undergo widespread realignment of their organizational and enforcement functions."[24]

As proposed in this book, the federal government would retain only those national forest and BLM lands of genuine national significance—perhaps some wilderness areas and a few other areas holding unique environmental, historical, cultural, or other assets from a national perspective. As a rough estimate, these federally retained lands might amount to about 20 percent of the current total of national forest and other federal land acreage in the West. The Forest Service and the BLM would be abolished, reflecting the outmoded character of their old centralized mission of scientific management. Any of their lands that were still retained at the federal level would be transferred to the National Park Service, the Fish and Wildlife Service, or to other federal agencies with more clearly defined missions. Perhaps some brand-new federal agency (or agencies) would be created to manage former national forest and BLM lands, say a federal wilderness management agency for those wilderness lands retained in the federal system.[25]

The federal government would still be heavily involved financially and in other ways, however, for a transitional period. As lands were transferred out of the federal system, the current federal spending to administer these lands would be converted into a block grant and made available to western states. Reflecting its temporary status, the block grant would decline over some appropriate period of time, perhaps ending altogether in, say, twenty years. Federal laws such as the Clean Water Act and the Endangered Species Act would continue to apply and to set binding targets for environmental quality where necessary—one might hope in improved versions from the current statutes. The federal government would also serve as a clearinghouse for information and the provider of technical expertise. Over time the federal model would gradually shift from regulator to provider of technical assistance.

The Western Water Policy Review Advisory Commission concluded that "the goal of privatizing certain federal assets . . . is laudable."[26] Yale law professor Robert Ellickson declares that "I urge the Federal Government to consider re-adopting the nation's land policy of the nineteenth century, a presumption that federal lands should be transferred into private ownership."[27] This recommendation can be applied to significant areas of national forests as well as to many dams and other water projects in the West. Some areas of the national forests have high timber growing potential, have been cut over in the past, and are well into a second cycle of reforestation with further timber harvesting planned at some point in the future. As timber managers, private industry has a much superior record on its own forest lands, as compared with the large financial losses—typical of public enterprises all over the world—incurred over the years by the Forest Service. Hence, those lands in the national forest system that have primarily a future of timber harvesting (although there is no need to exclude the possibility of considerable recreation and other nontimber uses occurring on these lands as well) should be transferred into private ownership. Many of these lands are in the Pacific Northwest where the Forest Service (and the BLM) own some of the prime timber growing lands in the world.

A privatization strategy should also encompass the possibility of turning over existing national forest lands to private nonprofit organizations. Organizations like the Nature Conservancy might do a much better job in managing for preservation, recreation, and other well-defined purposes. Local nonprofit organizations might be formed in many cases for the specific purpose of managing particular local areas of forest.

Perhaps the largest area of the existing national forest lands should be transferred to state ownership.[28] The western water commission also recommended more broadly in this regard that "it is desirable to transfer assets out of federal ownership in those situations in which the new owner can manage those assets as well as or better than, and at less cost than, the federal government." In considering this possibility, "the range of potential transferees should be broadened to include states or other nonfed-

eral entities with the financial and technical capabilities to own and manage such facilities or projects."[29] The management record of western states
with their own lands suggests that state ownership and management is in
fact often superior to federal management.[30]

Transfer of large parts of the existing national forests—that today can
cover in one state an area as large as 40 percent of Idaho—would not
necessarily represent a final resolution of land-tenure issues. The states,
in turn, could then have the equivalent of a great political and constitutional debate. The issue would be nothing less than the appropriate
political constitution to provide for a new manner of more genuinely
democratic governance of current federal lands—lands that are so vast
in area that even today they encompass on average one-half of the total
land area of the western states. Consistent with a philosophy of decentralization and acceptance of significant individual differences from
state to state, there is no reason to require at the federal level that state
constitutional debates should all produce the same outcome. Indeed,
there might be large differences from one western state to another in
the kind of ownership arrangements and the type of management of
the forest and range lands transferred to the states from federal ownership.

Each state would have to resolve questions such as the extent of
newly acquired lands to remain under direct state management.[31] Some
new state forest lands might be used to create new state parks or to add
to existing parks. Some lands might be turned over to other state agencies for "trust" land management, where the revenues would be dedicated to local schools or to other state or local beneficiaries. Many former federal forest lands, however, might eventually be transferred by
the state government to local governments. The local self-governing
forest units, as described in the short-run strategy above, might become
autonomous local governing units in the longer run. Existing county
and city governments might take ownership of still other forest lands.[32]

States might also choose to privatize many former national forest lands
outright.[33] It may not make sense for a state such as Utah today to have almost 70 percent of its land in government ownership (when federal, state,
and other government land holdings are all factored into the total). The
most logical forest lands for states to privatize would be lands with a high
commercial timber potential for long-run harvest rotations and no rare or
unique environmental assets. Since most of the economic return from
these lands would be internalized to the private owner, market incentives
would act to ensure efficient and effective management of the forests.
Where particularly significant nonmarket environmental considerations
came into play, governments could either employ regulatory mechanisms
or enter into voluntary financial arrangements to ensure the protection of

environmental values.

Why, if many national forest (and BLM district) lands might end up owned and managed at the local level, not simply transfer these lands directly to local authorities? Why involve state governments at all where the lands are to be locally owned? Yet the establishment of a regime of governance of former federal lands would be of great constitutional significance to each state. States would strongly and properly resist the federal imposition of a grand political design setting in place new constitutional arrangements for local democratic governance of much of the land area in a typical western state.

Constitutionally, the states and the federal government have equal sovereign status. Local governments, however, are creatures of state government, and as such the states can properly assert the right to establish their own political arrangements for local government. In short, politically and constitutionally, the route to more local forms of governance—perhaps built around watersheds or whatever—of former national forests (and BLM districts) must run, at least initially, through a federal transfer of large parts of the national forests and the BLM lands to state ownership.

CONCLUSION

The Western Water Policy Review Advisory Commission found that solutions to land and water resource problems in the West were unavoidably "to some degree, for better or worse, linked to our larger effort to improve the quality of government in the United States."[34] The manner of governance in the West has been greatly influenced by the pervasive presence of federal lands. It has resulted in a structure of governance unique in the United States, one that does not correspond to any theory of democratic government. The existing governance arrangements for the rural West are explainable only as a product of two centuries of American history.

As long as these governance arrangements functioned reasonably well, prudence might have dictated "leaving well enough alone," or a philosophy of "if it ain't broke, don't fix it." However, there is now close to universal agreement that the system is "broke." There is much less agreement about the causes and the changes that would be necessary to improve matters. Nevertheless, the failures of national forest and other federal natural resource management today, failures that inevitably extend to the broader governance arrangements for the rural West, are opening the way for a basic reconsideration of the instruments of rural resource management that the West has inherited from the past.

What is required is nothing less than the equivalent of a new constitutional convention for the rural West. The West has not had the self-confidence in the past to undertake such a formidable task. The large financial benefits of the federal presence have also been a major inhibiting factor. The time has come, however, for such a rethinking of western governance at a constitutional level. In order for this to work, a starting premise must be that the future ownership status of the existing national forests and other federal lands and natural resources that dominate the landscape of the rural West is a question to be resolved for most areas by the West itself.

NOTES

1. See also Robert H. Nelson, "Public Land Federalism: Go Away and Give Us More Money," in *Environmental Federalism*, ed. Terry L. Anderson and Peter J. Hill (Lanham, Md.: Rowman & Littlefield, 1997).

2. *Water in the West: Challenge for the Next Century*, Report of the Western Water Policy Review Advisory Commission (June 1998), p. 2-39.

3. Ibid., pp. 2-37, 3-39.

4. Ibid., p. 3-41.

5. Ibid., p. 3-41.

6. For a discussion of BLM's new regulations, see Bruce M. Pendery, "Reforming Livestock Grazing on the Public Domain: Ecosystem Management-Based Standards and Guidelines Blaze a New Path for Range Management," *Environmental Law* vol. 27 (1997).

7. See also Robert H. Nelson and Mary M. Chapman, *Voices from the Heartland: New Tools for Decentralizing Management of the West's Public Lands*, Points West—Special Report (Denver, Colo.: Center for the New West, December 1995).

8. This proposal is similar to ideas long advocated by Randal O'Toole. See Randal O'Toole, *Reforming the Forest Service* (Washington, D.C.: Island Press, 1988); see also "Reinventing the Forest Service," Special Issue of *Different Drummer* (Spring 1995).

9. The General Accounting Office recently studied examples of other nonfederal land management systems that operated on a more profitable basis than the Forest Service and also some of the obstacles to the Forest Service moving in such directions. See General Accounting Office, *Forest Service: Barriers to Generating Revenue or Reducing Costs*, GAO/RCED-98-58 (February 1998).

10. The broader movement in the United States today toward decentralization of environmental policy and management is reviewed favorably in Marc K. Landy, Megan M. Susman, and Debra S. Knopman, *Civic Environmentalism in Action: A Field Guide to Regional and Local Initiatives* (Washington, D.C.: Progressive Policy Institute, January 1999).

11. Tom Wolf, "Earnest About Changing the Way We Manage Lands," *The Seattle Times* (June 4, 1997).

12. *Options for the Forest Service 2nd Century: A Report to the American People by the Forest Options Group* (Portland, Ore.: Thoreau Institute, January 1999), executive summary. Available at <http://www.ti.org/2c.html>.

13. The more successful management of many state trust lands is examined in Jon A. Souder and Sally K. Fairfax, *State Trust Lands: History, Management, and Sustainable Use* (Lawrence: University Press of Kansas, 1996).

14. Marion Clawson and Burnell Held, *The Federal Lands: Their Use and Management* (Baltimore: Johns Hopkins University Press for Resources for the Future, 1957), p. 347.

15. Proposals for an independent federal timber corporation have been made, among others, by Dennis E. Teeguarden and Davis Thomas, "A Public Corporation Model for Federal Forest Land Management," *Natural Resources Journal* (April 1985); and John H. Beuter, *Federal Timber Sales* (Washington, D.C.: Congressional Research Service, Report 85-96, February 9, 1985), pp. 125–28.

16. *New Approaches for Managing Federally Administered Lands*, A Report to the Idaho State Board of Land Commissioners by the Federal Lands Task Force (Boise, Idaho: July 1998), pp. 12–15.

17. C. Phillip Weatherspoon and Carl N. Skinner, "Landscape-Level Strategies for Forest Fuel Management," in *Status of the Sierra Nevada, Volume II*, Sierra Nevada Ecosystem Project, Final Report to Congress (Davis: University of California, Wildland Resources Center Report No. 40, March 1997), p. 1485.

18. D. Bacon et al., *Strategic Assessment of Fire Management in the U.S. Forest Service*, unpublished Forest Service internal report (1995), cited in Weatherspoon and Skinner, "Landscape-Level Strategies for Forest Fuel Management," p. 1485.

19. The general problems of existing government policy with respect to natural hazards are discussed in Dennis S. Mileti, *Disasters by Design: A Reassessment of Natural Hazards in the United States*, A report to the National Academy of Sciences reflecting contributions of participants in the Assessment of Research and Applications on Natural Hazards (Washington, D.C.: John Henry Press, 1999).

20. U.S. Forest Service, *Course to the Future: Positioning Fire and Aviation Management* (Washington, D.C.: May 1995), p. 9.

21. U.S. Department of the Interior, U.S. Department of Agriculture, *Federal Wildland Fire Management: Policy and Program Review* (Washington, D.C.: December 18, 1995), p. iii.

22. Randal O'Toole, "Expect the Forest Service to Be Slowly Emasculated," *Seattle Times* (May 7, 1997).

23. See also Robert H. Nelson, *How to Dismantle the Interior Department* (Washington, D.C.: Competitive Enterprise Institute, June 1995); and Robert H. Nelson, *How and Why to Transfer BLM Lands to the States* (Washington, D.C.: Competitive Enterprise Institute, January 1996).

24. *Water in the West*, p. xvi.

25. See Robert H. Nelson, "The Public Lands," in *Current Issues in Natural Resource Policy*, ed. Paul R. Portney (Washington, D.C.: Resources for the Future, 1982).

26. *Water in the West*, p. 6-32.

27. Robert C. Ellickson, "Liberty, Property and Environmental Ethics," *Ecology Law Quarterly* vol. 21, no. 2 (1994), p. 402.

28. Management of state trust lands has been increasingly studied in recent years and has generally received positive reviews, relative to federal lands. See Sally K. Fairfax, Jon A. Souder, and Gretta Goldenman, "The School Trust Lands: A Fresh Look at Conventional Wisdom," *Environmental Law* Vol. 22, (1992), p. 797; Donald R. Leal, *Turning a Profit on Public Forests*, PERC Policy Series, Issue No. PS-4 (September 1995); and *Report to the Washington State Board of Natural Resources from the Independent Review Committee*, assisted by the Natural Resources Law Center, School of Law, University of Colorado (June 22, 1995).

29. *Water in the West*, pp. xxvi, 6-33.

30. See Donald R. Leal, "Making Money on Timber Sales," in *Multiple Conflicts over Multiple Uses*, ed. Terry L. Anderson (Bozeman, Mont.: Political Economy Research Center, 1994).

31. Lawrence J. MacDonnell, *Issues Related to Federal Land Divestiture*, Report to the Western State Land Commissioners Association (May 15, 1997).

32. For a general discussion of use of markets in environmental and land management, see Terry L. Anderson and Donald R. Leal, *Free Market Environmentalism* (Boulder, Colo.: Westview Press, 1991).

33. Various divestiture alternatives are examined in Marion Clawson, *The Federal Lands Revisited* (Washington, D.C.: Johns Hopkins University Press for Resources for the Future, 1983).

34. *Water in the West*, p. 3-44.

Conclusion

The Forest Service over the past quarter-century has stumbled from one proposed solution to another for its basic management problems, each attempt in turn failing. It has become ever clearer that the agency has become outmoded, grounded in a scientific management paradigm of the past, and is now unable to adjust to a new world in which its traditional operating assumptions and management principles no longer hold. The Forest Service is so confused today that it no longer knows the reason for its own existence. The only real mission of the agency now is institutional survival—protect the attractive jobs at good pay frequently found in rural western settings, jobs that many other Americans would like to have.

Answers to the problems of the national forests will have to be found at the state and local levels and in the private sector. There is today too much diversity of values around the United States to expect universal national answers to such value-laden issues as are posed by the management of the national forests. There is no reason why the management of each national forest should reflect the same social values—have the same basic objectives and policies—as every other forest. The fierce controversies today surrounding policy making for the national forests are partly the result of attempts to force the current value diversity of the American nation into a single forest management mold. That is one of the misguided legacies of the old scientific management design.

In the short run, devolution of the management authority for the national forests might take place within the existing federal system. This might well involve the creation of local self-governing forest units that are in large measure financially and managerially independent. In the longer run, most national forest lands, along with Bureau of Land Management (BLM) lands, should be transferred to the states and to the private sector. State governments can then devise an appropriate new constitutional regime for the governance of the former federal lands. Many of these lands might eventually end up owned and managed at the state and local level for various forms of dispersed recreational use. Substantial other portions of the former federal lands might end up being disposed of by the states into private ownership, where state and local regulations and other rules would still apply as needed.

It would be a political constitution for a newly democratic governance of former federal lands equal in total to almost one-half of the land area of the western United States—and one-quarter of the total land area of the United States as a whole.

Index

About the Author

Robert H. Nelson is a professor of environmental policy in the School of Public Affairs of the University of Maryland and senior fellow of the Competitive Enterprise Institute. From 1975 to 1993, he worked in the Office of Policy Analysis of the Department of the Interior in Washington, D.C., the principal policy office serving the Secretary of the Interior. He has written two other books on the topic of federal land and resource management: *Public Lands and Private Rights: The Failure of Scientific Management* (Rowman & Littlefield, 1995) and *The Making of Federal Coal Policy* (Duke University Press, 1983). Nelson's other books are *Reaching for Heaven on Earth: The Theological Meaning of Economics* (Rowman & Littlefield, 1991) and *Zoning and Property Rights: An Analysis of the American System of Land Use Regulation* (MIT Press, 1977). He is also the author of more than sixty articles in journals and other professional publications, including many on the management of lands and natural resources in the United States.

Nelson has been a visiting scholar at the Brookings Institution, the Woods Hole Oceanographic Institution, the Political Economy Research Center, and the Center for Applied Social Sciences at the University of Zimbabwe. He was senior research manger of the President's Commission on Privatization, senior economist of the Commission on Fair Market Value Policy for Federal Coal Leasing, and staff economist for the Senate Select Committee on Indian Affairs. Nelson is a columnist for *Forbes* magazine and has written for the *Washington Post, Los Angeles Times, Wall Street Journal, Weekly Standard,* and many other publications. He holds a Ph.D. in economics from Princeton University (1971).

About the Political Economy
Research Center

The Political Economy Research Center (PERC) is the nation's oldest and largest institute dedicated to original research that brings market principles to resolving environmental problems. PERC, located in Bozeman, Montana, pioneered the approach known as free market environmentalism. This approach is based on four main tenets: 1) private property rights encourage stewardship of resources; 2) government subsidies often degrade the environment; 3) market incentives spur individuals to conserve resources and protect environmental quality; and 4) polluters should be liable for the harm they cause others. PERC associates have applied the free market environmentalism approach to a variety of issues, including national parks, water marketing, chemical risk, private provision of wildlife habitat, public land management, and endangered species protection.

PERC's activities encompass three main areas: research and policy analysis, outreach, and environmental education. PERC associates conduct research, write books and articles, and lecture on the role of markets and property rights in environmental protection. PERC holds conferences and seminars for journalists, congressional staff members, state policy makers, business executives, and scholars. PERC also holds an annual free market environmentalism seminar for college students and sponsors a fellowship program that brings graduate students to PERC for three months of research and study on various environmental topics. PERC develops and disseminates environmental education materials for classroom use and provides training for kindergarten through twelfth-grade teachers.

In 1989, PERC organized the first of an annual conference series called the Political Economy Forum aimed at applying the principles of political economy to important policy issues. Each forum brings together scholars in economics, political science, law, history, and other disciplines to discuss and refine academic papers that explore new applications of political economy to policy analysis. The forum papers are then edited and published as a book in PERC's Political Economy Forum series. PERC believes that forums of this type can integrate cutting edge research with crucial policy issues.

From time to time, the series includes books not generated from PERC forums. These books are chosen based on their use of the free market environmentalism approach and their superior scholarship. This volume by Robert Nelson clearly fits both criteria. Nelson argues that the incentives facing the U.S. Forest Service make it impossible for the agency to practice scientific management. Focusing on the agency's forest fire policy, he contends that the Forest Service lacks a coherent vision and prefers to sponsor only fashionable environmental solutions. In *A Burning Issue*, Nelson makes a compelling case for abolishing the U.S. Forest Service and replacing it with a decentralized system to manage the protection of our national forests.

PERC hopes that scholarship such as this will help advice the environmental policy debate and looks forward to further volumes in this series.

ADY-8129

5/14/01

Armstrong
SD

565
N 46
2000